AF540255

ENVIRONMENTAL MANAGEMENT AND BUSINESS STRATEGIES

ENVIRONMENTAL MANAGEMENT AND BUSINESS STRATEGIES

By

Dr. SARBANI MITRA, MBA, Ph.D.
Sr. Lecturer & Coordinator
Department of Environment Management
Indian Institute of Social Welfare & Business Management
College Square West
Kolkata-700 073
e-mail: *sarbani_iiswbm@yahoo.co.in*

Dr. KRISHNA M. AGRAWAL, M.Sc., Ph.D.
Professor & Head
Department of Public Systems Management
Indian Institute of Social Welfare & Business Management
College Square West
Kolkata-700 073
e-mail: *km_agra@yahoo.com*

Dr. SATYAJIT DHAR, M.Com., Ph.D.
Reader & Head
Department of Business Administration
University of Kalyani
Kalyani, Nadia – 741 235
e-mail: *satyajitdhar@yahoo.co.in*

D P H

DISCOVERY PUBLISHING HOUSE PVT. LTD.
NEW DELHI-110 002

First Published-2009

ISBN 978-81-8356-469-4

Published by:

DISCOVERY PUBLISHING HOUSE PVT. LTD.
4831/24, Ansari Road, Prahlad Street
Darya Ganj, New Delhi-110002 (India)
Phone: 23279245 • Fax: 91-11-23253475
E-mail: dphbooks@rediffmail.com
dphtemp@indiatimes.com
website: www.discoverypublishinghouse.com

Printed at:

Sachin Printers
Delhi

Dedicated

to

Our Parents

FOREWORD

There are four reasons why every organization should take environmental factors into account in its management processes. Those four reasons are ethical, economical, legal and commercial. From ethical point of view, as human beings we have a duty to look after the world in which we live and to hand it on to our children in good shape. From economic point of view, conserving resources and not generating waste products or wasting energy means we save on cost. From legal point of view, more and more governments are passing laws to control how we interact with the environment. Therefore we need systems to make sure we stay within the law, otherwise we can be fined and damage our reputation. From commercial point of view, without evidence of an environmental management system, the number of customers prepared to trade will start to fall. On the other hand, by being able to demonstrate good environmental practice, new market opportunities may open up.

Accordingly, the beginning of 21st century have witnessed the fast changing business environment in our country and gradual changes in customers' expectations that have made it necessary to companies to take a proactive approach to deal with problems relating to environmental pollution control and management. Globally, the companies are faced with the challenge of integrating environmental considerations into their production and marketing plans. The major concern to environmental management is determining ways in which industrial action can be made compatible with nature. Further, it is attempted to aim at taking a holistic and integrated approach towards environmental management in corporate scenario for carrying capacity based sustainable development.

However, as it was found that Indian companies need to be more proactive in view of changing global business strategies, therefore it was felt to assess the present position of business practice in case of Indian companies regarding corporate environmental management and the level of proactiveness in management of environmental issues through appropriate policies and procedures. The inevitable questions that often confront us in this context are: how much environmental issues are being incorporated in business practice by Indian companies? Do they ever think of corporate social responsibility? How much proactive they are? These are the questions that do not have any ready answers. Now, incorporation of environmental issues means whether business strategy and operational procedure incorporates environmental issues. To be more specific, the first stage of addressing environmental issues in the business process would be making the operating units compliant with environmental regulations. Further, the process of compliance with environmental regulations would be incorporated in a holistic manner in process of the organization. So the entire business process would have a focus towards environmental issues.

The Book, *Environmental Management and Business Strategies*, authored by Dr. Sarbani Mitra, Dr. Krishna M. Agrawal and Dr. Satyajit Dhar, makes a commendable effort to choose certain aspects of business process including certain strategic issues (e.g., corporate mission, compliance with environmental regulations, quality certification, etc.) that may reflect the level of incorporation of environmental issues in business practice. Authors also tried to measure this level of integration by applying quantitative scores that was termed as environmental proactiveness score. Further, the authors categorized the business units in a matrix for better classification of units on the basis of environmental performance and other suitable criteria. They also analyzed the nature of variation in proactiveness among the units. Further, they attempted to explore the unit specific determinants that may explain the variation in proactiveness among the units.

It is highly expected that such kind of Book may provide some assistance to (a) corporate management who are in the top level to incorporate environmental issues into overall corporate strategy formulation and implementation at operational levels; (b) policy makers and the legislators who frame environmental regulatory policies and enact regulations; and (c) regulators who monitor and enforce such regulations. It is the modest hope from the side of the authors that the study might thereby show up the areas where there is scope of improving the quality of environmental performance of the industrial units.

Sandipan Mukherjee, IFS
Member Secretary
West Bengal Pollution Control Board
(Department of Environment, Government of West Bengal)
Paribesh Bhawan, Kolkata – 700 098

PREFACE

In the recent past corporate world had witnessed many-fold increase in the requirements of the environmental regulations in the business practice. Such requirements are likely to be further strengthened in the future. This warrants businesses to take more responsibility for the environmental damage that they create and to approach corporate environmental management in a more proactive way. Accordingly, at the beginning of 21st century, the biggest challenge to the interests of global business is the task of reconciling the demands of sustainable development and corporate strategy. In this context, it was interesting to study the position of industries in an emerging market economy like India. As environmental considerations are likely to be a source of quite profound changes in business practice, the present study attempted to provide managers the strategic plan for the environmental management.

Environmental management is emerging as an important area of research considering its impact on overall corporate performance. It is perceived that Indian Companies are not fully focussed in managing environment related issues. It appeared that there was further scope of exploring the condition of Indian companies. It was also found that no extensive work has yet been made in the Indian context attempting to measure the position of units in the field of environmental management and to assess the extent to which different unit specific determinants can explain the variations in such environmental performance. Also, previous work had hardly made any effort to identify the different environmental indicators for making the units proactive. In this context, it may be interesting to study the position of industries in an emerging market economy like India.

However, environmental regulations alone cannot solve the environmental problems. Implementation of regulations always remains as an issue. Gradually, awareness about environmental issues is increasing among policy makers and public in general. Therefore, environmental management is not only a compliance issue, but also it is a strategic business practice. There is wide scope of incorporation of environmental issues in business practice. Globally, green awareness, eco-friendly production, etc. become buzz words, which indicate heightened industry awareness on environmental issues. It may be due to prolonged activities of environmental activists.

The focus of this work was on incorporation of environmental issues in business practice. Incorporation of environmental issues means whether business strategy and operational procedure incorporates environmental issues. To be more specific, it was considered that the first stage of addressing environmental issues in the business process would be making the operating units compliant with environmental regulations. Further, the process of compliance with environmental regulations would be incorporated in a holistic manner in process of the organisation. So the entire business process would have a focus towards environmental issues. Accordingly, we had chosen certain aspects of business process including certain strategic issues (e.g., corporate mission, compliance with environmental regulations, quality certification, etc.) that may reflect the level of incorporation of environmental issues in business practice. We tried to measure this level of integration by applying quantitative scores. We termed this as environmental proactiveness score.

Accordingly, the present work deals with a very important aspect of corporate environmental management practices of different industrial units in India, a country that is on the threshold of emerging as one of the powerful economies in the presently globalising world. The underlying philosophy of this study is to explore empirically the position of industrial units in West Bengal regarding environmental management. It was desired to assess how far the units are proactive in management of environmental issues. In addition, it was desired to analyse the nature of variation in proactiveness score among the units. Further, it was attempted to explore the unit specific determinants (if any) that may explain the variation in proactiveness among the units. Once this analysis would be in hand, it would be easier to draw a framework where incorporation of environmental issues would make a proactive stance towards sustainable corporate planning and strategic management.

So, considering this work as a starting point of environmental proactiveness, it would lead in future to think of different ways and means to integrate the environmental issues into business practice that would be ultimately fruitful to the market entrepreneur to take strategic decision on economic development in a proactive way.

We would like to extend our thankful gratitude to Prof. P. K. Misra, Hon'ble Director, Indian Institute of Social Welfare and Business Management, Kolkata for giving us support throughout the period and allowing us to undertake this work and to use infrastructural and other facilities available at the Institute. We express our special gratitude to Professor S.C. Santra, Head, Department of Environment, University of Kalyani for his kind cooperation and encouragement. We would be failing in our duties, if we do not express our sincere thanks to the persons who have extended necessary support in spite of their busy schedule for providing highly informative documents related to the study. Specially, we are thankful to Dr. Sudip Banerjee, Former Chairman, West Bengal Pollution Control Board; Dr. Tapas K. Gupta, Chief Environmental Engineer, West Bengal Pollution Control Board, Kolkata; Mr. Nazeeb Arif, Secretary General, Indian Chamber of Commerce, Kolkata; Mr. S. N. Chakrabertty, Director, Indian Institute of Port Management; Mr. A.K. Ghosh, Chief of Production, Haldia Petrochemicals Ltd.; Mr. Amal Bhattacherjee, Senior Manager, Quality and SDCI, AREVA T&D India Limited, Kolkata; Mr. T.M. Joardar, Additional Manager (Mech.), Kolaghat Thermal Power Station; Mr. Sujit Basu, GM – HSE Cum Technical and Support, MCC PTA India Corporation Pvt. Ltd., Medinipur; Mr. T. K. Mitra, Operation Manager (Safety Dept), The Rifle Factory, Ishapore; and Mr. Kushal Bhowmick,

Sr. Manager (Environment), CESC Ltd., Southern Generating Station, Kolkata. We would want to acknowledge our debt of gratitude to a number of reputed libraries in the city of Kolkata and their staff members. These are the National Library, the British Council Library and the Central Library of the Indian Institute of Social Welfare and Business Management, Kolkata. Apart from providing materials they have also given some bibliographic leads.

Finally, but not the least important, we would like to thank our parents, spouses and children for their understanding and generosity. They have patiently borne with the neglect of even family chores and duties that our academic preoccupations have during the last few months forced on us. Their encouragement and the sacrificial giving of themselves have been exemplary.

Dr. Sarbani Mitra
Dr. Krishna M. Agrawal
Dr. Satyajit Dhar

CONTENTS

Part–IV

PART–I

1

INTRODUCTION

In the recent past corporate world had witnessed many-fold increase in the requirements of the environmental regulations in the business practice. Such requirements are likely to be further strengthened in the future. This warrants businesses to take more responsibility for the environmental damage that they create and to approach corporate environmental management in a more proactive way.

Numerous conventions and legislations have been hammered out, covering matters as the prevention and control of the environmental pollution and protection of environment from time to time throughout the world. Decisions to take appropriate steps for the preservation of the quality of air/water and control of air/water pollution have already been started since 1972, when India participated in the United Nations Conference on the Human Environment held in Stockholm. The forest and wildlife laws also have a long history and are the cumulative result of an increasing awareness of the compelling need to restore the catastrophic ecological imbalances introduced by the depredations inflicted on nature by human being. Gradually, the environmental appraisal of any industry/business was made mandatory under the provision of the environmental legislations to ensure the optimal utilisation of natural resources and minimisation of adverse impact on environment. For the purpose of grant of consent to establish and operate for the different industries, the Minimal National Standards (MINAS) and

Emission Standards were prescribed by the Central Pollution Control Board in consultation with the State Pollution Control Boards (Mohanty, 1997).

Accordingly, the beginning of 21st century have witnessed the fast changing business environment in our country and gradual changes in customers' expectations that have made it necessary to companies to take a proactive approach to deal with problems relating to environmental pollution control and management.

Globally, the companies are faced with the challenge of integrating environmental considerations into their production and marketing plans. The major concern to environmental management is determining ways in which industrial action can be made compatible with nature. When we say that business should contribute to the good of the society, it implies that business has an obligation both for stakeholders and environment. Here, the concept of corporate social responsibility comes up (Bowen, 1953). Further, it is attempted to aim at taking a holistic and integrated approach towards environmental management in corporate scenario for carrying capacity based sustainable development.

However, corporate strategy has been driven in the past by different forces viz. production pressures, personnel pressures, information pressures, etc. The beginning of 21st century shows clear signs of corporate strategy being driven by environmental pressures. Major changes in corporate strategy are clearly visible due to the increased environmental concerns of stakeholders and the belief that being 'green' pays through cost reduction and increased market entry (Bhargava and Welford, 1999).

Problem Identification

The following three problems had been identified that were associated with the incorporation of environmental issues in business practice:

First, very little was known about the extent of incorporation of environmental issues in business practice in case of Indian companies. Whereas, from the regulators' standpoint, this information is important in deciding whether the units are meeting the regulatory requirements; whether units are adopting specific precautionary/preventive measures to mitigate environmental pollution; whether the units have certification[1] or not.

Second, despite a high level of compliance, the management of units may be reluctant regarding commitment, proper communication, imparting motivation and training/ development to the employees regarding the environmental issues that would provide certain pieces of vital information which are relevant for decision making from the part of bottom level management and staff members.

Third, little empirical evidence was available regarding unit specific determinants, which might explain the variation, if any, in the extent of environmental performance.

Need of Integration of Environmental Issues in Business Practices

As environmental considerations are likely to be a source of quite profound changes in business practice, it was attempted to provide managers the strategic plan for the environmental management. Given the internal and external demands to improve the environmental performance of a company, those companies that achieve high standards of environmental performance are reaping benefits in the form of better productivity, reduced waste generation, energy conservation, regulatory compliance and a better image among their customers and in the market place. Moreover, a realisation has dawned that improving environmental performance can lead to cost savings and better efficiency which will in the long term enable companies to compete in the global marketplace. In the quest to generate dynamic competitive advantages, many firms in fact are looking for innovative ways and means to re-conceptualise their products and services (Sawhney and Jose, 2003).

Peter Drucker, a legend of modern management, enlightened "one is responsible for one's impacts whether they are intended or not. This is the first rule. There is no doubt regarding management's business". He further added, "Responsibility for socio impacts is a management's responsibility not because it is a social responsibility but because it is a business responsibility" (Drucker, 1975). So, it was here highlighted whether economic growth driven by business will help us to move towards a sustainable use of the world's environmental resources.

A good environmental profile is often more of an asset for a firm than a liability in the international market-place, notwithstanding somewhat higher production costs. Thus, entrepreneurs can be able to take decision where to reduce energy, how to recycle wastes, how to reduce the amount of product packaging, where to adopt a corporate environmental policy, where to conduct environmental audit, etc. Again, business would unambiguously raise welfare, if proper environmental policies were in place. Therefore, the biggest challenge to the interests of global business today is the task of reconciling the demands of sustainable development and corporate strategy.

The first Chapter (Chapter 1) under this Part mainly deals with genesis of corporate environmental management. Chapter 2 discusses about strategic dimensions of environmental management activities. Chapter 3 highlights environmental issues in the Indian business units. In Chapter 4 basic issues in assessment of environmental management in business practice are discussed.

NOTES

1. There are basically two type's certifications in the area of quality and environment management:

    (i) The ISO 9000 standards, that are quality standards, affect an organisation and its customers. These standards have been recognised as adding value to organisation's quality management programmes. The standards in the ISO 9000 series are: ISO 9001, ISO 9002 and ISO 9003.

    (ii) The ISO 14000 standards, that are environmental standards, have a greater reach and affect an organisation's relationship to its neighbours, nearby creatures and ecologies and ultimately human kind. In ISO 14000 series, the equivalent of the three ISO 9000 standards is ISO 14001. The ISO 14000 standards establish benchmarks for environmental management performance and describe the measures that industry must take to conform to these standards. ISO 14020 through 14024 deals with environmental labelling requirements, ISO 14040 through ISO 14043 deal with life-cycle assessment procedures and ISO 14060 (still under development) addresses environmental aspects of products. Moreover, Occupational Health and Safety Assessment Series (OHSAS 18001) have been developed to be compatible with the ISO 9001 (Quality) and ISO 14001 (Environmental) management system standards, in order to facilitate the integration of quality, environmental and occupational health and safety management system by organisations.

2

GENESIS OF CORPORATE ENVIRONMENTAL MANAGEMENT

Several studies have been conducted on corporate environmental management. Such studies include Madsen and Ulhoi (1996, 1997, 1999, 2001) and Madsen (2003) in the context of Danish industry; Ilinitch, Soderstrom and Thomas (1998) in the context of US; Wehrmeyer *et al.* (2002) in the context of United Kingdom and Germany; OECD (2004) in the context of Europe, North America and the Asia-Pacific region; Zhu and Sarkis (2004) in the context of Chinese enterprises; Takahashi and Nakamura (2005) and Ito (2006) in the context of Japanese companies; The Northern Ireland Eighth Environmental Management Survey (2006) in the context of Northern Ireland; Sohal and Zutshi (2006) and Zutshi (2006) in the context of Australia and New Zealand. Now, the question is: What should managers do to promote corporate greening[1]? Academic literature concerning corporate environmental management provides valuable insights into this question, but relatively few studies have been published on sufficiently concrete ideas based on which firms can formulate their action plans.

Corporate Environmental Management and Competitiveness

Madsen and Ulhoi (1996, 1997, 1999, 2001) made empirical study on corporate environmental management considering 500 Danish companies as sample size. According to Madsen and Ulhoi, the concept of corporate environmental and resource management has been developed to assist companies to reduce, evaluate, monitor and control the environmental impact. Implementation of this concept in business presents a challenge to management, since it implies a fundamental change in some of the ways of operating a company. Accordingly, the study characterised the actual situation of corporate environmental management in Danish companies. Madsen and Ulhoi (1996) contrasted different types of companies like reactive versus proactive ones. Madsen and Ulhoi (1997) carried out a more detailed analysis by means of a factor analysis to identify drivers in introducing environmental management. Madsen and Ulhoi (1999) described the overall situation of application of the various elements in corporate environmental management. Madsen and Ulhoi (2001) also evaluated environmental management practices in relation to the theory of stakeholder management. Statistical techniques were applied as well especially when differences in types or size of companies can be expected in characterising attitudes and the degree of environmental initiatives. Furthermore, it was considered to apply structural equation models in order to obtain a deeper insight into potential relationships.

The series of work of Madsen and Ulhoi (1996, 1997, 1999, 2001) was a major work regarding environmental proactiveness of business units. Their work was a pointer towards determinants that make drive introduction of environment management in business practice. However, they had not measured environmental performance of the business units quantitatively.

Now, the question was whether managers perceive corporate environmental initiatives as a challenge leading to new strategic options and, eventually, increased competitiveness, or whether they regard it as yet another burden. Madsen (2003) made an empirical study on corporate environmental management practices. Based on a number of surveys, his paper discussed contemporary trends in the implementation of environmental management system in Danish industry upto the beginning of the new millennium in an attempt to identify any related effects on competitiveness. Madsen (2003) added that the last decade or so had seen an increase in concern about environmental issues, especially in the West, where many unpleasant side-effects of industrial production had captured the headlines more and more often. This, in turn, has led to an increasing public and political focus on the negative consequences of present production and ways of life, which could threaten conditions for future generations. This has resulted in a spate of environmental legislations and agreements at international, regional, national and local levels, as well as voluntary initiatives. Business organisations tend to regard this either as yet another burden or as a new challenge. It is now more than a decade since mainstream industrial economists, namely Porter and van der Linde (1995) strongly opposed the reactive view that environmental regulations were just another burden that could erode competitiveness. Rather, they argued, by constantly looking for innovative solutions to increasing environmental regulations, companies would be able to tackle the challenge proactively, which could make them more, not less, competitive. The concept of corporate environmental management was introduced to help managers handle this new situation. The application of this concept has been described in terms of strategic advantages (for example, Welford and Gouldson, 1993; Welford, 1995; Ulhoi, 1997), which may lead to increased competitiveness. However, interest in implementing the principles behind corporate greening seems to have slowed of late, in part because of the perceived decreasing influence of various stakeholders, including customers (Madsen and Ulhoi, 2001). Madsen (2003) added that corporate environmental management can be considered as an attempt to translate the concept of environmental sustainability into an operational tool for company managers, since it is concerned with how companies analyse, handle and solve their environmental problems (for example, Ulhoi, 1997). But, as Welford (1995) pointed out, it is only a first step towards more universal sustainable attitudes and behaviour. Nonetheless, it is an important step, since it enables companies to go from reactive pollution prevention (end-of-pipe solutions) to a more proactive platform, where environmental issues are more or less integrated in all functional areas (clean-at-source solutions). Madsen's study concluded by saying that adopting the principles of corporate environmental management includes the formulation of an environmental strategy, which has clear relations to other strategic issues, such as corporate goals and product positioning. In other words, it must be considered as an element that can influence a company's competitive position. Reactive pollution prevention normally implies extra production costs: that is, a negative influence on competitiveness. On the other hand, a proactive attitude normally indicates an innovative climate. The result could be cost savings or improvements in a product's value, which in turn will make the company more competitive (Porter and van der Linde, 1995). However, it is important to note that the temporary adoption of a proactive environmental approach will not necessarily give a competitive advantage. A proactive environmental attitude requires continuous and dynamic development centred on organisational learning processes for new innovations to defend or improve the competitive position (Ulhoi, 1997). Madsen (2003) further added that another way of looking at the environment-competitiveness relationship is to compare a company's environmental performance with other. Accordingly, his paper was an excellent attempt to make a relationship between corporate environmental management performance and competitiveness. He tried to identify different elements of corporate environmental management. Yet, his discussion seemed to be of subjective nature.

Environmental Proactiveness of Business Units

Welford and Gouldson (1993) identified key environmental performance areas in organisations. These areas are 'the company and its products', 'direct environmental impacts', 'infrastructure' and 'external relations'. These areas were splitted into further sub-sections, giving a spectrum coverage of the company where 'the company and its product(s), processes, procedures and operations' cover areas such as the involvement and integration of the company in the supply chain and the product(s)' use and disposal; 'direct environmental impacts' areas include energy use and the impacts of the company on nature and ecosystems;

'infrastructure' environmental performance areas include buildings and management systems; 'external relations' environmental performance areas include education and environmental initiatives.

Welford and Gouldson logically pointed out the key determinants for environmental proactiveness. But, they did not demonstrate it by any case study that could reveal how those determinants would be integrated in operational practices to measure environmental performance of a business unit in real life situation.

Ashford and Meima (1993), Fiksel (1994) and James (1994) explored the principal drivers and beneficiaries of environmental performance. The general groups of principal drivers are: 'financial stakeholders' including investors; 'non-financial stakeholders' that include people, buyers, community demands, regulatory pressures, employee satisfaction, customer conscience; 'company systems' that cover cost minimisation, profitability improvement, competitive differentiation; and 'standardisation' that covers top quality management, programme requirements, international and national standards. Ashford and Meima (1993) explained that the environmental performance of the firm is the extent and effectiveness of actions which the firm takes to mitigate its environmental consequences.

Although Ashford and Meima, Fiksel and James critically identified the principal drivers for environmental proactiveness, their study seemed to be of more theoretical and subjective in nature than objective and practical-oriented.

Epstein (1995)'s study measured Corporate Environmental Performance as the best practices for costing and managing an Effective Environmental Strategy. Epstein (1995) identified ten indicators for corporations to measure their environmental performance. He added that environmental performance provides specific guidance on approaches to implementing a corporate environmental policy. The research report relied on a review of internal and public documents of 100 leading corporations, and interviews conducted at more than 30 companies. According to Epstein, CEOs have recognised the strong likelihood that in the next decade their corporations will be held responsible for post-consumer waste. This could occur in the form of "product take-backs," which will require companies to be responsible for the ultimate reuse, recycling, or disposal of the products they produce. Epstein stated that companies that have made a start in best practices for costing and managing an effective environmental strategy need to continue those practices to maintain their leadership position, because leadership in this arena brings competitive advantages and many of the laggards are beginning to make progress.

Epstein's study depicted a clear picture of the indicators for measuring environmental performance. The study was truly exceptional, as it directed the corporate manager to focus on those particular issues while considering the environmental management in the business practice. But the study did not measure the extent of relationship of each of those indicators to the environmental performance.

Global Environmental Management Initiative (1998) made a survey of tools (metrics) for measuring environmental performance of 41 companies. For the purpose, it used metrics that include lagging indicators, which measure outputs (such as pounds of pollutants emitted or discharged); leading indicators, which are in-process measures of performance; and environmental condition indicators, which measure the direct effect of an activity on the environment. The study revealed that metrics (tools) can measure the business value of environmental programmes or progress as well as the environmental performance of business operations. This can be particularly effective in demonstrating the value of environmental efforts to management. It can also provide data with which business units can design more efficient processes, decreasing material usage and environmental impacts while at the same time increasing yield and profitability. Selecting meaningful and effective tools for measuring environmental performance is becoming increasingly important due to the increasing costs of environmental operations; market, regulatory and public pressures; voluntary initiatives, such as the International

Chamber of Commerce Business Principles for Sustainable Development; and international standards, such as ISO 14001. The study also included trends in environmental performance measurement. The purpose of this study was to present a survey of environmental performance measurement tools (or "metrics") and present considerations for designing a metrics programme; selecting appropriate metrics; and for implementing, evaluating and improving such a programme. But, the study did not empirically explore the importance and the level of significance of each of those indicators to environmental proactiveness and business competitiveness.

Ilinitch, Soderstrom and Thomas (1998) used theoretical and empirical approaches to define corporate environmental performance (EP) and to consider how well existing measures operationalise the construct in the U.S. Interestingly, some popular environmental rating schemes seem to rely more heavily on public reaction to environmental events than on more precise and measurable outcome or process dimensions. The findings suggested a need for explicit environmental performance metrics in order to provide stakeholders with more reliable, consistent and accurate information for comparing companies and making key strategic decisions and regulating information about company performance. It has been argued that the accounting profession is an obvious candidate for establishing such metrics, since the domain of accounting typically includes measuring, communicating and regulating information about company performance. Expanding accountants' domain to include environmental performance can greatly contribute to the usefulness of environmental performance metrics.

Ilinitch, Soderstrom and Thomas put stress on environmental accounting and reporting for measuring environmental performance of business units. But the approach seemed to be of one-sided. It is logical that environmental accounting and reporting is a necessary condition for environmental proactiveness, but it is not the only one indicator. There are a number of indicators that are needed to be considered during incorporation of environmental issues in business practice.

Dehua, Chan and Liyin (2004) investigated the feasibility of developing an Environmental Performance Scoring System (EPSS) to measure a construction contractor's environmental performance through deployment of the proposed Environmental Performance Score (EPS). It was expected that the system will also assist contractors in diagnosing the causes of poor environmental performance to develop preventive measures. It was proposed that contractor who obtains a certain level of EPS is certified with a Green-Construction Award (GCA). It was estimated that the EPSS will provide a mechanism for determining the suitability of a contractor to receive a GCA.

Dehua, Chan and Liyin's approach to identify the Environmental Performance Scoring System is truly exceptional. If the same concept could be applied for whole business practice, it would provide a holistic view of business competitiveness due to consideration of environmental practices in operational processes of business units.

OECD (2004) also made an empirical study that focussed the extent to which 1509 companies in Europe (498), North America (518) and the Asia-Pacific region (493) provided internationally comparable information on the development and adoption of advanced environmental management practices. The structure reflected a simplified adaptation of the main elements of environmental management procedures in the sense that environmental management techniques are assumed to develop in three steps (environmental policy, environmental management system, environmental performance reporting). Under the first step of the issuance of an environmental policy statement, it was also mentioned that these observations need to be assessed against the background of considerable sectoral differences in corporate issuance of environmental policy statements. It was found that environmental policy statements almost invariably include a commitment to comply with the laws (95% of all companies), and that there are very limited geographic differences in this respect—although this does not take into account the difference between best practices and minimal legal requirements across the regions. It was explored that an interesting, but also potentially confusing, indicator regards companies' commitments to operate on higher standards than legally required. Another important indicator is the number of enterprises that allocate the responsibility for their environmental policy statements to the board level, and hence are perceived to attach a high level of managerial interest to them. Secondly, at more advanced levels of environmental practices, companies put in place formal management systems to control the environmental impacts of their operations. Respondents were requested to indicate the extent to which they had introduced different 'advanced management practices' (i.e. full-cost accounting, total quality management, etc.), and to rate the extent to which these were integrated with environmental management on a scale from 1 to 3. This will allow for an assessment of the 'value added' provided by environmental management relative to other management practices (i.e. does environmental accounting contribute to improved environmental performance in different areas beyond the contribution arising from the application of full-cost accounting?). The study also dealt with the relative importance of some of the relationships between environmental management system and the characteristics of the organisation and the market. Various tools have been developed to assist companies in implementing their EMSs, including Environmental Impact Assessment, Environmental Accounting and Auditing and Life Cycle Assessment. These tools may be employed for assessing and monitoring environmental impacts, setting a course of action and providing means of communication. Finally, a commitment to environmental performance reporting is integrated into most companies' environmental management system, but it is in practice often one of the last elements to be put into place. For the purposes of this study, environmental reporting refers to the practice of making information on environmental performance available to the public, whether in a stand-alone environmental report or included in the company's annual report. There are few widely accepted standards to help enterprises decide which information should be included in their environmental performance reports. In the absence of an agreed standard for environmental reporting, enterprises make their own choices as regards the scope and depth of their reporting. Four indicators of differences between the contents and scope of existing environmental performance reports are the publishing of quantitative data; whether performance is compared with targets; whether the report is verified by a third party; and whether the report includes environmental cost accounting.

OECD's study on development and adoption of advanced environmental management practices are really worthwhile for any business unit. If such kind of study could be undertaken in Indian perspective, it would be really helpful for regulators/ policy-makers as well as business units of India.

Takahashi and Nakamura (2005) made an empirical analysis on corporate greening processes within 193 large Japanese manufacturing firms. They stated that depending on the type of models that defined their framework, literature on corporate environmental management can be divided into two categories: economic models and sociological models. The economic models assume that firms perform rational actions in order to maximise their objective functions such as profits or firms' values. On the other hand, the sociological models assume that firms are firstly social groups that may not pursue profit maximisation, while the preconditions of their long-term existence make pursuit of survival a must. In several cases, studies employing sociological models segment a variety of firms into several stages to facilitate the differentiation of a firm's environmental progressiveness by assigning a stage to each company. Takahashi and Nakamura (2005) argued that generally, neither type of study has focussed on variables that corporate managers can manage in order to improve their firms' environmental management. Studies employing economic models usually choose variables that managers find difficult to change, such as firm size or industry sector. Studies employing sociological models often choose external variables such as social pressure or social norms. Accordingly, in this study, they have chosen variables that are linked to firms' organisational structures in environmental management and that can also be changed at will when firms' managers desire to do so. Possible relationships between firms' environmental organisational structures and corporate greening were examined using the qualitative comparative analysis (QCA) technique. Three dimensions of bureaucratisation (i.e., formalisation, centralisation and professionalisation) were chosen as the independent variables. They defined the dependent variable, corporate greening, as the development of corporate management wherein the corporate members exhibit a concern for the natural environment. They expected complex relationships between the independent variables (the three dimensions of bureaucratisation) and seven dependent variables (comparison with other companies, corporate strategy, decision making, new technology, sharing of ideas, necessity, culture). The analysis indicated that the bureaucratisation of environmental management generally promotes corporate greening. Different aspects of corporate greening require different factors or different combinations of the factors of bureaucratisation.

It was found that bureaucratisation of environmental management generally has a positive relationship with corporate greening and that the presence of one or two of the three dimensions of bureaucratisation may be sufficient for corporate greening to implement certain greening measures. Further, the positive relationship between the ISO 14001 certification and bureaucratisation elicits the view that implementing ISO 14001 EMS is the bureaucratisation of environmental management. This view is also supported by the ISO 14001 standard text itself.

Due to the nature of QCA, the study could not conduct a statistical test to check the statistical certainty of the results. The measurement of variables relies on a manager's perception and lacks reliability to a certain extent. The results of this study are applicable to firms that are either in the early stages of environmental management or at stages similar to those of the survey respondents' firms at the time of the survey. It should be pointed out, however, that even though environmental management by firms is a global movement, the style of implementing environmental management may be significantly affected by country culture.

However, Takahashi and Nakamura rightly mentioned about different unit specific determinants as dependent variables. Even, the attempt to make relationship between environmental organisational structures and corporate greening ushered a new era in the corporate environmental management study. But, they overemphasised the term 'bureaucratisation'. Corporate greening could be analysed based on some basic environmental indicators, which appeared to be missing in their study.

Consumers, corporations and the government are becoming more conscious of the importance of environmentally friendly business. Ito (2006) made a study on increase in environmental consciousness in Japanese business involving 1399 samples. It is explored that Japanese companies, realising the value of environmental conservation, are shifting their perception of conservation from social obligation to business opportunity. Under new initiatives for eco-friendly business, the study put stress on a number of variables viz., greater awareness on environmental management system, environmental accounting, environmental reporting, environmental ranking; financial support for eco-conscious financial products (financial institutions have been quick to offer environmentally related financial products to support capital investment in conservation) and eco funds (which invest in companies that excel in dealing with environmental issues or that offer superior environmental technology or services). Further, new regulatory frameworks are promoting greater awareness among corporations and consumers alike. The government, for example, developed a new framework where importance was given on environmental reports, environmental accounting, environmental labels, environmental management system, life cycle assessment, environmental performance ratings, support tools for small and midsised enterprises and environmentally compatible design. The study concluded by saying that a growing number of companies consider conservation an intrinsic part of business strategy and numerous methods have been devised to support investment in such companies.

However, the study did not provide clear guideline of how those indicators are integrated in operational practices in real life situation to measure the environmental performance of business units.

Sohal and Zutshi (2006) studied EMS adoption in the public sector in Australia. The objectives of the study were to demonstrate the government's commitment to lead by example by taking actions to reduce environmental impacts associated with its own operations; to contribute to the achievement of environmental outcomes through minimising the release of greenhouse gases, reducing wastes and conserving energy, and other resources; to drive cultural changes across government departments in relation to integrating environmental considerations into daily activities; to contribute to the achievement of efficiency gains and result financial savings by reducing the use of office-based resources; and finally, to maintain the state's leadership in transparency and openness in performance reporting by government departments. The study revealed that more exploratory and empirical research is required to document and enhance the understanding of the EMS adoption process in government departments. The objectives of the study were part of the state government's commitment to balance its social, environmental and economic goals.

However, Sohal and Zutshi put stress only one indicator i.e. EMS to measure environmental performance of the business units. There are a number of indicators to evaluate environmental proactiveness. If at least the prime indicators could be covered in the study, then it would provide an integrated and holistic approach.

The Northern Ireland Eighth Environmental Management Survey (2006) aimed to raise the profile of environmental issues amongst leading 200 companies, 26 local authorities, 19 health and social service trusts and the 5 education and library boards in Northern Ireland and encourage improvement in environmental management and performance. The Survey designed to test how well organisations have developed their approach to environmental management, assess how well they are performing and promote the commitment of senior managers to environmental issues. The Survey continued to place equal emphasis on environmental management and improving performance. With organisations from across the public and private sectors, the Survey provided a truly representative picture of how well environmental issues are dealt with by organisations in Northern Ireland. Consequently, the Survey put stress on major three parameters: Management (this section accounted for 50 per cent of the overall score and focusses on management arrangements within an organisation. It covered the basic principles of environmental management, such as having a well defined policy and objectives, but also took into account supply chain management and product stewardship), Performance (this section aimed to measure how well an organisation monitored its most significant environmental impacts and improved its performance. There were four questions: two core (energy and waste) and two free choice, allowing participants to focus on areas that are unique or important to them. All performance questions were equally weighted and the section as a whole accounted for 50 per cent of the overall score), Assurance (Participation in the Survey required 'sign-off' by a senior manager to provide assurance that adequate management processes were in place and that information provided was accurate and of an acceptable quality. It did not contribute to the overall score but is a requirement of participation). Even, to raise the profile of environmental issues among organisations in Northern Ireland and encourage improvement in environmental management and performance, the Northern Ireland Eighth Environmental Management Survey (2006) chose environmental policy, environmental audit, level of regulatory compliance, certification status, level of management bearing the responsibility to control environment department, employee awareness and training programme, etc. as prime environmental indicators. Finally, the balance between scores achieved in the management and performance sections of the Survey demonstrated that developing a robust approach to environmental management often leads to improvements in performance.

The Survey put stress on environmental indicators besides other management issues. It developed a framework to assess how far the environmental indicators improve the corporate performance. But it did not undertake cost-benefit analysis during consideration of environmental issues.

Zutshi (2006) made a study on implementation of EMS in Australian organisations (359 in Australia and 12 in New Zealand) certified with ISO 14001. The aim of the survey was to capture the experiences of Australian organisations with ISO 14001 implementation and to document any significant changes in EMS implementation process over the last four years. Similarly, the role of stakeholders (top management, employees and suppliers) was explored both during the EMS planning and implementation stages. The findings of this survey were also compared with a similar survey conducted in late 2000. Fifteen reasons for EMS adoption (on a five point Likert scale, where 1 = Not at all and 5 = To a very large extent) were listed in the questionnaire.

The limitation of this research was that it only focussed on three organisational stakeholders (top management, employees and suppliers) and not other external stakeholders such as customers, government agencies, non-government agencies, and the community.

NOTE

1. Corporate greening is the process by which companies can become more environmentally responsible in their operations. It describes a series of stages by which companies become progressively more environmentally conscious and reduce their impact on the natural environment.

3

STRATEGIC DIMENSIONS OF ENVIRONMENTAL MANAGEMENT ACTIVITIES

Facets of Environmental Issues

Khanna and Anton (2002) made a study on regulatory and market-based incentives in corporate environmental management involving 500 firms. It was investigated that the corporate approach to environmental protection has been evolving from a regulation-driven reactive mode to a more proactive approach involving voluntarily adopted management systems that integrate environmental concerns with traditional managerial functions. This new approach seeks to go beyond a confrontational "government-push" approach to relying on voluntary actions by firms themselves to improve their environmental performance, induced at least in part by public reaction (transmitted through well-functioning product and capital markets and citizen group efforts) to environmental information about firms. This trend towards self-regulation is also evident in the growing number of "business-led" initiatives being taken by firms to systematically integrate environmental considerations into their production decisions. These initiatives include the development of firm structured environmental management systems (EMSs), trade association programmes emphasizing codes of environmental management and international environmental management standards such as those set by ISO. These EMSs represent an organisational change within corporations and an internally motivated effort at environmental self-regulation by adopting management practices that integrate the environment into production decisions, identifying opportunities for pollution (wastes) reduction and implementing plans to make continuous improvement in production methods and environmental performance. Several hypotheses about the factors explaining the diversity in the environmental management system adopted by firms are tested using survey data. The analysis showed that the threat of environmental liabilities, high costs of compliance, market pressures and public pressures on firms with high on-site toxic emissions per unit output create incentives for adopting a more comprehensive environmental management system.

Khanna and Anton put stress on regulatory and market-based incentives in corporate environmental management. Their approach more highlighted the importance of environmental accounting in proactiveness of business units. If some more indicators could be analysed, that could give more integrated approach.

Wehrmeyer *et al.* (2002) made a comparative study of the environmental management activities and strategies adopted by about 2000 firms in the United Kingdom and Germany. As well as looking at what firms in the two countries do to manage their impact on the environment, the study asked what influences them do it, and what prevents them from doing more. The study provided a detailed statistical analysis resulting in the identification of environmental routines and strategies in UK and Germany. This identified significant relationships of different environmental management approaches and corporate environmental strategies with the explanatory factors—firm size, country location and sector membership (initially in the broad categories of service vs. manufacturing sector). It was tried to identify whether there are significant differences in strategic orientation or environmental management approach for different firm sizes. The study identified larger firms firstly more often pursue a 'compliance plus' strategy, and secondly, larger firms are able more often to create positive synergies of their environmental management activities with production in terms of, for example, reducing and better predicting costs and investments. The study also attempted to identify whether there is a link between sector membership [here 'sector coverage' refers to different industry segments producing food and tobacco products, metal products, machines and equipment, transport products, pulp and paper products (excluding timber industry, leather processing and recycling)] and the strategic orientation or environmental management approach of firms. The implication of these findings was that national environmental policy-making needs to take into account sectoral differences when aiming to encourage adoption of more proactive environmental strategies in firms.

Wehrmeyer *et al.*'s study showed a holistic and proactive approach towards environmental management. If the same could be undertaken in Indian perspective, it would definitely be useful for regulators for making policy changes and also for the business units to incorporate environmental issues into overall corporate strategy formulation and implementation at operational levels.

Magrini and Lins (2007) stated that for activities that have a high possibility of causing environmental accidents, like in the oil and gas sector, it is reasonable to expect the *environmental management* to be an important variable within the company's strategic planning. However, this is not always true. In some cases, a change in the companies' attitude, abandoning a reactive position and assuming a proactive one, only happens upon the occurrence of serious environmental accidents with strong repercussion in the media. For the company that was the object of study, these accidents gave rise to deep changes in its *environmental management*, culminating in investments of approximately US$ 2.6 billion in environment, health and security, from 2000 to 2004. This was the highest amount to date invested on these areas by an oil company. This case study aimed to discuss the integration between *environmental management* and strategic planning in the oil and gas sector over a period of 10 years (from 1995 to 2004) in order to make a contextual analysis of the period before and after the environmental accidents.

Magrini and Lins have concentrated only the enterprises where there is high possibility of accident. But small and medium scale industry had totally been overlooked.

Environmental and Economic Performance

Russo and Fouts (1997) stated that drawing on the resource-based view[1] of the firm, *environmental performance* and *economic performance* are positively linked and that industry growth moderates the relationship, with the returns to *environmental performance* higher in high-growth industries. They tested these hypotheses with an analysis of 243 firms over two years, using independently developed *environmental* ratings. Results indicated that 'it pays to be green' and that this relationship strengthens with industry growth.

Russo and Fouts's study is truly logical and exceptional to make a relationship between *environmental* and *economic performance*. But, they did not mention the individual importance of environmental indicators to measure the environmental performance of the business units.

Thornton, Kagan and Gunningham (2003) made an empirical study on pulp manufacturing industry which is a commodity industry and in which firms cannot easily capture and retain market advantages by developing a reputation for greenness. Hence most large improvements in *environmental performance* are linked to expensive investments in new technologies that in turn have been mandated, in effect, by periodic tightening of all firms' regulatory licences. While situations may be different and it is risky to generalise, other capital intensive, highly competitive, mature, highly scrutinised, heavy industries may resemble the pulp industry in the dynamics of *environmental* improvement. *Environmental* management makes a difference, even if it does not achieve the same kind of dramatic, abrupt improvement that results from equipment changes. Day-to-day incremental change can aggregate to significant effects over time, on the order of 50 per cent declines in emissions over a 15-year period. One implication of this analysis was that regulators would be well advised to identify industry leaders, find ways of rewarding them for their beyond compliance and management commitment efforts, and work closely with them in determining what innovations are feasible and can be made the basis of regulations for the entire industry.

Thornton, Kagan and Gunningham targeted only pulp manufacturing industry. The scope of the study would be broadened, if it could comparatively evaluate the environmental performances for different types of industry.

Zhu and Sarkis (2004) stated that globalisation results in both pressure and drivers for Chinese enterprises to improve their *environmental performance*. As a developing country, China has to balance *economic* and *environmental performance*. Green supply chain management (GSCM) is emerging to be an important approach for Chinese enterprises to improve *performance*, possibly on both these dimensions. Using empirical results from 186 respondents on GSCM practice in Chinese manufacturing enterprises, they examined the relationships between GSCM practice and *environmental* and *economic performance*. Using *regression analysis*, they evaluated the general relationships between specific GSCM practices and *performance*. They then investigated how two primary types of management operations philosophies-quality management and just-in-time (or lean) manufacturing principles, influence the relationship between GSCM practices and *performance*.

Zhu and Sarkis put stress on incorporation of environmental issues in supply chain management and accordingly, evaluated its relation with performance of the business units. But the study failed to highlight other functional areas of business units for the purpose of evaluation of *economic performance*.

Wagner (2005) addressed the question with regard to some specific industrial sectors, focusing on the influence of corporate *environmental* strategies (CESs). The two specific corporate *environmental* strategies discussed here are the end-of-pipe and the integrated pollution prevention approaches, as reflected by the actual physical *environmental performance* of the companies, and following the concept of *environmental* shareholder value. The research described applied multiple *regression analysis* to the data in order to understand the relationship between the *environmental* and *economic performance* of firms. The *analysis* took into account the influence of a number of important control variables.

Wagner's study was conducted targeting two strategies, from which the relationship between the *environmental* and economic *performance* of firms had been derived. But distinctly he did not mention any environmental indicator.

Schaltegger and Wagner (2006) provided an overview of how to manage the business case of sustainability. The study discussed the basic link between sustainability performance, competitiveness and economic success, introducing an inversely U-shaped relationship as a generic case. The study also presented the logical corollary of how to measure sustainability performance, business competitiveness and economic success conceptually and empirically, before introducing a framework for the interaction of factors explaining the relationship of sustainability performance and competitiveness. They explored that in a business company, successful management of sustainability performance is achieved only if the management of environmental and social issues is in line with increased competitiveness and economic performance. As a consequence, sustainability management requires an integration of environmental, social and economic management and thus, covers all the links between non-market and economic issues. It was stated that physical environmental performance indicators (EPIs) are one way to describe environmental aspects and thus, physical performance. Such physical EPIs can describe mass, energy or pollutant flows through the manufacturing process (e.g. the use of energy or water resources or the emissions of pollutants from processes or products), which constitute a direct relationship between companies and the environment. Physical EPIs can be quantitative (i.e. measured on a continuous, interval or ratio scale) as discussed in the life cycle assessment literature or qualitative (i.e. measured on a nominal scale; for example, when assessing whether a company is compliant with regard to specific emissions consent conditions). A fairly popular concept for linking environmental with economic performance is the concept of eco-efficiency measuring value added in relation to environmental impact added or the environmental impact caused per monetary unit earned. Sustainability performance measures can thus, embrace the dimensions of sustainability in a more or less integrative manner. The choice of measure may vary substantially depending on the exact question, industry and company considered and on what factors are parts of the respective analysis. With regard to the other core concept, business competitiveness, a first approximation could be to use measures of economic performance such as measures of short-term profitability operationalised in terms of common financial performance ratios. One reason for using economic performance measures instead of indicators of competitiveness might be the difficulty of defining and measuring competitiveness in one dimension.

Schaltegger and Wagner (2006) made a quantitative evaluation of environmental performance of business units. The study truly assessed the relationship of sustainability performance and competitiveness. But it did not put stress on scoring of independent indicators of environmental performance that would ultimately lead towards sustainability.

NOTE

1. The resource-based view (RBV) is an economic tool used to determine the strategic resources available to a firm. The fundamental principle of the RBV is that the basis for a competitive advantage of a firm lies primarily in the application of the bundle of valuable resources at the firm's disposal (Wernerfelt, 1984). To transform a short-run competitive advantage into a sustained competitive advantage requires that these resources are heterogeneous in nature and not perfectly mobile. Effectively, this translates into valuable resources that are neither perfectly imitable nor substitutable without great effort (Prahalad and Hamel, 1990; Hoopes, 2003). If these conditions hold, the firm's bundle of resources can assist the firm sustaining above average returns.

4

ENVIRONMENTAL ISSUES IN THE INDIAN BUSINESS UNITS

At the outset, it may be mentioned that Indian studies on environmental performance related issues are not very extensive. Only a few studies (Gupta and Goldar, 2003; Chakrabarti and Mitra, 2005; Pahuja, 2006; etc.) have examined the environmental issues in the context of Indian business units. For the purpose of our discussion we have bifurcated those studies into two parts, namely environmental management related issues and environmental accounting and finance related issues.

Environmental Management Related Issues

Agrawal and Mitra (2004) made an assessment of prospects of implementation of Environmental Management System in Indian Industries. The prime objective of the study was to evaluate that the ISO 14000 standards are used as intended, and not as a barrier to trade, especially in the Indian context. The study was also intended to highlight the potential benefits and threats of the EMS to encourage the new companies to go for ISO 14001 certification. The study involved a sample survey through structured questionnaire that was conducted among a number of ISO 14001 certified companies covering major industrial sectors viz., power plants, petrochemicals, cement, textile, pulp and paper, automobile, etc. located in the eastern and northern part of the country. The analysis revealed that the main reasons in order of priority for adopting EMS were to improve image of the company, to achieve cost reduction by minimising waste and pollution, to account for the social responsibility and to gain competitive advantage. The most common difficulty reported to implement EMS was defining the full range of environmental aspects, lack of top management commitment and provision of inadequate budget.

Agrawal and Mitra put stress on only one prime indicator (EMS) of proactiveness of business units. So, such study could be considered as a starting point to analyse the attempt of firms to be proactive in environmental management.

Dutta, Agrawal and Mitra (2004) put stress on incorporation of environmental management into the overall business strategy and accordingly, developed a strategic framework for corporate environmental management that depicted how environmental consideration leads corporate entrepreneurs to reshape the strategic planning for the purpose of achieving corporate image and for gaining competitive advantage. They stated that corporate entrepreneurs have begun to realise that 'green issues' or 'green management' is not a passing fad but is here to stay even in the developing country like India. Strategies associated with corporate environmental management, and integrating a systems-based approach into those strategies, is the road down which should be followed. So, companies are now taking a more positive attitude to environmental regulations. Tighter environmental policy will impact on the costs of industry; however, increasingly, a high level of environmental protection will become not only a policy objective of its own, but also a precondition of industrial expansion. In this respect, a new impetus towards a better integration of policies aiming at consolidating industrial competitiveness and at achieving a high level of protection of the environment is necessary in order to make the two objectives fully mutually supportive. Some companies have even begun to realise that they can influence the regulations that are introduced, in such a way as to increase competitive advantage. One way of doing this is by moving beyond compliance, in anticipation of future legislations and converting what might have become legislations into voluntary codes of conduct. Such a strategy enables a company to minimise the disruption caused by complying with new regulations, and to seize market opportunities. Tackling environmental problems requires a concerted and cooperative effort. The balancing of the economic growth/environmental trade-off is likely to determine the success of any policies. But there also needs to be concerted and cooperative political motivations. There will be those who will argue, therefore, that the attainment of an effective and concerted environmental policy will require political and economic union. Significant environmental improvement will only be attained with the cooperation and commitment of producers.

Dutta, Agrawal and Mitra explained about the strategic decisions to incorporate environmental issues in business practice. But the study did not mention the quantitative techniques to incorporate those issues in business practice. Also, they did not attempt to measure the environmental performance of business units.

Chakrabarti and Mitra (2005) made an empirical study on cost-benefit analysis of air pollution control technology in Indian perspective. For the purpose, eight secondary lead smelting units in Picnic Garden and four in Kankurgachi were surveyed. The objective of the study was to compare the costs incurred by the firms for the installation of the pollution abatement technology with the benefit obtained from it. The study also aimed to suggest a methodology to measure the efficiency of the evolved technology. The use of air pollution control technology is a measure for maintaining the balance in the environment, which obviously has two sides, it creates values and it imposes costs. To a producer in a smelting unit the investment for the installation of any abatement technology along with its operation and maintenance cost is an additional one over and above the cost of production. Regarding running costs, the different components include cost of maintenance, cost of electricity and cost of replacement of bags. On the other hand, benefit may be obtained from the use of device in two ways, by preserving heat for the use of improved 'vatti' required for operating the device which saves the consumption of fuel i.e. coal, an important input and by reusing the dust collected with the help of cyclone/impact separator and bag filter as input. A profit maximising producer or private investor takes the investment decision regarding control technology by taking into account the net profit at the margin. From this point of view, it is the involved cost and the generated profit that are crucial variables in determining the choice of control technology. So this study was an attempt in estimating the net benefits that was achieved by the units and society at large, from the adoption of control device, even though it involves additional installation cost. The findings of the study helped the other units to undertake similar investment decisions regarding the adoption of the developed technology. It was also revealed that apart from the financial profitability considerations, this system involves also considerable social and environmental significance for the workers and the immediate neighbourhood surrounding the units.

Chakrabarti and Mitra's study is truly exceptional to attempt to undertake cost-benefit analysis of control technology taking into consideration of only one type of business unit (smelting). The other units operating in different industry segments had not been considered here.

Environmental Accounting and Finance Related Issues

Gupta and Goldar (2003) conducted an event study to examine the impact of environmental performance of 17 large pulp and paper, 15 automobile and 18 chlor alkali firms in India on their stock prices. They explored that the dissemination of knowledge about weak environmental performance of companies tends to lower the return to investors holding the stocks of such companies. The study undertook a life cycle assessment (LCA) beginning from raw material procurement to product recycling that was used to study the environmental impact of a firm. It should also be noted, however, that the weights assigned to various criteria vary substantially across the three sectors based on their inherent characteristics. For instance, in the case of pulp and paper firms, maximum weight was given to procurement of raw material and production phases, whereas for automobile firms highest weight was assigned to the product use phase. This reflects the implicit assumption that environmental impacts of different sectors occur at different stages of the life cycle. It is also important to note that such study benchmarks environmental performance against 'theoretical best practice' for the various components/criteria. In other words, companies/plants/products are not rated against current environmental norms, standards or regulations but against an ideal best practice. In fact, full compliance with current environmental regulations merely fetches a score of 2 on a 10 point scale. Specifically, such rating uses the following scores on a 10 point scale for each component/criterion: Indian average/standard/legal requirement 2, global best practice 8, theoretical best practice 10. In other words, wherever a domestic source specific discharge standard exists it is taken as the lowest benchmark (2 points). In case there is no such standard as in the case of SO_2 emissions, the average discharge for all plants in the sample is taken as the lowest benchmark and below average performance is given zero, the best performance gets 8 and there is a linear scale between 2 and 85. The points given to global best practice and theoretical best practice reflect an incentive for better environmental performance. It is, therefore, important to bear in mind that the rating emphasises over-compliance with current standards or practices. The aim of the study was to investigate whether the capital market in India responded significantly to the announcement of the ratings of plants belonging to these industries and the nature of this response. For the purpose, market model was used for carrying out an event study.

The study pointed to the fact that capital markets react to environmental news and thus, create incentives for pollution control in both developed and emerging market economies. The study found that the market generally penalises environmentally un-friendly behaviour as announcement of weak environmental performance by firms lead to negative abnormal returns to the extent of 43 per cent. A positive correlation is found between positive abnormal returns to a firm's stock and the level of its environmental performance. These findings should be viewed as further evidence of the important role that capital markets could play in environmental management, particularly in developing countries where environmental monitoring and enforcement are weak.

In sum, the study lends credence to the view that even in emerging market economies such as India, capital markets can: (i) leverage monitoring and enforcement activities, (ii) act as an additional environmental pressure point on firms, and (iii) create incentives for participation in voluntary environmental programmes.

Gupta and Goldar highlighted the impact of environmental performance of specific types of industry on their stock prices. So, their findings might not match irrespective of all industry segments.

Pahuja (2006) made a study on accountants' response to environmental accounting and reporting challenges in Indian perspective. The main objective of the study was to analyse the problems and challenges in the area of environmental accounting and reporting. Environmental reporting means incorporation of environmental issues into annual reports or other statements prepared by corporate entities. An attempt has also been made to examine the need for a specific regulatory framework (including accounting guidelines, principles and standards) in this area. Opinions of 101 senior Chartered Accountants (CAs) were obtained on the issues raised in the study. The study found out that due to growing social and legal pressures in recent years, a business has to take care of environment around it. Establishment of a good EMS helps in maintaining clean and green environment around the factories, controlling pollution emission and thereby meeting legal standards in this area. The study also explored that few adjustments may be required to make the current financial accounting framework more comprehensive to cover specific environmental accounting issues. It was also identified that there is a need for some separate standard on environment and some important accounting standards need to be revised to deal with specific environmental accounting problems like depreciation of environmental assets or measurement of environmental benefits. The study reinforced a great need for development of a separate conceptual framework and a standard on environmental accounting and reporting to help companies in properly identifying, measuring, recognising and disclosing relevant environmental costs, benefits, assets, liabilities and contingencies. The need for introducing mandatory environmental reporting in India has also been felt. The regulatory authorities and accounting profession in India has to respond to the issue of environmentalism and help the companies in dealing with environmental matters in the books of accounts.

Pahuja's study was undertaken targeting a number of senior chartered accountants. The responses from the management level who are dealing the environmental issues were totally absent. Therefore, the result seemed to be one-sided in nature.

5

BASIC ISSUES IN ASSESSMENT OF ENVIRONMENTAL MANAGEMENT IN BUSINESS PRACTICES

Basic issues in assessment of environmental management in business practices reviewed in the preceding sections are summarised below:

Selection of Environmental Indicators

A considerable number of studies have been undertaken to select the indicators for assessing the proactiveness. In the field of environmental performance, some authors used the term environmental performance indicators (EPIs), which are presented briefly as follows:

Welford and Gouldson (1993) identified key environmental performance areas in organisations, which are 'the company and its products', 'direct environmental impacts', 'infrastructure' and 'external relations'. Further, 'the company and its product(s), processes, procedures and operations' cover areas such as the involvement and integration of the company in the supply chain and the product(s)' use and disposal; 'direct environmental impacts' areas include energy use and the impacts of the company on nature and ecosystems; 'infrastructure' environmental performance areas include buildings and management systems; 'external relations' environmental performance areas include education and environmental initiatives.

According to Ashford and Meima (1993), Fiksel (1994) and James (1994), some of the principal environmental drivers are: 'regulatory pressures', 'cost minimisation', 'profitability improvement', 'competitive differentiation', 'top quality management', 'environmental programme requirement', 'international and national standards', etc.

Epstein (1995) identified ten indicators for corporations to measure their environmental performance. Those are: 'corporate environmental strategy', 'integrating environmental concerns into product design systems', 'systems for identifying, organising, and managing *environmental* impacts', 'information systems for internal reporting', 'internal environmental auditing systems', 'external environmental reporting and external environmental audits', 'costing systems', 'capital budgeting systems', 'integrating environmental impacts into performance evaluation systems' and 'implementing a corporate environmental strategy'.

Global Environmental Management Initiative (1998) used a number of 'lagging indicators', which measure outputs (such as pounds of pollutants emitted or discharged) and a number of 'leading indicators', which are in-process measures of performance, and some 'environmental condition indicators', which measure the direct effect of an activity on the environment.

Ilinitch, Soderstrom and Thomas (1998) considered 'environmental accounting and reporting' as one of the most important environmental indicators.

OECD (2004) identified 'environmental policy', 'environmental management system' and 'environmental performance reporting' as three major indicators of company's efforts at improving the environmental performance of business units. Besides these, they also considered 'companies' commitment' to operate on higher standards and 'managerial interest' for taking care of environmental issues as other important indicators.

Takahashi and Nakamura (2005) chose 'formalisation', 'centralisation' and 'professionalisation' as the independent variables of corporate greening.

Ito (2006) put stress on a number of indicators viz., 'environmental management system', 'environmental accounting', 'environmental reporting', 'environmental ranking', 'financial support for eco-conscious financial products' and 'eco funds'. Besides these, they also considered 'environmental labels', 'life cycle assessment', 'environmental performance ratings', 'support tools for small and midsized enterprises', 'environmentally compatible design' as the other variables.

Sohal and Zutshi (2006) identified some critical success factors (viz., 'top management commitment', 'implementation support', 'proper communication', 'awareness amongst personnel', etc.) as primary indicators.

The Northern Ireland Eighth Environmental Management Survey (2006) chose 'environmental policy', 'environmental audit', 'level of regulatory compliance', 'certification status', 'level of management bearing the responsibility to control environment department', 'employee awareness', 'training programme', etc. as prime environmental indicators.

Zutshi (2006) identified a number of indicators namely 'improving corporate image', 'identification of potential areas for improvement', 'making compliance with existing regulatory requirements', 'pressure from customers', 'communication with employees', 'taking employee suggestions and feedback', 'employee training', 'initiating environmental policy and EMS supporting programmes', etc.

Assignment of Weights

In some studies, environmental performance indicators have been weighted on the basis of their relative importance to the environmental proactiveness. The weights used have either been determined by the researcher or taken from previous studies. While in some other studies, unweighted indicators have been used. In such an index, equal weight, i.e. 'one' has been assigned to each environmental performance indicator of the environmental proactiveness on the assumption that all the environmental performance indicators are equally important to arrive at proactiveness score (for example, the Northern Ireland

Eighth Environmental Management Survey, 2006, where all environmental performance questions were equally weighted and the section as a whole accounted for 50 per cent of the overall score). Any weighted index may involve an element of subjectivity, but it may facilitate the true measurement of the score recognising perceived importance of different primary indicators to overall environment management. It is most unlikely that each primary indicator has equal weightage in framing a real life environment policy.

Stating in the same tune, Business in the Environment and KPMG Peat Marwick (1992) depicted an example of the method of calculating weightings in the form of an index of emissions. In addition, it was stated that the weighting factor is subjective and will ultimately change over time due to the priorities of the decision maker. Global Environmental Management Initiative (1998) arguing in the same tune, put weightage of each performance level based on priority during the evaluation of environmental performance. In the study of Gupta and Goldar (2003), the weights assigned to various criteria were varied substantially across the sectors based on their inherent characteristics. For instance, in the case of pulp and paper firms, maximum weight was given to procurement of raw material and production phases, whereas for automobile firms highest weight was assigned to the product use phase. Wier *et al.* (2005) also used weighted environmental effects indices to form one environmental performance score for each family type and product type. Fiksel (1994) stated that there is no universal weighting scheme that will suit the needs of diverse organisations and each industry and/or company should develop a scheme that suits its business characteristics.

Awarding Score

For awarding score to different environmental performance indicators, most researchers have followed a dichotomous procedure in which an environmental performance indicator has been awarded its assigned weight or score (i.e. 'one' in the case of unweighted index and a weighted score in the case of weighted index), if it was present (eg. Wehrmeyer *et al.*, 2002; Wagner, 2005;

Schaltegger and Wagner, 2006). On the other hand, if the environmental performance indicator was not present, and it was found that the indicator was applicable to the concerned company, a score 'zero' has been awarded (eg. Ilinitch, Soderstrom and Thomas, 1998; Thornton, Kagan and Gunningham, 2003; Ito, 2006; The Northern Ireland Eighth Environmental Management Survey, 2006). However, a few researches have awarded score to environmental performance indicators on the basis of their merit of environmental proactiveness (Rice, 1993; Russo and Fouts, 1997; Gupta and Goldar, 2003; Dehua, Chan and Liyin, 2004; Zhu and Sarkis, 2004; Takahashi and Nakamura, 2005; Zutshi, 2006).

To deal with environmental management and performance, The Northern Ireland Eighth Environmental Management Survey (2006) put stress on major three parameters: Management, which section accounted for 50 per cent of the overall score; Performance, which section as a whole accounted for 50 per cent of the overall score; Assurance, which section did not contribute to the overall score but is a requirement of participation.

Rice (1993) produced a scorecard with a simple weighting scale for various categories of environmental performance areas of 'very important', 'important', 'slightly important' and 'not important'. This produced later a ranking of companies through the use of values that ranged from zero (worst) to ten (best) for performance in 20 key environmental areas.

Gupta and Goldar (2003) in their study on impact of environmental performance of firms on their stock prices mentioned that full compliance with current environmental regulations merely fetches a score of 2 on a 10 point scale. Specifically, such rating uses the following scores on a 10 point scale for each component/criterion: Indian average/standard/legal requirement 2, global best practice 8 and theoretical best practice 10. In other words, wherever a domestic source specific discharge standard exists, it is taken as the lowest benchmark (2 points). In case there is no such standard as in the case of SO_2 emissions, the average discharge for all plants in the sample is taken as the lowest benchmark and below average performance is given zero, the best performance gets 8 and there is a linear scale between 2 and 85. The points given to global best practice and theoretical best practice reflect an incentive for better environmental performance. It is, therefore, important to bear in mind that the rating emphasizes over-compliance with current standards or practices.

To measure corporate greening, Takahashi and Nakamura (2005) put weightage each of the statements or presence of environmental indicators by rating them on a 1-5 Likert-type scale (1 = do not agree at all, 2 = do not agree, 3 = neutral, 4 = agree, 5 = strongly agree). Similarly, to undertake a study on implementation of EMS, Zutshi (2006) put weightage each of the environmental indicators by rating them on a five point Likert scale, where 1 = Not at all and 5 = To a very large extent.

Number of Sample Units

There are considerable variations in the number of sample companies in each study. For example, Epstein (1995) has taken 30 sample companies; Madsen and Ulhoi (1996, 1997, 1999, 2001) have taken a sample of 500 companies; Russo and Fouts (1997) have taken 243 firms; Global Environmental Management Initiative (1998) has taken 41 sample companies; Khanna and Anton (2002) have taken 500 sample units; Wehrmeyer et al. (2002) have taken about 2000 sample units; Gupta and Goldar (2003) have taken 50 sample companies; OECD (2004) has taken 1509 sample companies; Zhu and Sarkis (2004) have taken 186 respondents; Chakrabarti and Mitra (2005) have taken 8 sample units; Takahashi and Nakamura (2005) have taken 193 sample companies; Ito (2006) has taken 1399 samples; Pahuja (2006) has taken 101 respondents; The Northern Ireland Eighth Environmental Management Survey (2006) has taken 250 sample companies; Zutshi (2006) has taken 371 sample companies; and so on.

Industry Type

In general, almost all studies have not focused on any specific industry, with a few exceptions like the study of Thornton, Kagan and Gunningham (2003) who have studied on pulp manufacturing industry; Chakrabarti and Mitra (2005) who have studied on secondary lead smelting units; Sohal and Zutshi (2006) who have studied on public sector; The Northern Ireland Eighth Environmental Management Survey (2006) studied on leading companies besides local authorities, health and social service trusts, education and library boards; Zutshi (2006) who has studied on ISO 14001 certified organisations; Magrini and Lins (2007) who have studied on oil and gas sector. Many of these studies have excluded certain industry segments because of their special nature of reporting requirements. For example, Gupta and Goldar (2003) have kept out industry like thermal power, ferrous metal, food and beverage; etc.

Selection of Unit Specific Determinants

The number of unit specific determinants that have been examined as potential predictors (considered as explanatory or independent variable) of the extent of environmental proactiveness (considered as dependent variable), vary under different studies.

Selection of unit specific determinants has been guided by a number of considerations. In some studies, unit specific determinants have been purely theory driven, such as, studies conducted by Ashford and Meima (1993); Welford and Gouldson (1993); Fiksel (1994); James (1994). In such studies one or more relevant theories have been identified and based on that or those theories, unit specific determinants have been selected. In some other studies, selection of unit specific determinants has been based on survey of both theoretical literatures and empirical studies.

In previous studies, the major unit specific determinants that were used as possible predictors in explaining the variations in environmental proactiveness include total turnover, company size, nature of industry segment, total capital investment and nature of ownership of the unit. In this regard, Ashford and Meima (1993), Fiksel (1994) and James (1994) considered unit specific determinants namely, financial stakeholders including investors; non-financial stakeholders including buyers, community demands, employee satisfaction, customer conscience; company systems including competitive differentiation. Madsen (2003) considered corporate goals, product positioning, cost savings, improvement in a product's value as unit specific determinants. OECD (2004) considered unit specific determinants namely, multi-facility, change in sales, profitability, primary customers (final consumers/other), market scope (local or national/regional or global), head office (domestic/foreign), government incentive. Takahashi and Nakamura (2005) considered unit specific determinants namely, comparison with other companies, corporate strategy, decision making, new technology, sharing of ideas, necessity and culture. Schaltegger and Wagner (2006) considered unit specific determinants namely, competitiveness, profitability/returns, market position or stock market valuation, return on sales, return on owners' capital employed, return on equity.

In several studies (Madsen and Ulhoi, 2001; Wehrmeyer *et al.*, 2002; OECD, 2004; Takahashi and Nakamura, 2005; Ito, 2006), the association between corporate size and environmental proactiveness has been tested. Size of the reporting company has been measured in one or more ways. In some of those studies, corporate size has been measured in terms of total capital investment by Firth (1979); Epstein and Young (1998), HaBler and Reinhard (2000).

Further certain studies have used size as an independent variable to find out its significance as a unit specific determinant. For ex., Cerf (1961); Singhvi and Desai (1971); Buzbi (1975) and Inchausti (1997) have used size variable as unit specific determinant to explain quality of disclosure in annual reports of the company and measured corporate size in terms of total assets. Some researchers like Stanga (1976); Cooke (1989); Ahmed and Nicholls (1994); Raffournier (1995); Marston and Robson (1997); Papas (2002) have measured corporate size in terms of sales. A few researchers like Tai *et al*. (1990) have measured corporate size in terms of number of shareholders on the reporting company. Besides, corporate size can be measured in terms of number of employees (Patton and Zellanka, 1997; OECD, 2004), in terms of shareholders' equity (McNally *et al.*, 1982; Epstein and Young, 1998; Repetto and Austin, 2001; Wagner, 2005), in terms of market capitalisation (Hossain *et al.*, 1994) and in terms of profitability (Wehrmeyer *et al.*, 2002).

Most empirical studies have found significant and positive association between the corporate size and environmental proactiveness, suggesting that extent of environmental proactiveness increases with increase in size of firm. It was explored from the theoretical reasoning on the differences in environmental management between large and small firms (Henriques and Sadorsky, 1996; Bradford, 2000) that there is a significant difference in environmental performance score due to the different sizes of surveyed units. An empirical study was also made by Wehrmeyer *et al.* (2002) who tried to identify whether there are significant differences in strategic orientation or environmental management approach for different firm sizes. The study was also in the same tune identifying larger firms firstly more often pursue a 'compliance plus' strategy, and secondly, larger firms are able more often to create positive synergies of their environmental management activities with production in terms of, for example, reducing and better predicting costs and investments. OECD (2004) revealed that there is a statistically significant relationship between facility size and proactiveness.

Some studies have tested the association of the nature of industry segment with the extent of environmental proactiveness. Madsen and Ulhoi (1996, 2001) attempted to assess environmental proactiveness for different type of companies like reactive versus proactive ones. Wehrmeyer *et al.* (2002) attempted to identify whether there is a link between sector membership [here 'sector coverage' refers to different industry segments producing food and tobacco products, metal products, machines and equipment, transport products, pulp and paper products (excluding timber industry, leather processing and recycling)] and the strategic orientation or environmental management approach of firms. The implication of these findings was that national environmental policy-making needs to take into account sectoral differences when aiming to encourage adoption of more proactive environmental strategies in firms. Takahashi and Nakamura (2005), also uttering in the same tune, stated that there is a link between type of industry segment and environmental proactiveness.

Russo and Fouts (1997) stated that drawing on the resource-based view of the firm, they posited that environmental performance and economic performance are positively linked and that industry growth moderates the relationship, with the returns to environmental performance higher in high-growth industries.

Some studies (Wehrmeyer *et al.*, 2002) have tested the association of the country location with the extent of environmental proactiveness.

Gupta and Goldar (2003) explored that there is a significant positive correlation between the estimated abnormal return to a firm's stock and the environmental score. This was the first attempt to examine the impact of public disclosure of environmental performance on the financial performance of firms for a developing economy.

OECD (2004) revealed that there is a statistically significant positive relationship of environmental proactiveness with the facility being part of a multi-facility firm, profitability, market being international, head office being overseas, the presence of a quality management system and regulatory incentives being provided to introduce an EMS. On the contrary, there is a statistically significant negative relationship of environmental proactiveness with the firm primarily selling to final consumers.

Takahashi and Nakamura (2005) explored that bureaucratisation (in terms of formalisation, centralisation and professionalisation) of environmental management generally has a positive relationship with corporate greening and that the presence of one or two of the three dimensions of bureaucratisation may be sufficient for corporate greening to implement certain greening measures. Further, the positive relationship between the ISO 14001 certification and bureaucratisation elicits the view that implementing ISO 14001 EMS is the bureaucratisation of environmental management. This view is also supported by the ISO 14001 standard text itself.

Some researchers have predicted a negative association between the nature of ownership and the extent of environmental proactiveness. Earnhart and Lizal (2006) analysed the effects of ownership structure on corporate environmental performance.

Statistical Tools

To examine the association between several unit specific determinants (independent variables) and the extent of environmental proactiveness (dependent variable), various statistical analyses have been made. In some studies the matched-pair statistical procedures have been used to test the difference between environmental performance scores of two country locations or two/more groups of sample firms. Some have relied on ANOVA, Z-testing and chi-square testing, while student's t-test has been used by some others. Bivariate statistical analyses have also been used by some researchers.

To make the examples more exhaustive and pertinent, Zhu and Sarkis (2004); Wagner (2005) followed regression analysis, while Gupta and Goldar (2003) have introduced the use of Ordinary Least Squares (OLS) regression to estimate a linear relationship between the return of any security and the return of the market portfolio.

Zhu and Sarkis (2004) used regression analysis to evaluate the general relationships between specific green supply chain management practices and environmental performance.

Wagner (2005) applied multiple regression analysis in order to understand the relationship between the environmental and economic performance of firms.

Besides the regression analysis, different researchers have examined environmental proactiveness in the varied statistical ways. Some major ones are as follows:

Madsen and Ulhoi (1997) carried out a detailed analysis by means of a factor analysis to identify drivers in introducing environmental management in business practice.

Global Environmental Management Initiative (1998) produced a scatter diagram by graphically plotting a site's environmental performance evaluation (EPE) score against its risk score.

Wehrmeyer *et al.* (2002) made data analysis through three distinct stages—the basic features of environmental management in the manufacturing sectors of two countries Britain and Germany were evaluated using descriptive statistics (such as percentages and frequency distributions). This was followed by principal component analysis/cluster analysis and the corresponding sensitivity analysis, to identify and establish underlying patterns in firm behaviour. This was done by interpreting homogeneous factors/clusters in the numerical dataset, which were then analysed in the third stage by using ANOVA to identify significant relationships of different environmental management approaches and corporate environmental strategies with the explanatory factors viz., firm size, country location and sector membership.

Gupta and Goldar (2003) conducted an event study to examine the impact of environmental performance of firms in India on their stock prices. Schaltegger and Wagner (2006) opined that event studies assess market responses after a positive or negative environmental event and are part of a broader strand of research which assesses the response of capital markets on events related to specific companies or industrial sectors.

Takahashi and Nakamura (2005) examined possible relationships between firms' environmental organisational structures and corporate greening using the qualitative comparative analysis (QCA) technique. They expected complex relationships between the independent variables (three dimensions of bureaucratisation i.e., formalisation, centralisation and professionalisation) and seven dependent variables (comparison with other companies, corporate strategy, decision making, new technology, sharing of ideas, necessity, culture). They defined the dependent variable, corporate greening, as the development of corporate management wherein the corporate members exhibit a concern for the natural environment. The QCA can handle only binary variables, not multichotomous ones. In particular, the QCA analysed binary variables, 0 (no)/1 (yes), using the Boolean logic. To use the data collected in the survey, they transformed responses on a 1-5 scale as responses with a score of '1' to '3' are transformed into '0' and responses with a score of '4' and '5' are transformed into '1'. Responses marked 'do not know' are transformed into '0'. The analysis indicated that the bureaucratization of environmental management generally promotes corporate greening. Different aspects of corporate greening require different factors or different combinations of the factors of bureaucratisation.

Some researchers took help of portfolio studies that analyses real or model portfolios of environmentally proactive and environmentally reactive companies, and compare their respective returns. They have however, been criticised as only focussing on average performance (Schaltegger and Wagner, 2006).

However, empirical evidences have not always supported the theoretical predictions of the associations between the extent of environmental proactiveness and independent variables considered in previous studies. In many cases, empirical results have not been consistent with the theoretical predictions, particularly with respect to association between environmental proactiveness and (a) nature of industry segment, (b) nature of ownership, (c) age of the unit, (d) ratio of permanent employees out of total workers. Variability across studies is also found with regard to the extent of association between environmental proactiveness and independent variables. Schaltegger and Wagner (2006) stated that most empirical research in this field is based on more or less sophisticated regression analyses searching for correlations. The findings are very mixed, which is not surprising given that the databases are mostly limited in the number of companies and issues considered as well as in the time period considered. Furthermore, it is rarely clarified what kind of causal link is expected and there is no overarching theoretical framework to structure the analysis provided. Regression analyses have generally not provided the clear proof or sufficiently significant and generalisable results that the researchers were seeking. For instance, research on the influence of EMAS and ISO 14000 certified environmental management system has not been able to demonstrate a clear link to the companies' economic performance in terms of their industry average, although many company examples have been analysed and described.

Even, Schaltegger and Wagner (2006) mentioned that an increasingly popular empirical approach is to work with case studies. Case studies allow specific causal links and circumstances to be investigated in more depth, but they remain limited in their generalisation for other companies and industries.

Argument

The discussion on environmental management and corporate greening suggests a straight forward relation between the visibility of environmental issues and firm-level environmental proactiveness. To the extent that environmental issues become visible and urgent within a particular industry they may invoke response from important stakeholders (customers, authorities, media and so forth) and thus, influence the competitive fate of the firm (Mitchell, Agle and Wood, 1997; Hoffman, 1999). In order to pre-empt stakeholder response, the firm will tend to become increasingly proactive as environmental issues become more visible (Madsen and Ulhoi, 1996; Sharma and Vredenburg, 1998). Thus, environmental proactiveness implies corporate initiative to address environmental issues in strategic planning and business practice so that any harmful reaction from government, public in general and other related parties may be averted. However, we have found a number of gaps in the discussion on environmental proactiveness made in the preceding section.

First, a good number of studies have been undertaken on environmental issues, but very few of them have focussed on the environmental performance of the existing units.

Secondly, majority of the studies were based on the foreign industries.

Thirdly, the number of environmental performance indicators examined in the discussion on environmental proactiveness, except a few cases, is subjective, narrow and theoretical, making the scope of their works limited. Welford and Gouldson (1993) have not demonstrated the environmental proactiveness by any case study that could reveal how those determinants would be integrated in operational practices to measure environmental performance of a business unit in real life situation. The studies of Ashford and Meima (1993), Fiksel (1994) and James (1994) seemed to be of more theoretical and subjective in nature than objective and practical-oriented. Epstein (1995)'s study did not evaluate the extent of significance of each of those indicators to the environmental performance of the business units. Madsen and Ulhoi (1996, 1997, 1999, 2001) and Madsen (2003) had not used quantitative measurement of environmental performance. Russo and Fouts (1997) did not mention the individual importance of environmental indicators that are considered to measure the environmental performance. Global Environmental Management Initiative (1998) did not empirically explore the importance and the level of significance of each of the environmental indicators to proactiveness and business competitiveness. Khanna and Anton (2002)'s approach more highlighted the importance of environmental accounting in proactiveness of business units. If some more indicators could be analysed, that could give more integrated approach. Gupta and Goldar (2003) highlighted the impact of environmental performance of specific types of industry on their stock prices. So, their findings may not match irrespective of all industry segments. The scope of the study undertaken by Thornton, Kagan and Gunningham (2003) would be broadened, if it could comparatively evaluate the environmental performances for different industry segments. Zhu and Sarkis (2004) put stress on incorporation of environmental issues in supply chain management and accordingly, evaluated its relation with performance of the business units. But the study failed to highlight other functional areas of business units for the purpose of evaluation of economic performance. Chakrabarti and Mitra (2005)'s study is truly exceptional to attempt to undertake cost-benefit analysis of control technology applicable to a particular type of units and taking into consideration of only one type of business unit (smelting). The other units operating in different industry segments have not been considered here. Takahashi and Nakamura (2005) overemphasised the term 'bureaucratisation', though corporate greening could be analysed based on some basic environmental indicators, which appeared to be missing in their study. Ito (2006) did not provide clear guideline of how the environmental indicators are integrated in operational practices in real life situation to measure the environmental performance of business units. Schaltegger and Wagner (2006) did not put stress on scoring of independent factors of environmental performance that would ultimately lead towards sustainability. Sohal and Zutshi (2006) put stress only one indicator i.e. EMS to measure environmental performance of the business unit. If at least the prime indicators could be covered in the study, then it would provide an integrated and holistic approach. The Northern Ireland Eighth Environmental Management Survey (2006) did not undertake cost-benefit analysis during consideration of environmental issues. Zutshi (2006) only focussed on three organisational stakeholders (top management, employees and suppliers) and not other external stakeholders such as customers, government agencies, non-government agencies, and the community. In the study of Magrini and Lins (2007), the status of small and medium scale industry have totally been overlooked.

It is worthwhile to mention here that OECD (2004)'s study on development and adoption of advanced environmental management practices are really worthwhile for any business unit. If such kind of study could be undertaken in Indian perspective, it would be really helpful for regulators/policy-makers as well as business units of India. Similarly, Wehrmeyer *et al.* (2002)'s study showed a holistic and proactive approach towards environmental management. If the same could be undertaken in Indian perspective, it would definitely be useful for regulators for making policy changes and also for the business units to incorporate environmental issues into overall corporate strategy formulation and implementation at operational levels.

Fourthly, many studies discussed about environmental performance indicators, but none, except Welford and Gouldson (1993), OECD (2004), Takahashi and Nakamura (2005) and the Northern Ireland Eighth Environmental Management Survey (2006) has highlighted the key environmental performance indicators that are needed to make the company environmentally proactive, to raise the profile of environmental issues among organisations and to encourage improvement in environmental management and performance.

For measuring the extent of environmental proactiveness, most of the studies have applied unweighted indicators ignoring the relative importance of different environmental performance indicators to arrive at proactiveness score.

While awarding scores to different environmental performance indicators, most of the researchers have focused too much on a binary presentation. They have considered 'have the facility' and 'not having the facility' i.e. 'yes' or 'no' type response, as the two mutually exclusive events and consequently, have ignored the fact that degree of environmental performance score details of some environmental performance indicators might vary across the companies. Such result would hinder to go to detail in-depth analysis by size, or nature of industry segment, etc. Thus, scoring was made without considering the possibility of partial proactiveness, i.e. previous studies (though such empirical studies are very few in numbers) may be successful to explore the portfolio of 'excellent' and 'poor' units in terms of environmental proactiveness, but it would fail to find out the detail of the units that lie in between these two spectra. As a result from management perspective, it would be difficult to take strategic decision based on only two extreme positions of the units.

Previous studies (except Wehrmeyer *et al.*, 2002) have failed to explore how the environmental performance of the units varies based on nature of different industry segments.

For studies in the Indian context, the following observations merit consideration:

First, no extensive empirical study has yet been undertaken to measure the extent of environmental performance of the existing Indian companies.

Second, these studies have not attempted to determine the unit specific determinants that could explain the variations in the extent of environmental proactiveness.

Third, no detailed investigation has been made to identify the portfolio of the units that would explore the specific industry segment that will be helpful to take strategic decision from the management perspective in future.

Implication

In the view of the above arguments, it is urgently needed to assess the awareness of the existing units about the environmental issues and incorporation of those issues in the corporate mission and policies. It is also required to analyse the level of implementation and problem of implementation of environmental management system in the actual business practice; and also to assess the level of compliance with extant environmental regulations by the business. It is the time to explore the position of sample units regarding environmental management; compare benefit against cost due to incorporation of environmental issues in business; and assess empirically how far the sample units are proactive in management of environmental issues. Hence, continuous monitoring and research are required to examine how corporate sectors are coping with the changing needs of economy and society.

In this Part (Part-I), it was attempted to review the incorporation of environmental issues in business practice to align strategies with environmental concern. It led us to make arguments in respect of environmental proactiveness. In the next Part we would focus on the conceptual and theoretical aspects of corporate environmental management in the belief that the concept developed in the foregoing pages regarding the methodological and substantive aspects of environmental proactiveness would help us on evaluation of environmental proactiveness of different units in India and abroad.

6

REFERENCES

Agrawal, K. M. and Mitra, Sarbani (2004), 'Assessment of Prospects of Implementation of Environment Management System in Indian Industries', in Mallikarjun, M. and Chugan, Pawan K. (2004) (ed.), *Prastavana*: Souvenir of Nirma International Conference on Management (NICOM – 2004), pp. 62-63, Proc. of NICOM – 2004 on *Managing Trade, Technology and Environment*, Institute of Management, Nirma University of Science and Technology, Ahmedabad, January 2-4, 2004.

Ahmed, K. and Nicholls, D. (1994), 'The Impact of Non-Financial Company Characteristics on Mandatory Disclosure Compliance in Developing Countries: The Case of Bangladesh', *International Journal of Accounting*, 29, pp. 62-77.

Ashford, N. A. and Meima, R. (1993), 'Designing the Sustainable Enterprise Summary Report', *The Greening of Industry Network*, Second International Research Conference, Cambridge, Massachusetts, Quoted in Welford, Richard (1996), *Corporate Environmental Management: Systems and Strategies*, Universities Press (India) Limited, Hyderabad, pp. 151-157.

Bhargava, Sangeeta and Welford, Richard (1999), 'Corporate Strategy and the Environment: the Theory', in Welford, Richard (1996) (ed.), *Corporate Environmental Management: Systems and Strategies*, Universities Press (India) Limited, Hyderabad, pp. 13-32.

Bhattacharyya, Dipak Kumar (2003), *Research Methodology*, Excel Books, New Delhi, p. 57.

Bowen, Haward R. (1953), *Social Responsibility of Businessmen*, Harper and Brothers, New York, p. 169.

Bradford, D. (2000), 'Motivating SMEs Towards Improved Environmental Performance', *The IPTS Report*, Institute for Prospective Technological Studies, Seville, No. 41, pp. 25-29.

Business in the Environment and KPMG Peat Marwick (1992), 'A Measure of Commitment – Guidelines for Measuring Environmental Performance', *Business in the Environment and KPMG Peat Marwick*, Quoted in Welford, Richard (1996), *Corporate Environmental Management: Systems and Strategies*, Universities Press (India) Limited, Hyderabad, p. 156.

Buzbi, S.L. (1975), 'Company Size, Listed Versus Unlisted Stocks, the Extent of Financial Disclosure', *Journal of Accounting Research*, 13(1), Spring, pp. 16-37.

Cascio, J., Woodside, G. and Mitchell, P. (1996), *ISO 14000 Guide*, McGraw-Hill, New York, Quoted in Bishop, Paul L. (2000), *Pollution Prevention: Fundamentals and Practice*, McGraw Hill, Singapore, p. 255.

Cerf, A.R. (1961), *Corporate Reporting and Investment Decision*, University of California Press, Berkeley, p. 12.

Chakrabarti, Dr. Snigdha and Mitra, Dr. Nita (2005), *A Report on Cost-Benefit Analysis of Air Pollution Control Technology—A Case Study of Secondary Lead Smelting Industry*, Funded by West Bengal Pollution Control Board, Kolkata.

Cooke, T. E. (1989), 'Disclosure in the Corporate Annual Reports of Swedish Companies', *Accounting and Business Research*, 19(74), Spring, pp. 113-124.

Dehua, W., Chan, Edwin H. W. and Liyin, S. (2004), 'Scoring System for Measuring Contractor's *Environmental Performance*', *Journal of Construction Research, Vol. 5, Issue 1*, pp. 139-147.

Drucker, Peter F. (1975), *Management Task, Responsibilities, Practices*, Allied Publishers Private Ltd., New Delhi, p. 314.

Dutta, A.K., Agrawal, K.M. and Mitra, Sarbani (2004), 'Trade and Corporate Environmental Management Strategies—An Analysis in Indian Perspective', in Mallikarjun, M. and Chugan, Pawan K. (2004) (ed.), *Managing Trade, Technology and Environment*, 1st ed., Excel Books, New Delhi, pp. 579-588, Proc. of Nirma International Conference on Management (NICOM – 2004) on *Managing Trade, Technology and Environment*, Institute of Management, Nirma University of Science and Technology, Ahmedabad, January 2-4, 2004.

Earnhart, Dietrich and Lizal, Lubomir (2006), 'Effects of Ownership and Financial *Performance* on *Corporate Environmental Performance*', *Journal of Comparative Economics, Vol. 34, Issue 1*, pp. 111-129.

Epstein, Mark (1995), 'A Sound *Environmental* Policy Adds to Financial Success', *Corporate Board*, Vol. 16, Issue 95, p. 26.

Epstein, Marc J. and Young, S. David (1998), 'Improving *Corporate Environmental Performance* through Economic Value Added', *Environmental Quality Management*, Vol. 7, Issue 4, pp. 1-7.

Fiksel, J. (1994), 'Quality Metrics in Design for Environment', *Total Quality Environmental Management*, Winter, pp. 181-192, Quoted in Welford, Richard (1996), *Corporate Environmental Management: Systems and Strategies*, Universities Press (India) Limited, Hyderabad, pp. 151-159.

Firth, M. (1979), 'The Impact of Size, Stock Market Listing and Auditors on Voluntary Disclosure in Corporate Annual Reports', *Accounting and Business Research*, 9(36), Autumn, pp. 273-280.

Global Environmental Management Initiative (1998), *Measuring Environmental Performance: A Primer and Survey of Metrics in Use* [http://www.gemi .org/MET_101 .pdf, visited on 21st November 2006].

Gupta, Shreekant and Goldar, Bishwanath (2003), 'Do Stock Markets Penalise Environment-Unfriendly Behaviour? Evidence from India', *Centre for Dèvelopment Economics*, Working Paper No. 116 [http://www.cseindia. org/ programme/industry/pdf/stock_market.pdf, visited on 21st November 2006].

HaBler, Robert and Reinhard, Dirk (2000), '*Environmental*-Rating: An Indicator of *Corporate Environmental Performance*', *Greener Management International, Issue 29, p. 18.*

Henriques, I. and Sadorsky, P. (1996), 'The Determinants of an Environmentally Responsive Firm: An Empirical Approach', *Journal of Environmental Economics and Management*, 30, pp. 381-395.

Hoffman, A. J. (1999), 'Institutional Evolution and Change: Environmentalism and the U.S. Chemical Industry', *Academy of Management Journal*, 42(4), pp. 351-371.

Hoopes, D. G., Madsen, T.L., Walker, G. (2003), 'Guest Editors' Introduction to the Special Issue: Why is There a Resource-Based View? Toward a Theory of Competitive Heterogeneity', *Strategic Management Journal*, 24, p. 891.

Hossain, M., Tan, L.M. and Adams, M. (1994), 'Voluntary Disclosure in An Emerging Capital Market: Some Empirical Evidence from Companies Listed on the Kuala Lumpur Stock Exchange', *International Journal of Accounting*, 29, pp. 334-351.

Huijbregts, Mark A. J., Rombouts, Linda J. A., Hellweg, S., Frischknecht, R., Hendriks, A. J., van de Meent, D., Ragas, Ad. M. J., Reijnders, L., Struijs, J. (2006), 'Is Cumulative Fossil Energy Demand a Useful Indicator for the *Environmental Performance* of Products?' *Environmental Science & Technology*, Vol. 40, Issue 3, pp. 641-648.

Ilinitch, Anne Y., Soderstrom, Naomi S. and Thomas, Tom E. (1998), 'Measuring *Corporate Environmental Performance*', *Journal of Accounting and Public Policy, Vol. 17, Issue 4/5,* p. 383.

Inchausti, B. G. (1997), 'The Influence of Company Characteristics and Accounting Regulations on Information Disclosed by Spanish Firms', *The European Accounting Review*, 6(1), pp. 45-68.

Ito, Misako (2006), 'Environmental Consciousness Increases in Japanese Business', *JETRO Japan Economic Report*, Topic Report, Japanese Economy Division [http://www.jetro.go.jp/en/market/trend/special/pdf/jer0606-1e.pdf, visited on 21st November 2006].

James, P. (1994), *Business Strategy and the Environment*, 3, 2, pp. 59-67, Quoted in Welford, Richard (1996), *Corporate Environmental Management: Systems and Strategies*, Universities Press (India) Limited, Hyderabad, p. 151.

Khanna, Madhu and Anton, William Rose Q. (2002), 'Corporate Environmental Management: Regulatory and Market-Based Incentives', *Land Economics*, University of Wisconsin Press, Vol. 78, No. 4, pp. 539-558 (20) [http://www.ingentaconnect.com/content/wisc/lec/2002/000000 78 /00000004/art00006, visited on 21st November 2006].

Lu, W.M. and Lo, S. F. (2007), 'A Benchmark-Learning Roadmap for Regional Sustainable Development in China', *Journal of the Operational Research Society*, Vol. 58, Issue 7, pp. 841-849.

Madsen, H. and Ulhoi, J. P. (1996), 'Environmental Management in Danish Manufacturing Companies: Attitudes and Actions', *Business Strategy and the Environment*, 5, pp. 22-29.

Madsen, H. and Ulhoi, J. P. (1999), 'Industry and the Environment: A Danish Perspective', *Industry and Environment*, 22, pp. 35-37.

Madsen, H. and Ulhoi, J. P. (2001), 'Integrating Environmental and Stakeholder Management', *Business Strategy and the Environment*, 10, pp. 77-88.

Madsen, Henning (2003), 'Have Trends in Corporate Environmental Management Influenced Companies' Competitiveness?' *Greener Management International* [http://goliath.ecnext.com/coms2/summary_0199-3498784_ITM, visited on 21st November 2006].

Madsen, Henning and Ulhoi, John P. (1996, 1997, 1999, 2001), *Analyses of Corporate Environmental Management: Methodological Aspects* [http://isi.cbs.nl/iamamember/CD2/pdf/574.PDF, visited on 21st November 2006].

Madsen, H., Sinding, K. and Ulhoi, J. P. (1997), 'Sustainability and Corporate Environmental Focus: An Analysis of Danish Small and Medium Sized Companies', *Managerial and Decision Economics*, 18, pp. 443-453.

Magrini, Allessandra and Lins, Luiz dos Santos (2007), 'Integration Between *Environmental Management* and Strategic Planning in the Oil and Gas Sector', *Energy Policy*, Vol. 35, Issue 10, pp. 4869-4878.

Marston, C.L. and Robson, P. (1997), 'Financial Reporting in India: Changes in Disclosure Over the Period 1982 to 1990', *Asia-Pacific Journal of Accounting*, 4(1), June, pp. 103-139.

McNally, G.M., Eng, L.H. and Hasseldine, C.R. (1982), 'Corporate Financial Reporting in New Zealand: An Analysis of User's Preference, Corporate Characteristics and Disclosure Practices for Discretionary Information', *Accounting and Business Research*, 13, Winter, pp. 11-20.

Mitchell, R.K., Agle, B.R. and Wood, D.J. (1997), 'Toward a Theory of Stakeholder Identification and Salience: Defining the Principle of Who and What Really Counts', *Academy of Management Review*, 22, pp. 853-886.

Mohanty, S.K. (1997), *Universal's Environment & Pollution Law Manual*, Universal Law Publishing Co. Pvt. Ltd, Delhi, pp. 27-87.

OECD, Directorate for Financial and Enterprise Affairs (2004), 'Overview of Corporate Environmental Management Practices', *Roundtable on Corporate Responsibility: Encouraging the Positive Contribution of Business to Environment through the OECD Guidelines for Multinational Enterprises* [http://www.oecd. org/dataoecd/12/29/31967893.pdf, visited on 21st November 2006].

Pahuja, Shuchi (2006), 'Accountants' Response to Environmental Accounting and Reporting Challenges in an Emerging Economy: A Study of India', in Sahay, B. S., Stough, R. R., Sohal, A. and Goyal, S. (2006) (ed.), *Green Business*, Allied Publishers Pvt. Ltd., New Delhi, pp. 281-310.

Papas, Antonios A. (2002), 'An Assessment of Mandatory Disclosure in the Annual Reports of Greek Companies', *Indian Journal of Accounting*, 32, June, pp. 1-14.

Patton, J. and Zellanka, I. (1997), 'An Empirical Analysis of the Determinants of the Extent of Disclosure in Annual Reports of Joint Stock Companies in the Czech Republic', *The European Accounting Review*, 6(4), pp. 605-626.

Porter, M. E. and van der Linde, C. (1995), Quoted in Madsen, Henning (2003), 'Have Trends in Corporate Environmental Management Influenced Companies' Competitiveness?' *Greener Management International* [http://goliath.ecnext.com/coms2/summary_0199-3498784 _ITM, visited on 21st November 2006].

Prahalad, C.K. and Hamel, G. (1990), 'The Core Competence of the Corporation', *Harvard Business Review*, Vol. 8, No. 3, pp. 79-91.

Raffournier, B. (1995), 'The Determinants of Voluntary Financial Disclosure by Swiss Listed Companies', *The European Accounting Review*, 4(2), pp. 261-280.

Repetto, Robert and Austin, Duncan (2001), 'Quantifying the Impact of *Corporate Environmental Performance* on *Shareholder* Value', *Environmental Quality Management*, Vol. 10, Issue 4, pp. 33-44.

Rice, F. (1993), 'Who Scores Best on the Environment', *Fortune*, July 26, pp. 104-111, Quoted in Welford, Richard (1996), *Corporate Environmental Management: Systems and Strategies*, Universities Press (India) Limited, Hyderabad, p. 155.

Russo, Michael V. and Fouts, Paul A. (1997), 'A Resource-Based Perspective on *Corporate Environmental Performance* and Profitability', *Academy of Management Journal*, Vol. 40, Issue 3, p. 534.

Sarantakos, S. (1998), *Social Research*, Macmillan Press, London, 2nd ed., p. 224, Quoted in Ahuja, Ram (2003), *Research Methods*, Rawat Publications, New Delhi, pp. 216-217.

Sarkar, Runa (2006), 'Corporate Environmental Behaviour: A Comparative Study of Firms in the Indian Paper Industry', in Sahay, B.S., Stough, R. R., Sohal, A. and Goyal, S. (2006) (ed.), *Green Business*, Allied Publishers Pvt. Ltd., New Delhi, pp. 35-58.

Sawhney, Aparna and Jose, P.D. (2003), 'The Greening of Business Strategy: From Compliance to Competitive Advantage', *IIMB Business Review*, p. 132.

Schaltegger, Stefan and Wagner, Marcus (2006), 'Managing and Measuring the Business Case for Sustainability-Capturing the Relationship Between Sustainability Performance', *Business Competitiveness and Economic Performance*, Greenleaf Publishing [http://www.greenleaf-publishing.com, visited on 21st November 2006].

Sharma, S. and Vredenburg, H. (1998), 'Proactive Corporate Environmental Strategy and the Development of Competitively Valuable Organisational Capabilities', *Strategic Management Journal*, 19 (6), pp. 729-754.

Sheldon, Christopher and Yoxon, Mark (1999), *Installing Environmental Management Systems: A Step-by-Step-Guide*, Earthscan Publications Ltd., London, p. 120.

Singhvi, S. and Desai, H. B. (1971), 'An Empirical Analysis of the Quality of Corporate Financial Disclosure', *The Accounting Review*, 46(1), January, pp. 129-138.

Singleton, R.A. and Straits, B. C. (1999), *Approaches to Social Research*, Oxford University Press, New York, 3rd ed., p. 259, in Ahuja, Ram (2003), *Research Methods*, Rawat Publications, New Delhi, pp. 216-217.

Sohal, Amrik and Zutshi, Ambika (2006), 'EMS Adoption in the Public Sector: Experiences from Australia', in Sahay, B. S., Stough, R.R., Sohal, A. and Goyal, S. (2006) (ed.), *Green Business*, Allied Publishers Pvt. Ltd., New Delhi, pp. 253-267.

Stanga, Keith G. (1976), 'Disclosure in Published Annual Reports', *Financial Management*, Winter, pp. 42-50.

Tai, B., Au Yeung, P. K., Kwok, M. and Lau, I. (1990), 'Non-compliance with Disclosure Requirements in Financial Statements: The Case of Hong Kong Companies', *The International Journal of Accounting*, 25(1), pp. 99-112.

Takahashi, Takuya and Nakamura, Masao (2005), 'Bureaucratisation of Environmental Management and Corporate Greening: An Empirical Analysis of Large Manufacturing Firms in Japan', *Corporate Social Responsibility and Environmental Management*, Wiley InterScience (www.interscience.wiley.com), 12, pp. 210-219 [http://pacific.commerce. ubc.ca/nakamura/nakamura_csrem_2005.pdf, visited on 21st November 2006].

The Northern Ireland Eighth Environmental Management Survey (2006), *Business in the Community*, ARENA Network, Northern Ireland [http://www.bitc.org.uk/regions/bitc_in_your_region/northern_ irela nd/programmes/environment/survey.html, visited on 21st November 2006].

Thornton, D., Kagan, Robert A. and Gunningham, N. (2003), 'Sources of *Corporate Environmental Performance', California Management Review, Vol. 46, Issue 1,* pp. 127-141.

Ulhoi, J. P. (1997), Quoted in Madsen, Henning (2003), 'Have Trends in Corporate Environmental Management Influenced Companies' Competitiveness?' *Greener Management International* [http://goliath. ecnext.com/coms2/summary_0199-3498784_ITM, visited on 21st November 2006].

Wagner, Marcus (2005), 'Sustainability and Competitive Advantage: Empirical Evidence on the Influence of Strategic Choices Between *Environmental* Management Approaches', *Environmental Quality Management*, Vol. 14, Issue 3, pp. 31-48.

Wehrmeyer, W., Wagner, M., Pacheco, C. and Schaltegger, S. (2002), *Environmental Management Strategies: Britain and Germany Compared*, Anglo-German Foundation for the Study of Industrial Society, London [http://www.agf.org.uk/pubs/pdfs/1336 web.pdf, visited on 21st November 2006].

Welford, R. J. (1995), Quoted in Madsen, Henning (2003), 'Have Trends in Corporate Environmental Management Influenced Companies' Competitiveness?' *Greener Management International* [http://goliath. ecnext.com/coms2/summary_0199-3498784_ITM, visited on 21st November 2006].

Welford, R.J. and Gouldson, A. P. (1993), *Environmental Management and Business Strategy*, Pitman Publishing, London, Quoted in Welford, Richard (1996), *Corporate Environmental Management: Systems and Strategies*, Universities Press (India) Limited, Hyderabad, p. 152.

Wernerfelt, B. (1984), 'The Resource-Based View of the Firm', *Strategic Management Journal*, 5 (2), p. 172.

West Bengal Pollution Control Board (2004-2005), *Annual Report*, Part II, Annexure IV, pp. 143-160.

Wier, M., Christoffersen, Line B., Jensen, T., Pedersen, Ole G., Keiding, H., Munksgaard, J. (2005), 'Evaluating Sustainability of Household Consumption-Using DEA to Assess *Environmental Performance', Economic Systems Research, Vol. 17, Issue 4,* pp. 425-447.

Zhu, Quinghua and Sarkis, Joseph (2004), 'Relationships Between Operational Practices and *Performance* Among Early Adopters of Green Supply Chain Management Practices in Chinese Manufacturing Enterprises', *Journal of Operations Management*, Vol. 22, Issue 3, pp. 265-289.

Zutshi, Ambika (2006), 'Environmental Management System Implementation in Australian Organisations', in Sahay, B.S., Stough, R.R., Sohal, A. and Goyal, S. (2006) (ed.), *Green Business*, Allied Publishers Pvt. Ltd., New Delhi, pp. 311-325.

PART–II

7

ENVIRONMENTAL LEGISLATIONS AND BUSINESS PRACTICES

With the rapid economic growth during the last few decades, the utilisation of natural resources and generation and disposal of wastes have increased exponentially to a point where the livelihood of physical constraints has become evident. Consequently, there are a growing number of increasingly urgent environmental problems to be tackled. During '50s through '60s people all over the world became more concerned about the quality of their environment. However, the doctrine of "the common heritage for mankind", the key behind all types of environmental thinking and actions had emerged in 1930s and was incorporated in the laws in 1950s (Timothy, 1995). The significance of this doctrine lies in accepting obligation by the present generation to act as trustees of the natural and human heritage so as to enhance the biological and spiritual life of its descendants (Paliwal, 2002, p. 62). Thus, the Environmental Revolution in 1968 indicates the start of modern man's concern with the environment. At the dawn of the 21st century, man has to deal with his legacy. Man realizes that it is no longer acceptable to create wealth without consideration of the immediate and longer term effects that such activities have on the environment (Rostron, 2001).

'Environmental law' is the law relating to the use, protection and conservation of the three environmental media of earth, air and water. This law expresses itself in rules of environmental regulation (primarily the domain of public authorities) and environmental liability which are concerned with attributing responsibility to meet the costs and consequences of environmental harm, and for past environmental wrong doing, international or otherwise (Hughes *et al.*, 2002, p. 3).

Thus, the multitude of potential sources of environmental contamination by industry or by products of industry has, over recent years, led to an ever-increasing level of regulations aimed at minimising environmental damage and threats to public health (Bishop, 2000, p. 147). All around the world the governments have enacted environmental rules and regulations to monitor the developmental activities from the environmental point of view. The countries such as the USA, the UK, Canada, Germany, Norway, the Netherlands, Philippines, etc. have led the world community in this direction, which is reflected by their efforts in this area (Paliwal, 2002, p. 62). Yet, some lacunae in the policies and legislations exist which needs further amendment (Khitoliya, 2005, p. 25).

The objectives of this Chapter are to show the general trends in environmental laws, where it is going and what the issues may be in the future; to put environmental laws into its wider context and to explain some of the basic issues needed to understand how environmental laws work. This is an attempt to put the problem of environmental degradation into perspective. If we can comprehend how the laws have responded to this problem, then we are at least someway towards its solution.

Need of Environmental Regulations

The first and foremost step in the establishment of Environmental Management System is the adherence to the legislative requirements in the organisation (Roy, 1998, p. 267). The Charter of Economic Rights and Duties of States of 1974 stated: "The protection, preservation and the enhancement of the environment of the present and future generation is the responsibility of all States. All States have the responsibility to ensure that the activities within their jurisdiction or control do not cause damage to the environment of other States or of areas beyond the limits of national jurisdiction. All States should cooperate in evolving international norms and regulations in the field of the environment" (Chaturvedi and Chaturvedi, 1998, p. 18). Therefore, to create an awareness about the current norms and projected environmental restrictions under which organisations may have to operate in future, management should give highest priority on this subject (Roy, 1998, p. 267).

In this context, it would be relevant to refer to the environmental problems that are faced in India. Projected in great detail in the 6th Five Year Plan document of Government of India, these may be summarised as under (Ramesh, 2000, pp. 234-235; Khitoliya, 2005, pp. 2-4):

(i) **Air and noise pollution:** A CPCB Pollution inventory of Delhi shows quite clearly that vehicles cause 70 per cent of air pollution in Delhi which is the fourth most polluted city in the world. Noise pollution is now-a-days a growing menace.

(ii) **Water pollution:** Experts have estimated that 20 years from now approximately $^{1}/_{3}$rd of the world's population will suffer from water crisis.

(iii) **Solid and hazardous wastes:** According to a report of the Ministry of Environment and Forests (MoEF), more than 5 million tones of hazardous wastes are generated every year in India, apart from more than 25 million tones of municipal solid wastes per annum.

(iv) **Land degradation and water depletion:** It is estimated that 175 million hectares out of the country's total land area of 304 million hectares (nearly 60 per cent of the available land area) is subject to different levels of environmental problems.

(v) **Threats to biodiversity and ecosystems:** Unplanned development and relentless pressure on the natural environment have resulted in loss and disappearance of several species and ecosystems in India.

(vi) **Soil erosion:** India is losing about 6,000 million tonnes of top soil per annum through water erosion. The acuteness of the problem strikes when one realises that it takes several thousand years for Mother Earth to generate half an inch of top soil on its surface.

(vii) **Problems related to human settlements:** Unhygienic and insanitary living conditions in rural and urban settings and unplanned growth of human settlements have had a negative impact on the environment and health of man.

(viii) **Degradation of forests:** Denudation of forests for a number of economically advantageous activities, promotion of monoculture, forest encroachments and poaching have reduced our natural carbon sink to no more than 12 per cent of the land area as against the target of 33 per cent prescribed by the National Forest Policy of 1952.

(ix) **Population:** From 340 million at the time of independence 1947, India's population has nearly trebled crossing the billion mark and current official projections are that by 2016, within 20 years, the number will cross the level of 1.25 billion.

The above problems, leading to the environmental crisis we are in, are interrelated and a number of factors are responsible for causing the same. The plan document cites poverty and underdevelopment and the negative effects of the very process of development as the major causes for the environmental problems. In addition, over-consumption, the demographic factor and lack of environmental education have contributed in no small measure to the problem. Further, inadequacies in policy formulations; legislative short-sightedness and administration; ignoring, to the point of neglecting, native intelligence and indigenous systems; and over-reliance on Anglo-Saxon jurisprudential inspirations in law-making and enforcement are the major contributing factors for poor, inefficient and ineffective environmental management that has led to the current state of environment (Ramesh, 2000, p. 235).

Basis of Environmental Regulations

The roots of environmental regulations in the United Kingdom lie in planning law, whose task is to provide a framework for the orderly management of the changing use of land, and in public (or environmental) health law which is virtually exclusively concerned with protection of human beings. Over the last decade and half, these roots have become entwined with the growth of ideas – often emanating from Brussels – that the environment itself is deserving of protection, and indeed the Environmental Protection Act 1990 was specifically declared to be a measure to protect the environmental media of land, air and water in addition to human health (Hughes *et al.*, 2002, p. 17).

But does it matter whether the rules of environmental laws reflect underlying principles and, ultimately, moral concerns? The answer must be 'yes', for without some basis in principle individual laws are no more than mere reactions to individual perceived problems lacking coherence, and likely to result in anomalies (Hughes *et al.*, 2002, p. 17). These principles are: *sustainable development, the precautionary principle* and *the polluter pays principle*. These are supplemented by a number of subsidiary principles to be considered in due course.

I. **Sustainable Development:** The World Conservation Strategy (IUCN 1980) argued that: 'development and conservation are equally necessary for our survival' and the report of the World Commission on Environment and Development (Brundtland Commission) (WCED, 1987) argued that sustainable development means global economic development sufficient to meet current needs while allowing future generations to achieve their needs: what is done now should not prevent future generations from pursuing their legitimate options.

II. **The Precautionary Principle:** It is not always possible, and rarely easy, to know what environmental consequences may, at some unknown future date, flow from particular uses of the environment and its resources, or from particular industrial, or agricultural processes, nor the ways in which they may happen. This may be labeled the 'principle of uncertainty'. The laws could require:

   1. cautious progress until a process/project is judged 'innocent';

2. ordinary progress until findings of 'guilt' are made; or
3. no progress until intensive research has been conducted into a proposed process and its innocence has been demonstrated.

It is No. 3 above, which represents the strongest formulation of the 'precautionary principle'.

III. **The Polluter Pays Principle:** This principle was developed by the Organisation for Economic Co-operation and Development (OECD) in 1902. Where a process is found to have unwanted consequences, questions arise as to who should 'pay' for them. In some cases, it may not be easy to identify a responsible individual and it may be considered to be economically and administratively more efficient in such circumstances to place the responsibility for, and costs of 'clean up' measures, on some other body. This has been true of the water industry where water suppliers have borne the cost of purifying water affected by nitrates, applied by farmers, which have leached into ground and surface waters. It has been thought preferable to impose costs on water suppliers rather than to disrupt food production.

Best Practicable Environmental Option (BPEO): It was initially developed as an idea by the Royal commission on Environmental Pollution in their 5th Report (Cmnd[1] 6371). They returned to the matter in their 10th and 11th reports (Cmnd 9149[2] and 9675[3]), defining it as 'the use of different sectors of the environment to minimise damage overall' and finding 'the optimum combination of available methods ...... so as to limit damage to the environment to the greatest extent achievable for a reasonable and acceptable total combined cost to industry and the public purse' (Hughes *et al.*, 2002, p. 27). BPEO is clearly a concept which links legal and economic thinking and could be given wide application in environmental laws.

Having discussed the basis of environmental regulations briefly, we proceed to discuss the environment related regulations in a detailed manner in the next section of this Part. Accordingly, the first and second Chapters (Chapter 8 and 9) under this Part focus on environmental legislations in global and Indian context respectively. These chapters trace the evolution of statutory controls from their historical routes. It discusses the legal, regulatory and policy issues concerning air pollution. It also describes the policy framework and legal processes involved in dealing with water pollution. It explains the laws surrounding wastes. It deals with the regulatory processes involved in dealing with contaminated land, recycling/reuse, incineration and import/export. It deals with the laws and policies of integrated pollution control. It specifically describes the background to the laws, its application to certain processes, and offences and remedies. It also mentions the role of regulatory agencies in this regard. It also critically reviews the requirement and impact of major environmental legislations for businesses. Finally, the last Chapter (10) explores some strategic techniques to make compliance with environmental regulations that would ultimately lead to incorporation of environmental issues in business practice.

NOTES

1. The concept of 'best practicable environmental option' (BPEO), designed to assist decision-taking in situations where controlling pollution in one environmental medium (for example, air) can lead to increased pollution in another (for example, water) was introduced in the Fifth Report: Air Pollution Control: An Integrated Approach (Cmnd 6371), published in January 1976.
2. The Tenth Report: Tackling Pollution-Experience and Prospects (Cmnd. 9149), published in February 1984, contained a wide-ranging review of priorities for the future and the action that was needed to combat new and growing forms of pollution. It made a number of recommendations, particularly about coastal and air pollution, public access to information and the development of environmental policy in the European Community. The government responded to the Report in Pollution Paper No. 22, published in December 1984.
3. The Eleventh Report: Managing Waste: The Duty of Care (Cmnd. 9675), published in December 1985, was concerned with the handling and disposal of wastes (other than radioactive wastes). Its principal recommendation was that all those who produce wastes should have a 'duty of care' to ensure that their wastes were subsequently managed and disposed of without harm to the environment. The government's response to the Report was published as Pollution Paper No. 24 in September 1986.

8

ENVIRONMENTAL LEGISLATIONS IN GLOBAL CONTEXT

Historical Development

A brief chronology of the major global environmental movement is discussed as follows, which is based on the analysis of experts in the area (Nicholson, 1972; Kolinsky, 1984; McCormick, 1995; Chaturvedi and Chaturvedi, 1998; Rostron, 2001; Hughes *et al.*, 2002; Paliwal, 2002; Khitoliya, 2005):

- In 1863, Britain passed the first broad-ranging air pollution law in the world and created the first pollution control agency.
- The first international agreement on the environment was signed in 1886; today there are more than 300, most of which have been signed since 1960.
- 1945-1961, the post-Second World War era, is the period of conservation and reconstruction:
  - The concurrent International Union for the Protection of Nature (IUPN)/UNESCO Conference–the International Technical Conference on the Protection of Nature (ITC) (Lake Success, 22-29 August, 1949) focussed on education and human ecology.
  - Between 1948 and 1956, influenced by the Commission of Ecology's warnings that people should be aware of the ecological consequences of their activities, IUPN's

interests gradually broadened to include conservation and in 1956 its name has been changed to the International Union for Conservation of Nature and Natural Resources (IUCN).

- 1962-1970 is the age of the Environmental Revolution.
  - In the USA the Clean Air Act of 1963 was the first national legislation aimed at air pollution control followed by Clean Water Act in 1972.
- 1968-1972 is the era of prophets of doom, when three issues in particular were focused: pollution, population growth and technology.
  - In June 1972, the United Nations Conference on the Human Environment was held in Stockholm. It aimed to "create a basis for comprehensive consideration within the United Nations of the problems of the human environment", and to "focus the attention of governments and public opinion in various countries on the importance of the problem" (UN Economic and Social Council, 1968).
- 1970-1986 is the era of politics and activism, when new environmentalism began to be translated into political action by governments: new laws, new environmentalism intensified, public concerns were increasingly reflected in changes in public policy at the national level.
  - In 1956-60, only four major pieces of national environmental legislations were passed in Organisation for Economic Cooperation and Development (OECD) member states; by contrast, 10 were passed in 1961-65; 18 in 1966-70; and 31 in 1971-75 (OECD, 1979). As of August 1971, 12 countries (Australia, Britain, Canada, France, West Germany, India, Japan, Kenya, New Zealand, Singapore, Switzerland and the United States) had either planned or implemented reorganisation of their environmental programmes (Council on Environmental Quality, 1971); by June 1972, the number had reached 25 (11 of

them in LDCs); by 1985, more than 140 countries had created national environmental agencies (World Environment Center, 1983).

- During 1972-1990, there was arrival of the greens.
  - Dissatisfied with the response of conventional ideologies, new green parties emerged to challenge the old order. The first were founded in Tasmania and New Zealand in 1972; by 1991, more than 35 countries had national green parties, of which 22 had elected members to their national legislatures. In response, many of the older established parties rewrote their environmental policies and began to take notice of the green vote.
  - By the 1980s, there was a realisation that long term planning was needed to deal with new problems and the concept of sustainability was developed. This led to a growing number of policy initiatives at an international, European and domestic level.
  - To achieve sustainability, the "Vienna Convention" to prevent the depletion of ozone layer was conducted in 1982, followed by "Montreal Protocol" in 1987.
  - In 1987, the World Commission on Environment and Development (WCED) reiterated the concept of sustainable development and stated that there should be cooperation on a world-wide basis.
  - The initiatives of the 1974 legislation were continued by UK by enacting the Water Act, 1989 which is now found as the Water Industry Act, 1991 and the Water Resources Act, 1991.
- The Stockholm Conference resulted in the creation of the United Nations Environment Programme (UNEP) (1972-1992). UNEP successfully brought nearly 140 countries and 14 UN agencies together to confront pollution and coastal degradation in shared seas.

- The Environmental Protection Act 1990 of UK marked a further major step forward in this process in that it was concerned with production of the environment and not just public health, and it introduced a generalized concept of 'the environment', which applies throughout many of its provisions, as being the media of air, land and water. This process continued as a result of the Environment Act 1995, with an encouragingly more integrated notion of environmental protection being introduced by further legislation in 1999.
- In 1992, United Nations Conference on Environment and Development (UNCED) held at Rio de Janeiro, with a view to provide a new global commitment to sustainable development, promised on the interconnectedness of human activity and the environment. This was followed by the Kyoto Protocol to the United Nations Framework Convention on Climate Change and Buenos Aires' Conferences on measures to tackle global warming.
- A voluntary programme, Environment Audit and Management Scheme (EAMS), was launched by European Union in 1993. It encouraged firms to reduce the environmental impacts of their operations. Participation in EAMS increased the credibility of environmental issues and resulted in preliminary measures to improve the environmental performance.

It is primarily a history of the movement and sets out both to describe the key events in the evolution of that movement and to provide analysis that helps explain that evolution and place it in its broader context. Its central argument is that environmentalism must be seen not simply as a series of separate national movements, but as part of a cumulative, broad-ranging, long-term change in human attitudes arising as a reaction to industrialism and leaving almost no society untouched. It also argues that few environmental problems can be addressed by individual states acting alone, but that we must develop regional and global policies that recognize the regional and global links between cause and effect.

Environmental Legislations

The widespread globalisation of business and industry in recent years has led to a need to be intimately aware of international laws and regulations, as well as federal, state, and local ones (Bishop, 2000, p. 177). A multitude of laws have been designed specifically to control environmental degradation. There are widespread variations in regulations relative to environmental issues among countries. The USA has made a commendable progress in this area, although, it was UK that first legislated first broad ranging air pollution law. Taking the USA as a case, we describe laws that are enacted to tackle various environmental menaces. Laws, that are pertinent to industries and other businesses (Bishop, 2000, p. 150), are mentioned as follows:

Laws Pertaining to Clean Air

Clean Air Act (CAA): The first law established to protect and enhance the quality of the nation's air resources in USA were passed in 1955. CAA was amended in 1967, 1970 1977 and 1990 (Bishop, 2000, p. 150).

Laws Pertaining to Clean Water

Clean Water Act (CWA): The Federal Water Pollution Control Act, popularly known as CWA, is the primary federal legislation that protects the nation's surface waters. The law was originally passed in USA in 1948, and it was subsequently amended in 1972, 1977, 1981, and 1987. It is currently under review again (Bishop, 2000, p. 157).

Safe Drinking Water Act (SDWA): As the CWA was designed primarily to protect the nation's surface waters, in 1974 the SDWA was enacted in USA to manage potential contamination threats to groundwater. Subsequently it was amended in 1986 and 1996 (Bishop, 2000, p. 159).

National Environmental Policy Act (NEPA): NEPA of 1969 established national policies and goals for the protection of the environment. It also provided the framework for the government to assess the environmental effects of its actions and the progress made toward improving environmental quality (Bishop, 2000, p. 159).

Laws Pertaining to Hazardous Materials and Wastes

Toxic Substances Control Act (TSCA): TSCA was passed in 1976 to empower the USEPA to obtain information on all new and existing chemical substances and to control any of these substances determined to cause an unreasonable risk to public health or the environment. This Act was subsequently amended in 1986 and 1990 (Bishop, 2000, pp. 160-161).

Resource Conservation and Recovery Act (RCRA): Until 1976, hazardous wastes were regulated under the Solid Waste Disposal Act of 1965, which dealt primarily with the disposal of non-hazardous wastes. RCRA rewrote the previous legislation and provided the framework for national programmes to achieve environmentally sound management of both hazardous and non-hazardous wastes (Bishop, 2000, p. 162).

Hazardous Materials Transportation Act (HMTA): The HMTA of 1975 was designed to improve the federal regulatory and enforcement authority to protect the public adequately against risks to life and property which are inherent in the transportation of hazardous materials in commerce (Bishop, 2000, p. 172).

Laws Pertaining to Pollution Prevention

Pollution Prevention Act (PPA): The goal of PPA of 1990 is to shift the nation's waste strategy from the control of wastes after its generation to the reduction of wastes at its source (Bishop, 2000, pp. 175-176).

Laws Pertaining to Occupational Hazards

Occupational Safety and Health Act (OSHA): The OSHA was enacted in 1970 and amended in 1990. Inspection of factories by regulatory agencies began in England in the early 19th century in response to public protest against the working conditions for women and child labourers. Later governments adopted regulations against unhealthful and dangerous working conditions (Bishop, 2000, p. 174).

9

ENVIRONMENTAL LEGISLATIONS IN INDIAN CONTEXT

Evolution

In India, the concern for environment was first echoed in the 1970's, following the United Nations Stockholm Conference on environment. The Indian constitution contains specific provisions for environmental protection under the chapters of directive principles of state policy and fundamental duties. Right to a wholesome environment is a fundamental right (Khitoliya, 2005, pp. 27-28). It is also worthwhile to mention here that the Constitution of India incorporated strong commitment to protection of environment. Article 48A of the Constitution entrusts upon the State to take measures to protect and improve the environment and to safeguard the forests and wildlife of the country. Article 51A (g) makes it a fundamental duty of every citizen to protect and improve the natural environment, including forests, lakes, rivers and wildlife and to have compassion for living creatures (Paliwal, 2002, p. 65).

The alien rulers in India did take measures to maintain the standards of hygiene and sanitation in the metropolitan cities, like Calcutta, Madras and Kanpur as also in the Cantonment areas for the protection of the defence personnel by enacting various Nuisances Acts, Municipality Acts, and a number of Building Codes. The Calcutta Municipal Act, 1951 contains special provisions to prohibit the fouling of water. After independence, the State of Uttar Pradesh was the first to establish its Effluent (Control) Board Act, in 1955. In 1970, the State of Maharashtra enacted its Water Pollution Control Act which stood as the model for the national law styled as the Water (Prevention and Control of Pollution) Act of 1974 (Chaturvedi and Chaturvedi, 1998, p. 37).

In order to provide a point in the structure of the Government where environmental aspects could receive the deserved attention on an integrated manner, the National Committee on Environmental Planning and Coordination (NCEPC) was established in February 1972 (Chaturvedi and Chaturvedi, 1998, p. 21). Prime objectives of the Committee were to advise on environmental problems and to make recommendations for their improvement.

In pursuance of the recommendations made by the Tiwari Committee constituted for recommending legislative measures and administrative machinery for ensuring environmental protection, a separate Department of Environment was set up in November, 1980 under the Ministry of Science and Technology, Government of India to act as a nodal agency for environmental protection and eco-development work and to carry out environmental appraisal of development projects.

A comprehensive law to control and prevent water pollution was passed in 1974. The Central Government enacted an air pollution prevention and control law in 1981. After "Bhopal Gas Tragedy" (December 2/3, 1984) and after "Oleum gas leakage" from Sri Ram Food and Fertiliser Industry, New Delhi it was felt that there should be some laws which could deal with such emergent situations. Accordingly, the Environment (Protection) Act was passed in 1986 to provide an integrated approach to deal with the environmental pollution problems (Shastri and Trivedi, 1997, p. 278). The series of rules developed under this umbrella legislation, to regulate movement of hazardous substances, wastes dumping, etc., appear to have broadened its vision and areas of activity.

Thus, the Water (Prevention and Control of Pollution) Act, 1974; The Water (Prevention and Control of Pollution) Cess Act,

1977; The Air (Prevention and Control of Pollution) Act, 1981; and the Environment (Protection) Act, 1986 are the principal legislations enacted to control and combat pollution in the post-Stockholm era. Major Indian Environmental Acts, Rules and Regulations are grouped in Exhibit 9.1 according to the purposes and are listed chronologically in accordance with their year of enactment. While there are specific legislations and administrative authorities (Pollution Control Boards – both at the central and state levels) dealing with water and air pollution, the Environment (Protection) Act governs their functioning and provides the procedures and mechanisms for their implementation. Detailed sets of rules and notifications were issued from time to time to regulate coastal zone, hazardous wastes and biomedical wastes management (Ramesh, 2000, p. 246).

EXHIBIT 9.1
INDIAN ENVIRONMENTAL ACTS, RULES AND NOTIFICATIONS

Air Pollution Related:

1. The Air (Prevention and Control of Pollution) Act, 1981 (14 of 1981)

   The Air (Prevention and Control of Pollution) Amendment Act, 1987 (47 of 1987)
2. The Air (Prevention and Control of Pollution) Rules, 1982
3. Ozone Depleting Substances (Regulation) Rules, 2000

Noise Pollution Related:

4. Noise Pollution (Regulation and Control) Rules, 2000
5. Noise Pollution (Regulation and Control) (Amendment) Rules, 2002

Water Pollution Related:

6. Orissa River Pollution Prevention Act, 1953
7. The River Boards Act, 1956
8. Maharashtra Prevention of Water Pollution Act, 1969
9. The Water (Prevention and Control of Pollution) Act, 1974 (6 of 1974)

(Contd...)

The Water (Prevention and Control of Pollution) Amendment Act, 1988 [53 of 1988]

10. The Water (Prevention and Control of Pollution) Rules, 1975
11. The Water (Prevention and Control of Pollution) Cess Act, 1977 (36 of 1977)
12. The Water (Prevention and Control of Pollution) Cess (Amendment) Act, 1991 (53 of 1991)
13. The Water (Prevention and Control of Pollution) Cess Rules, 1978
14. The West Bengal Ground Water Resources (Management, Control and Regulation) Act, 2005

Solid and Hazardous Wastes Management Related:

15. Bhopal Gas Leak Disaster (Processing of Claims) Act, 1985
16. Hazardous Wastes (Management and Handling) Rules, 1989

    Hazardous Wastes (Management and Handling) Amendment Rules, 2000
17. The Manufacture, Storage and Import of Hazardous Chemical Rules, 1989

    The Manufacture, Storage and Import of Hazardous Chemical (Amendment) Rules, 2000
18. Manufacture, Use, Import, Export and Storage of Hazardous Micro-Organisms, Genetically Engineered Organisms or Cells Rules, 1989
19. The Public Liability Insurance Act, 1991 (6 of 1991)
20. The Public Liability Insurance Rules, 1991
21. The National Environment Tribunal Act, 1995 (27 of 1995)
22. The National Environment Appellate Authority Act, 1997 (2 of 1997)
23. Bio-Medical Waste (Management and Handling) Rules, 1998
24. Re-cycled Plastics Manufacture and Usage Rules, 1999

(Contd...)

Re-cycled Plastics Manufacture and Usage Amendment Rules, 2002

25. Municipal Solid Wastes (Management & Handling) Rules, 2000
26. Batteries (Management & Handling) Rules, 2001

Environment Protection Related:

27. The Mines and Minerals (Regulation and Development) Act, 1947
28. The Factories Act, 1948

    The Factories Amendment Act, 1987
29. The Industries (Development and Regulation) Act, 1951
30. The Environment (Protection) Act, 1986 (29 of 1986)
31. The Environment (Protection) Rules, 1986

Notifications

- Environment (Siting for Industrial Projects) Rules, 1999–Notification
- Environment (Protection) Second Amendment Rules, 2002
- G. S. R. 489 (E) – The Environment (Protection) Third Amendment Rules, 2002
- S.O. 727 (E) and S.O. 728 (E) – Amended EPA Notification of MoEF number S. O. 83 (E), 84 (E) dated 16th February, 1987 – published on 10th July, 2002
- S. O. 729 (E) and S. O. 730 (E) – Amended EPA, 1986 dated 10th July, 2002
- EIA Notification of 27th January 1994
    - Amended EIA Notification of 27th January 1994 – dated 21st November, 2001
    - Amended EIA Notification of 27th January 1994 – dated 13th June, 2002

(Contd...)

- ❑ Amended EIA Notification of 27th January 1994 – dated 15th September, 2006

➤ Central Ground Water Board Authority, 1992 – Notification

➤ The Prevention and Control of Pollution (Uniform Consent Procedure) Rules, 1999 (Draft)

Forest and Wildlife Related:

31. The Mysore Destructive Insects and Pests Act, 1917
32. The Andhra Pradesh Agricultural Pests and Diseases Act, 1919
33. The Indian Forest Act, 1927 (16 of 1927)
34. The Assam Agricultural Pests and Diseases Act, 1954
35. The Uttar Pradesh Agricultural Diseases and Pests Act, 1954
36. The Kerala Agricultural Pests and Diseases Act, 1958
37. The Insecticides Act, 1968
38. The Forest (Conservation) Act, 1980 (69 of 1980)

    The Forest (Conservation) (Amendment) Act, 1988 (69 of 1988)
39. The Forest (Conservation) Rules, 1981
40. National Forest Policy, 1988
41. New Biodiversity Bill, 2000
42. The Wildlife (Protection) Act, 1972 (53 of 1972)

    The Wild Life (Protection) (Amendment) Act, 1982 (23 of 1982)

    The Wild Life (Protection) (Amendment) Act, 1986 (28 of 1986)

    The Wild Life (Protection) (Amendment) Act, 1991 (44 of 1991)

    The Wild Life (Protection) (Amendment) Act, 1993 (26 of 1986)

(Contd...)

43. The Wildlife (Transaction and Taxidermy) Rules, 1973
44. The Wildlife (Stock Declaration) Central Rules, 1973
45. The Wildlife (Protection) Licensing (Additional Matters for Consideration) Rules, 1983
46. The Wildlife (Protection) Rules, 1995
47. The Wildlife (Specified Plants – Conditions for Possession by Licensee) Rules, 1995
48. The Wildlife (Specified Plant Stock Declaration) Central Rules, 1995

Coastal Zone Related:

49. Coastal Regulation Zone – Notification dated May 21, 2002
50. Coastal Zone Management Authority – Notifications
51. The Coast Guard Act, 1978

Miscellaneous:

52. Shore Nuisance (Bombay and Kolaba) Act, 1853 (XI of 1853)
53. The Northern India, Canal and Drainage Act, 1873 (VIII of 1873)
54. The Land Acquisition Act, 1894
55. The Indian Fisheries Act, 1897
56. The Bengal Smoke Nuisance Act, 1905
57. The Bombay Smoke Nuisance Act, 1912
58. The Poisons Act, 1919
59. The Motor Vehicles Act, 1939

    The New Motor Vehicles Act, 1988
60. The Bihar Waste Lands (Reclamation, Cultivation and Improvement) Act, 1946
61. The Acquisition of Land for Flood Control and Prevention of Erosion Act, 1955
62. The Atomic Energy Act, 1962

(Contd...)

63. The Gujarat Smoke Nuisance Act, 1963
64. The Constitution (Forty-Second Amendment) Act, 1976

Regulatory Framework of Environmental Legislations in India

There are more than 300 central and state statutes, having bearing on environmental protection. However, many of these legislations are dedicated to different objectives, where the environmental provisions are only incidental. In the following section, an overview of contemporary principal environmental laws in India have been discussed, which is based on analysis of experts in the area (Rosencranz *et al.*, 1991; Jadhav and Bhosale, 1995; Mohanty, 1997; Roy, 1998; Paliwal, 2002; Khitoliya, 2005).

➢ Acts/Rules Relating to Water Pollution

The Water (Prevention and Control of Pollution) Act, 1974 (6 of 1974): This Act has been enacted by Parliament under Article 252 of the Constitution to provide for the prevention and control of water pollution and the maintaining or restoring of wholesomeness of water, for the establishment, with a view to carrying out the purposes, of Boards for the prevention and control of water pollution, for conferring on and assigning to such Boards' powers and functions relating thereto and for matters connected therewith. In exercise of the powers conferred by Section 63 of the Act, the Central Government after consultation with the Central Board for the prevention and control of water pollution has prescribed **the Water (Prevention and Control of Pollution) Rules, 1975**. The Rules mainly deal with detail procedure for proper enforcement of the Act.

The Water (Prevention and Control of Pollution) Cess Act, 1977 (36 of 1977): This is an Act to provide for the levy and collection of a cess on water consumed by persons carrying on certain industries and by local authorities, with a view to augment the resources of the Central Board and the State Boards for the prevention and control of water pollution constituted under the Water (Prevention and Control of Pollution) Act, 1974. In exercise of the powers conferred by Section 17 of the Act, the Central Government has prescribed **the Water (Prevention and Control**

of Pollution) Cess Rules, 1978 to operationalise the Act. The Rules mainly deal with detail procedure for proper enforcement of the Act.

➢ Acts/Rules Relating to Air Pollution

The Air (Prevention and Control of Pollution) Act, 1981 (14 of 1981): This Act has been enacted under Article 253 of the Constitution, following the United Nations Conference on the Human Environment held at Stockholm, 1972 to take appropriate steps for the preservation of the natural resources of the earth which, among other things, include the preservation of the quality of air and control of air pollution. The Act's objective is to implement the decisions of the Conference to alleviate the "detrimental effect of air pollution on the health of the people as also on animal life, vegetation and property." **The Air (Prevention and Control of Pollution) Rules, 1982** mainly deal with detail procedure for proper enforcement of the Air (Prevention and Control of Pollution) Act, 1981.

➢ Acts/Rules Relating to Environment Protection

The Environment (Protection) Act, 1986 (29 of 1986): This Act clearly drew its inspiration from the proclamation adopted by the United Nations Conference on the Human Environment, 1972 to take appropriate steps for the protection and improvement of human environment. In fact, this has been enacted under Article 253 of the Constitution after the Bhopal disaster[1]. Section 3(1) of this Act empowers the Government of India "to take all such measures as it deems necessary or expedient for the purpose of protecting and improving the quality of the environment and preventing, controlling and abating environmental pollution". In this Act, the Centre has been authorised to set new national standards for maintaining environmental quality (ambient standard) and also the standards for controlling emissions and effluent discharges; to prescribe procedures for hazardous wastes and chemicals management; to regulate the location of industries; to establish safeguards to prevent accidents; to collect and disseminate information on environmental pollution. This Act is the first Act to empower the Central Government authority to issue direct written orders, to close, prohibit, or regulate any industry, operation or process or to stop or regulate the water and electric supply or any other service. Later these powers have also been included in the Air Act, 1981 and the Water Act, 1974 through amendments. In exercise of powers conferred by Sections 6 and 25 of the Act, **the Environment (Protection) Rules 1986** have been made by the Central Government. The Rules mainly deal with standards of emission or discharge of environmental pollutants; prohibition and restriction on the location of industries; prohibition and restriction on the handling of hazardous substances in different areas; etc.

➢ Rules Relating to Handling of Hazardous Substances

Hazardous Wastes (Management and Handing) Rules, 1989: In exercise of the powers conferred by Sections 6, 8 and 25 of the Environment (Protection) Act, 1986 (29 of 1986), the Central Government has prescribed the Hazardous Wastes (Management and Handling) Rules, 1989. The Rules mainly deal with responsibility of the occupier for handling of wastes; grant of authorisation for handling hazardous wastes; detail procedure of packaging, labelling, transport and import of hazardous wastes; etc. Hazardous Wastes (Management and Handing) Rules, 1989 has been amended to **the Hazardous Wastes (Management and Handing) Amendment Rules, 2000.**

The Manufacture, Storage and Import of Hazardous Chemical Rules, 1989: In exercise of the powers conferred by Sections 6, 8 and 25 of the Environment (Protection) Act, 1986 (29 of 1986), the Central Government has prescribed the Manufacture, Storage and Import of Hazardous Chemical Rules, 1989. The Rules mainly deal with general responsibility of the occupier during industrial activity; transitional provisions; preparation of on site emergency plan by the occupier; etc. The Rules have been amended to the **Manufacture, Storage and Import of Hazardous Chemical (Amendment) Rules, 2000.**

The Public Liability Insurance Act, 1991 (6 of 1991): This Act was enacted for the purpose of providing immediate relief to the persons affected by accidents occurring while handling hazardous substances. As per the provisions of this Act, the insurance policy of amount more than paid-up capital of the industry but less than Rs. 50 crores have to be taken up by the owner of the industry before starting handling of specified hazardous substances to give the relief in case of death or damage to property from an accident occurring while handling of hazardous substances.

The National Environment Tribunal Act, 1995: In 1995, the Parliament passed 'The National Environment Tribunal Act, 1995' with the object of providing for strict liability for damages arising out of any accident occurring while handling any hazardous substance and for the establishment of a National Environmental Tribunal for effective and expeditious disposal of cases arising from such accidents, with a view to give relief and compensation for damages to persons, property and the environment and for matters connected therewith or incidental thereto.

Role of PCB and Other Government Bodies

For enforcing environmental regulations, role of certain Government bodies require special mention. On the basis of the recommendations of the Tiwari Committee on legislative measures and administrative mechanisms to ensure environmental protection, the Government of India constituted a separate Department of Environment (DoE) effective from November 1, 1980 to be the center stage for planning, promoting and coordinating programmes related to the environment. Subsequently, a full-fledged Ministry of Environment and Forests (MoEF) was constituted in 1985, to oversee these functions at the national level (Chaturvedi, 1997, p. 4).

MoEF is the nodal agency at the Central level for planning, promoting and coordinating the environmental programmes, apart from policy formulation. A number of enforcement agencies assist MoEF in executing the assigned responsibilities as specified in the "Allocation of Business Rules" (Chaturvedi, 1997, p. 5). In April, 1997, MoEF issued a notification requiring environmental clearance of industrial projects by Central or State Governments (Paliwal, 2002, p. 67). The Central Board for prevention and control of water pollution was established in September 1974 for the purpose of implementing provisions of the Water (Prevention and Control of Pollution) Act, 1974. Subsequently, the State Pollution Control Boards were constituted to implement the Act in respective states of the Indian Union. Thereafter, the Central/ State Pollution Control Boards were also given the responsibility of implementing other specific enactments relating to the environment. The executive responsibilities for the industrial pollution prevention and control are primarily executed by the Central Pollution Control Board at the Central level, which is a statutory authority, attached to MoEF. The State Departments of Environment and State Pollution Control Boards are the designated agencies to perform these functions at the State level. The organisational network of environmental management in India is shown in Figure 9.1. The agencies responsible for environmental management and their key functions are listed in Table 9.1 (Chaturvedi, 1997, p. 5).

Fig. 9.1

Organisational Structure for Environmental Management in India

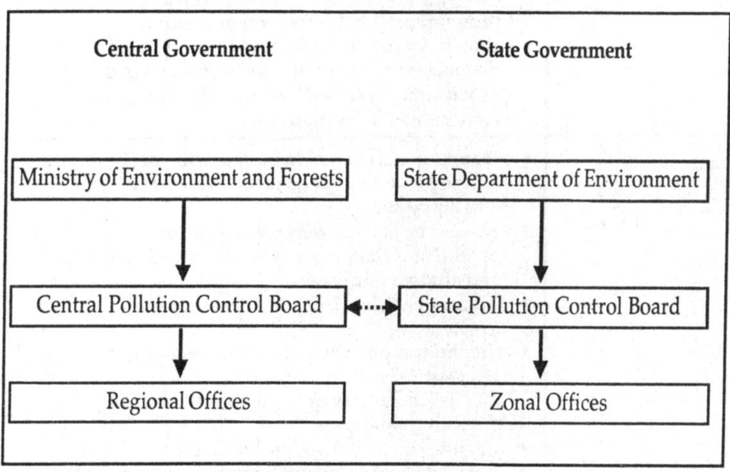

Source: Chaturvedi (1997, p. 7)

Table 9.1: Key Functions of the Agencies Responsible for Environmental Management

Name of the Agency	*Key Functions*
Ministry of Environment and Forests	• Environment policy planning • Ensure effective implementation of legislations • Monitoring and control of pollution • Eco-development • Environmental clearances for industrial and development projects • Environmental research • Promotion of the environmental education, training and awareness • Coordination with concerned agencies at the national and international levels • Forest conservation, development and wildlife protection • Biosphere reserve programme
Central Pollution Control Board	• Promote cleanliness of streams and wells • Advise the Central Government on the matters concerning prevention, control and abatement of water and air pollution • Coordinate and provide technical and research assistance to State Boards • Information dissemination, training and awareness • Lay down, modify or annul the standards for a stream or well, and for air quality, etc. • Planning and execution of nation wide programmes for the prevention, control of abatement of water and air pollution • Ensure compliance with the provisions of the Environment (Protection) Act, 1986 and other environmental legislations
State Pollution Control Board	• Planning and execution of state wide programmes for the prevention, control or abatement of water and air pollution • Advise the State Government on prevention, control and abatement of Water and Air pollution and siting of industries • Information dissemination, training and awareness • Ensure compliance with the provisions of the relevant Acts • Lay down, modify or annul the effluent and emission standards • Ensure legal action against defaulters • Evolve techno-economic methods for treatment, disposal and utilisation of the effluent

Source: Chaturvedi (1997, p. 6)

Enforcing Regulations – Present Scenario

Recently Supreme Court of India has emphasised on the need to strengthen some institutional machinery to enforce anti pollution laws across the state. For the purpose, Government of India was suggested to set up special courts (i.e. Green Bench) exclusively to deal with cases relating to violations of environmental laws. The Supreme Court has also suggested that chemical industries should not be treated at par with the other industries, rather they should be treated separately (Roy, 1998, p. 271).

Under the major environmental legislations viz., the Water Act (1974); the Air Act (1981) as well as E(P)A (1986), very wide powers have been given to the Central Government. It has the powers to issue directions for the closure, prohibition or regulation of any industry, operation or process and to regulate the supply of electricity or water. It is suggested that the Central Government should make use of these powers to ensure that the industries do not pollute the environment in any manner. Section 7 of the E(P)A which provides that no person carrying any industry operation or process shall discharge or emit any environmental pollutant in excess of the prescribed standards, is in consonance with the "fundamental duty" of every citizen to protect and improve the environment. Section 15 of the E(P)A is a very important section as it provides for deterrent punishment for the violation of the Act (i.e. fine upto Rs. 1,00,000/- and/or imprisonment upto 5 years which might be extended if the violation gets continued). Similar penalties have been imposed under the Water and Air Act in case of the violation of provisions of these Acts. However, the deterrent effect of Section 15 is reduced by the Section 24(2) of the Act which provides that where an act or omission constitutes an offense under this Act as well as under any other Act, there the offender shall be punished under other Act and not under this Act. It is suggested that this anomaly should be removed by amending the laws suitably and by retaining the deterrent effect of the laws. Another good feature of the E(P)A is that the company or the government departments or their in-charge for the conduct of business can also be held liable and punished under this Act. Thus, it will be making the person in-charge more vigilant in the discharge of his duties. Khitoliya (2005, p. 335) mentioned that the Section 19 of E(P)A should be amended and the requirement of giving notice of sixty days should be done away with. It has been seen in India that most of the environmental litigations have come up as a result of public interest litigation under the writ jurisdiction. In view of the importance of the environment protection, people should be encouraged to bring to the court those cases where there is a violation of anti-pollution laws or where any activity has resulted in the environmental harm.

Problems with Implementation

A survey of the Indian Laws revealed that there are more than 300 enactments relating to the environment passed either by the Central Government or by the State Governments. Yet, this plethora of environment laws has not been able to check the environmental degradation and eco-system imbalances (Shastri and Trivedi, 1997, pp. 277-278). Further, the environmental movement has been far from homogeneous. At the local and national level, debates rage about the causes of the environmental crisis and about the appropriate responses; should policies change to deal with problems as they arise, or is the key a fundamental reordering of human attitudes towards the biosphere and even towards each other? (McCormick, 1995)

The present discussion, therefore, endeavours to identify and articulate some anomalies in implementation of pollution related laws in India. Bandyopadhyay (1998, p. 290) highlighted that the emission level norms set by the Pollution Control Board do not adequately discriminate between large and small units. They go generally by command and control system keeping the emission level under certain norms. For instance, large power stations even when fitted with modern pollution control devices and despite having high efficiencies cause total emission per year which may be high compared to small unsophisticated plant. But the small plants which have neither adequate financial backup to incur an additional cost nor proper infrastructure to accommodate a sophisticated pollution control device are also commanded to install electrostatic precipitator (ESP). Some of the small plants which have spreader stoker or chain grate stoker boilers, inherently by virtue of the design of the boilers, generate mostly bottom ash. Fly ash generated by these boilers may be at the most of the order of 20 per cent. Hence, over a period of time the quantum of pollution from the small plants is much less compared to large power plants even though these plants are fitted with sophisticated pollution control devices. However, in advanced countries like United States, this factor has been given due consideration and the pollution laws have been formed in such a way that the control is done on area wise rather than on individual units. Also the individual units are controlled on the basis of total quantum of pollutants in an emission created in a year rather than on the percentage of the pollutants in an emission. Some authorities feel that this is the most rational way to control pollution.

It is evident that under the present way of regulatory compliance many industries may become unviable because installation of sophisticated pollution control equipment is either technically not possible or commercially not viable especially in small and medium scale units. It will inhibit laudable economic enterprise as well as violate critical environmental constraints. As an alternative, the process of adaptive environmental management and policy design should be offered, which integrates environment with economic and social understanding at the very beginning of the design process in a sequence of steps during the design phase and after implementation.

There are at least two basic difficulties that can be identified with the present approach. First, the fundamental properties of any development or policy are set very early in the design stage. If problem arises because the original context is too narrow, any fundamental redesign is extremely difficult unless there is extraordinary pressure. Ultimately confrontation is generated as different groups identify clear conflicts with their own interests.

The second major problem with present protective and reactive response is that it makes the practice of environmental assessment arbitrary, inflexible and unfocussed. Each issue is often dealt with as if it were unique and as the environmental consequence would be separated from the economic ones. Deleterious social and economic impact can be induced through ecological forces that if recognized early, could at times be turned to human's benefit rather than simply suppressed and ignored.

Similarly, Furtado (1991) identified that the present environmental regulations have been found to be inadequate to ensure sustainable livelihoods in the developing countries due to poor and unreliable database; scarce skilled and technical expertise; weak understanding of local, provincial and national-ecological and economic dynamics; and ignorance of regional and global ecological and economic inter-linkages.

NOTE

1. On the night of December 2nd and 3rd, 1984, a Union Carbide plant in Bhopal, India, began leaking 27 tons of the deadly gas methyl isocyanate. None of the six safety systems designed to contain such a leak were operational, allowing the gas to spread throughout the city of Bhopal. Half a million people were exposed to the gas and 20,000 have died to date as a result of their exposure. More than 1,20,000 people still suffer from ailments caused by the accident and the subsequent pollution at the plant site.

10

COMPLIANCE WITH ENVIRONMENTAL LEGISLATIONS AND BUSINESS PRACTICES

Regarding enactment of laws, the law-making bodies would try to enforce it to the extent possible. Hence, it is imperative for business units to make adequate arrangement so that adverse consequence for non-compliance is kept at minimum. Further, a number of studies show that there is scope of improving business performance through incorporation of environmental initiatives in business practice. It is pertinent to mention here that a set of descriptive and procreative techniques can provide the skeleton for policy design that can integrate economic, ecological and environmental understanding. Therefore, to incorporate environmental issues in business practice and to reduce environmental pollution, business should comply with environmental legislations. Accordingly, on the basis of different approaches made by Jadhav and Bhosale (1995), Shastri and Trivedi (1997, p. 281), Bandyopadhyay (1998, p. 291), Roy (1998, p. 267), Ramesh (2000, p. 248), Paliwal (2002, pp. 156-157), Khitoliya (2005, pp. 14-15), following major ways may be explored for such incorporation:

- Each business unit needs to establish policies, programmes and practices for conducting operations in an environmentally sound manner to recognise environmental management as among the highest corporate priorities and as a key determinant to sustainable development. It is also required to integrate these policies, programmes and practices fully into each business segment as an essential element of management in all its functions.

- Each business unit needs to continue to improve corporate policies, programmes and environmental performance, taking into account technical advancements/ developments, consumer needs and community expectations.
- Involvement of various stakeholders and creating appropriate environmental awareness among them are necessary to tackle the environmental issues effectively.
- In order to protect the environment, the precautionary measures should be explored on priority basis.
- There is a need to incorporate provisions to force the corporate sector to disclose the authentic facts about environmental activities and to provide for verification of the facts disclosed.
- Awareness among the consumers for purchasing only products that are produced from the factories which have adopted EMS need to be popularised.
- Each unit needs to develop and provide products and services that have no undue environmental impact and are safe in their intended use, that are efficient in their consumption of energy and natural resources, and that can be recycled, reused, or disposed off safely.
- Each unit needs to develop, design and operate facilities and conduct activities taking into consideration the efficient use of energy and materials, the sustainable use of renewable resources, the minimisation of adverse environmental impact and wastes generation, and the safe and responsible disposal of residual wastes. It also needs to assess the requirement of installation of the pollution control equipments and effluent treatment plants. Concrete efforts are needed to measure the effluent flow and quantity of effluents discharged outside the premises.

- Each unit needs to educate, train and motivate employees to conduct their activities in an environmentally responsible manner.
- Each unit needs to advise, and where relevant, educate customers, distributors and the public in the safe use, transport, storage and disposal of products provided; and to apply similar consideration to provision of services.
- Each unit requires to foster openness and dialogue with employees and public, anticipating and responding to their concerns about the potential hazards and impacts of operations, products, wastes or services, including those of trans-boundary or global significance.
- As a prerequisite all potential polluters must obtain consent to establish before initiating any action for setting up of new business/trade or planning for expansion/modernisation. Whereas in case of a large unit, business house should submit Environmental Impact Assessment (EIA) and Environmental Management Plan (EMP) to the State/Central Government for environmental clearance of the project.
- Each unit needs to take base line data regarding existing environmental status viz., ambient air quality, meteorological data, surface and ground water quality, noise levels, terrestrial ecology to provide the reference for assessing the trend in the pollution level.
- Each unit needs to measure environmental performance; conduct regular environmental audits and periodically provide appropriate information to the board of directors, shareholders, employees, the authorities and the public. It also needs to prepare an Environmental Statement and submit to the Pollution Control Board.
- Each unit needs to develop and maintain, where significant hazards exist, emergency preparedness plans in conjunction with emergency services, relevant authorities and local community, recognising potential transboundary impacts.

- Periodic review of the laws should be obligatory for the lawmakers to examine at regular intervals their continued suitability and durability, besides ensuring that they keep pace with constitutional amendments.
- Codification and consolidation of pollution-control laws, that do away with the repetitions, overlaps, dogging the existing laws, is the need of the hour.

However, some industrialists may think that environmental pollution control is the anti-thesis of the industrial development. But, in reality, environmental pollution control and industrial development are complementary to each other and they are the two sides of the same coin. Therefore, the pseudo impression formed in the minds of the industrialists must be driven out first and they must be made to think that their efforts to keep the environment clean is not a statutory obligation imposed on them, but it is a great service rendered by them to the human race not only for the present but also for the future (Shastri and Trivedi, 1997, p. 157). Unless the industrialists take the task of environmental pollution control very seriously, there is going to be a lull in the industrial development and danger to the human race. Any industrial development without environmental pollution control would create innumerable insurmountable difficulties which can never be solved. Therefore, the problem of environmental pollution is a very serious problem and has to be tackled by all sections of the society with utmost sincerity.

In this Part (Part-II), it was attempted to throw light on the need of environmental regulations followed by the discussion on the basis of environmental regulations. It tried to draw an overview of environmental legislations and conventions/treaties coming on the way of the businesses in global and Indian context. It also mentioned the role of various regulatory agencies and requirement and impact of major environmental legislations for businesses. Finally, it attempted to explore some strategic techniques to make compliance with environmental regulations that would ultimately lead to incorporation of environmental issues in business practice.

Based on this, subsequent Part of this study would try to explore different models that are advocated to incorporate environmental issues in business practice. We hope that the theoretical discussions made in the foregoing sections regarding the legislative aspects of environmental proactiveness would help us to keep a correct pace towards a sustainable approach in corporate practices.

11

REFERENCES

Bandyopadhyay, Sriparna (1998), 'Pollution Control Measure in India: Some Anomalies', in Roy, Dilip (1998) (ed.), *Environmental Management with Indian Experience*, A. P. H. Publishing Corporation, New Delhi.

Bishop, Paul L. (2000), *Pollution Prevention: Fundamentals and Practice*, McGraw-Hill International Editions, Singapore.

Chaturvedi, A. K. (1997), *Indian Environmental Legislation: Guide for Industry and Businesses*, Confederation of Indian Industry, New Delhi.

Chaturvedi, Dr. R. G. and Chaturvedi, Dr. M. M. (1998), *Law on Protection of Environment and Prevention of Pollution (Central and States)*, The Law Book Company (P) Ltd., Allahabad.

Cmnd 6371 (1976), 'Fifth Report: Air Pollution Control: An Integrated Approach', *Royal Commission on Environmental Pollution*, HMSO, London.

Cmnd 9149 (1984), 'Tenth Report: Tackling Pollution – Experience and Prospects', *Royal Commission on Environmental Pollution*, HMSO, London.

Cmnd 9675 (1985), 'Eleventh Report: Managing Waste: The Duty of Care', *Royal Commission on Environmental Pollution*, HMSO, London.

Council on Environmental Quality (1971), *Environmental Quality 1971*, US Government Printing Office, Washington DC, p. 28, Quoted in McCormick, John (1995), *The Global Environmental Movement*, John Wiley & Sons Ltd., England, 2nd edition, p. 155.

Furtado, Jose I. Dos Remedios (1991), 'Ecologically Based Strategies for Conservation and Development in the Tropics', *Ecological Research*, 6: pp. 157-174, Quoted in Khitoliya, R. K. (2005), *Environmental Protection and the Law*, A.P.H. Publishing Corporation, New Delhi, p. 19.

Hughes, D., Jewell, T., Lowther, J., Parpworth, N. and Prez, Paula de (2002), *Environmental Law*, Lexis Nexis Butterworths Tolley, United Kingdom, 4th ed.

Jadhav, H. V. and Bhosale, V. M. (1995), *Environmental Protection and Laws*, Himalaya Publishing House, Bombay, p. 160.

Khitoliya, R. K. (2005), *Environmental Protection and the Law*, A.P.H. Publishing Corporation, New Delhi.

Kolinsky, Eva (1984), 'The Greens in Germany: Prospects of a Small Party', *Parliamentary Affairs* 37: 4, Autumn 1984, pp. 434-447, Quoted in McCormick, John (1995), *The Global Environmental Movement*, John Wiley & Sons Ltd., England, 2nd Edition, p. 203.

McCormick, John (1995), *The Global Environmental Movement*, John Wiley & Sons Ltd., England, 2nd edition, p. xiv.

Mohanty, S.K. (1997), *Universal's Environment & Pollution Law Manual*, Universal Law Publishing Co. Pvt. Ltd., Delhi.

Nicholson, Max (1972), *The Environmental Revolution*, Hodder & Stoughton, London, p. 196, Quoted in McCormick, John (1995), *The Global Environmental Movement*, John Wiley & Sons Ltd., England, 2nd edition, p. 45.

Organisation for Economic Cooperation and Development (1979), *The State of the Environment in OECD Member Countries*, OECD, Paris, Quoted in McCormick, John (1995), *The Global Environmental Movement*, John Wiley & Sons Ltd., England, 2nd edition, p. 155.

Paliwal, U.L. (2002), *Environment Audit*, Indus Valley Publications, Jaipur.

Ramesh, M.K. (2000), 'Environmental Legislation and Implementation in India', in Chary, S. N. and Vyasulu, Vinod (2000) (ed.), *Environmental Management: An Indian Perspective*, Macmillan India Limited, New Delhi.

Rosencranz et al. (1991), *Environmental Law and Policy in India: Cases, Materials and Statutes,* N.M. Tripathy Private Ltd., Bombay, Quoted in Khitoliya, R.K. (2005), *Environmental Protection and the Law,* A. P. H. Publishing Corporation, New Delhi, p. 52.

Rostron, Jack (2001), *Environmental Law for the Built Environment,* Cavendish Publishing Limited, UK, p. 1.

Roy, Dilip (1998), *Environmental Management with Indian Experience,* A.P.H. Publishing Corporation, New Delhi.

Shastri, Satish and Trivedi, Manjoo Bala (1997), 'Environmental Laws in India: How Effective It Is?' in Sinha, Rajiv K. (1997) (ed.), *Environmental Crisis and Humans at Risk (Priorities for Action),* Ina Shree Publishers, Jaipur.

Timothy, O'Riordon (1995), 'Managing the Global Commons', *Environmental Science for Environmental Management,* Longman Group Limited, England, Quoted in Paliwal, U. L. (2002), *Environment Audit,* Indus Valley Publications, Jaipur, p. 62.

UN Economic and Social Council (1968), Annexes, Agenda Item 12 (Doc E/4466/Add.1) at 2, ECOSOC, New York, Quoted in McCormick, John (1995), *The Global Environmental Movement,* John Wiley & Sons Ltd., England, 2nd Edition, pp. 107-108.

WCED (1987), *Our Common Future*: Report of the World Commission on Environment and Development, Oxford University Press, Oxford, p. 400, Quoted in Khitoliya, R. K. (2005), *Environmental Protection and the Law,* A.P.H. Publishing Corporation, New Delhi, p. 19.

World Environment Center (1983), *The World Environment Handbook,* WEC, New York, Quoted in McCormick, John (1995), *The Global Environmental Movement,* John Wiley & Sons Ltd., England, 2nd Edition, p. 155.

PART–III

12

INCORPORATION OF ENVIRONMENTAL ISSUES IN BUSINESS

Businesses are at the core of the environmental debate and are central both to the pollution problem and to the solution (Kumar, 1999, p. 1). Accordingly, the environment has been incorporated into business decisions and firms today have realised that it can pay to be green (Sawhney and Jose, 2003, p. 130). Not only is it ethical for a company to improve its environmental performance, but it is sound business practice (Kumar, 1999, p. 2).

In the late 1980s and the 1990s, there was a shift towards more preventive regulations and an increasing awareness of 'eco-efficiency' concepts such as waste minimisation and energy efficiency. This coincided with a move towards improved quality management and hence companies began to look for technologies that brought environmental and/or workplace benefits along with quality and efficiency improvements (Hillary, 2001, p. 167). Consequently, firms are now moving away from reactive end of the pipeline process solutions to proactive ones of identifying and preventing environmental damages or even using environmental attributes for product differentiation (Sawhney and Jose, 2003, p. 130). It is now clear, however, that the demands placed upon industry to improve its environmental performance will continue to grow. Companies which respond to this challenge will see themselves at the forefront of industry, developing new products in new markets and gaining a competitive edge over their competitors.

As 'strategy' is the determination of the basic long-term goals and objectives of an enterprise and the adoption of courses of action necessary for carrying out these goals, in order to achieve competitive advantage based on sustainable principles, companies need to develop effective strategies which translate actions into benefits, improving their environmental performance and addressing the environmental demands placed upon them by stakeholders. By incorporating the increasingly important environmental dimension into the decision-making processes of the firm, managers can seek to reduce costs and address the opportunities offered by increased public environmental concern within a dynamic marketplace. Thus, environmental management and product innovation can help firms keep ahead of their competitors by creating market niches or creating new market demand for environmentally differentiated products in markets that would otherwise have been purely competitive.

Thus, it is perceived that incorporation of environmental issues in business practice gives an edge to the entity, and benefits of such incorporation generally exceeds the related costs. Against this backdrop, we have tried to explore some of the findings/ recommendations of different authors that prescribe different models for such incorporation. The core objective of the analysis is to gain an understanding of the models that are advocated to incorporate environmental issues in business strategy.

The first Chapter (Chapter 13) under this Part focuses on different models that are advocated to incorporate environmental issues in business strategy. Chapter 14 discusses about various tools required for incorporation of environmental issues in business practice. Chapter 15 highlights different success stories illustrating application of those models. Chapter 16 critically reviews various issues that need to be addressed for implementation of such incorporation.

13

MODELS FOR INCORPORATION OF ENVIRONMENTAL ISSUES IN BUSINESS STRATEGY

In this section, we have discussed insights of different contemporary models propounded by some eminent researchers that are advocated to incorporate environmental issues in business strategy. For the sake of convenience, before presenting those models, we have first discussed the importance of such concept in business practice and finally, highlighted different models arranging in the order of focussing on various inputs stepwise that are to be incorporated in the business process to get the sustainable output.

There is no doubt that environmental considerations will open new business opportunities in the development of new technology (Lozada and Mintu-Wimsatt, 2004, p. 189).

Though, manufacturing organisations are usually driven by product sales and the resultant net profits, yet, Bishop (2000, p. 277) has pointed out that many companies in recent years have realised the importance of considering the environmental impacts of their manufacturing processes and products. Consumers, in increasing numbers, are demanding environmental accountability from producers and often are making purchasing decisions based on the "greenness" of a company. By conducting and implementing Life Cycle Assessments (LCAs) and publicising the results, companies can show that they are concerned about the environment.

Thus, increasingly, companies are realising they need to change the way they 'do business', by becoming more open and accountable for their activities, in order to meet the growing demands made of them from stakeholders and government. Companies need to identify and communicate with their stakeholders, to consider and act on their needs, and to involve them fully in corporate business. Companies must also begin to fully integrate economic viability with environmental responsibility and social accountability (core values) to make their operations more sustainable. To complete the picture, external reporting is necessary to communicate the company's performance on its core values to all stakeholders (Hillary, 2001, pp. 204-205).

New environmental laws have pushed some firms into thinking more widely about how they do business and integrating environmental considerations into their own activities. At the core of any environmental strategy has to be a consideration of ethical issues associated with doing business. That requires industry to be more open, honest and credible than it has been in the past. In this context, Kumar (1999, p. 12) stated that we need to search for new economic paradigms which stress the importance of environmental issues and integrate ever-wider ethical aims.

To incorporate environmental issues in business practice, companies began adopting systems that produce better quality products; maximise material yield and minimise losses; use less energy and water; take up less space on the shop floor; are simpler and cheaper to operate and maintain; are inherently cleaner, producing less pollution and improving shop floor conditions (Hillary, 2001, p. 167).

According to Hart (2005), business units need to address strategic issues regarding environment. A vision need to be developed and three stages of environmental strategy may be helpful:

Stage I: Pollution prevention: The first step for most companies is to make the shift from pollution control to pollution prevention. Pollution control means cleaning up waste after it has been created. Pollution prevention focuses on minimising or eliminating waste before it is created.

Stage II: Product stewardship: Product stewardship focuses on minimising not only pollution from manufacturing but also all environmental impacts associated with the full life cycle of a product. As companies in stage one move closer to zero emissions, reducing the use of material and production of waste requires fundamental changes in underlying product and process design.

Stage III: Clean technology: Companies with their eye on the future can begin to plan for and invest in tomorrow's technologies. The simple fact is that the existing technology base in many industries is not environmentally sustainable. The chemical industry, for example, while having made substantial headway over the past decade in pollution prevention and product stewardship, is still limited by its dependence on the chloride molecule (Many organochlorides are toxic or persistent or bioaccumulative). As long as the industry relies on its historical competencies in chlorine chemistry, it will have trouble making major progress towards sustainability.

Beaumont, Pederson and Whitaker (1993) drew from Industry Structure Analysis Framework as advocated by Porter (1985) to analyse the nature of competition with regard to the environment in any particular industry. The Porter's Model is given in Figure 13.1.

Undoubtedly, the green revolution has been responsible for a number of new market entrants. For example, companies manufacturing greener and cleaner products have increased the threat of substitutes such as replacements for CFCs and aerosols etc. In addition, greening of industry strategies have brought about changed relationships between companies and their suppliers and buyers. And within some industries the environment has brought about new levels of competition and rivalry. The two by two matrix shown in Figure 13.2 sums up Beaumont, Pederson and Whitaker's strategic environmental framework. It shows the various options available to companies for achieving competitive advantage (Welford, 1996).

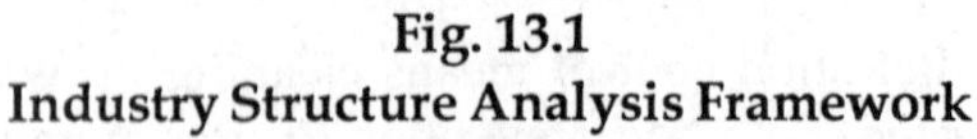

Fig. 13.1
Industry Structure Analysis Framework

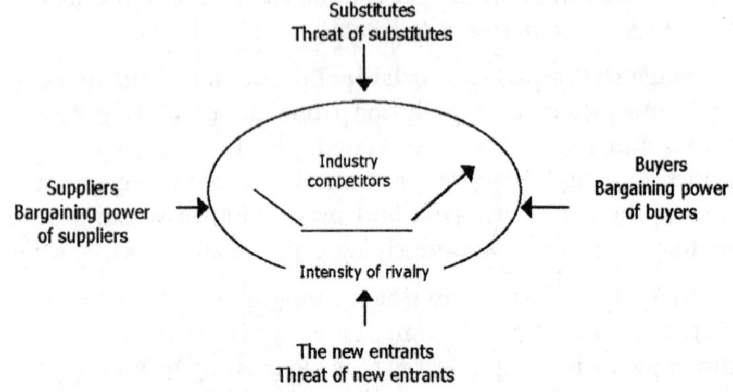

Source: Porter, 1985.

Fig. 13.2
Alternative Positions to Achieve Competitive Advantage

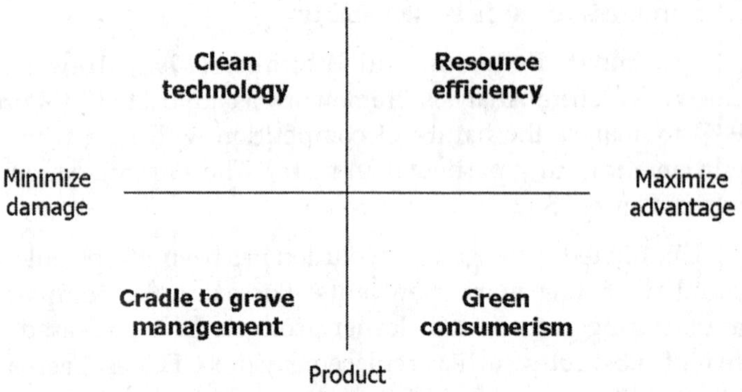

Source: Beaumont, Pederson and Whitaker, 1993.

Hutchinson and Hutchinson (1996, p. 149) also highlighted the technique of waste minimisation. Waste can be prevented by a reduction at source, product changes, and on-site recycling of waste and material recovery. Such a waste minimisation strategy (Figure 13.3) involves six stages:

Fig. 13.3
A Waste Minimization Strategy

Source: Hutchinson and Hutchinson, 1996, pp. 150-151.

- *Commitment to action:* Companies need to have a policy commitment to waste minimisation, senior management support, clear objectives and a strategy with targets and timescales.
- *Organisation for action:* Organisation for action covers the need for the establishment of a multidisciplinary team, appropriately trained, led by the project champion and reporting to senior management.
- *Audit and review:* The waste audit involves a review of process and ensuring that there are comprehensive and up-to-date process diagrams.
- *Options for improvement:* Options should be costed and prioritised. Some may involve simple procedural changes and good housekeeping, while others require capital investment and/or research and development.
- *Action:* This covers the implementation of the programme of changes with the setting of targets and timescales.
- *Feedback-monitoring and targeting:* It involves review of the results of the changes and the identification of further

opportunities. Waste minimisation is a journey rather than a destination with monitoring and targeting being a feedback loop for continually assessing performance.

Another well-used model in strategic management is the 7S concept (Waterman, Peters and Philips, 1980), which links Structure, Systems, Style, Staff, Skills and Strategy with the internal Shared values (Figure 13.4). This model helps our understanding of strategic eco-management. All elements of the company are to be assessed through the internal value of sustainable development and the ethics of social responsibility. The effects of this are felt throughout every aspect of the company's operations and strategy. The 7S eco-framework provides an excellent holistic eco-model for placing green issues right at the center of all internal decision-making.

Fig. 13.4
7S Eco-Framework

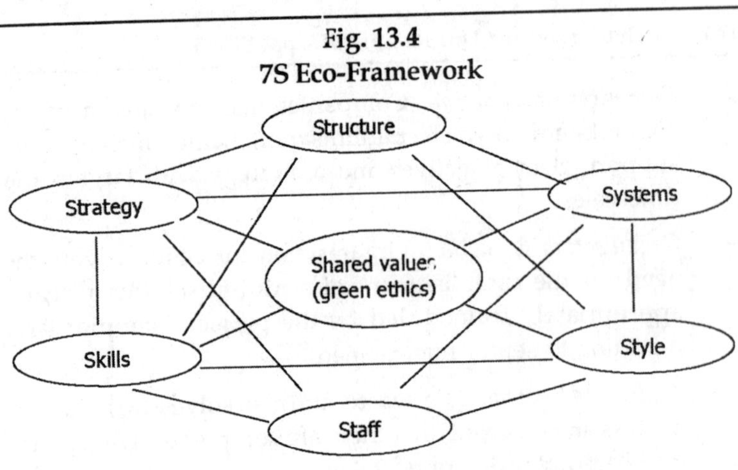

Source: Waterman, Peters and Philips, 1980.

Further, it is recognised in Figure 13.5 that, before a business can change to a 'sustainable business', it is essential that a strategic approach is taken towards the environment. To do this, first of all the staff at all levels of the organisation should be involved. This can be achieved by creating environmental awareness and training. Secondly, the organisation's culture should be changed and developed. Thirdly, cleaner and more efficient processes and technology should be developed (Hutchinson, 1992; Irwin and

Fig. 13.5

Strategic Framework for Environmental Management

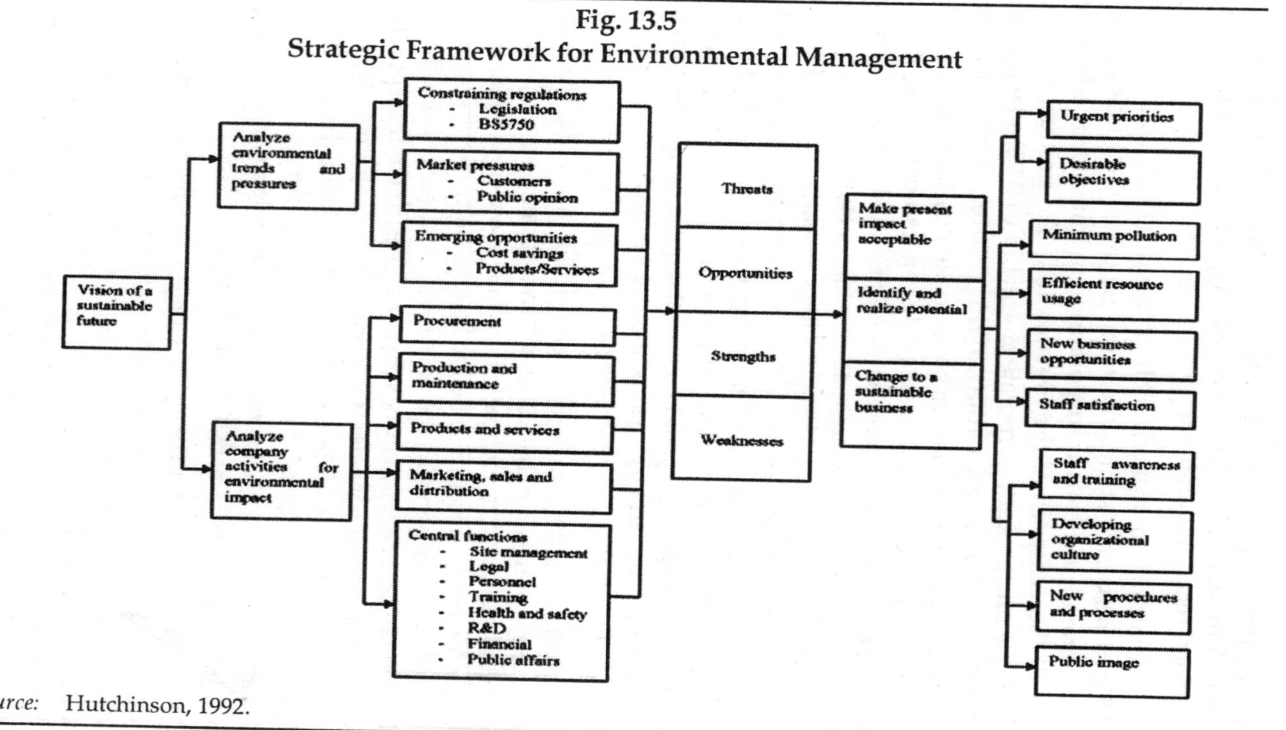

Source: Hutchinson, 1992.

Hooper, 1992). Finally, an organisation should have a clean public image. A number of stakeholders, ranging from employees to the investors, react favourably to this.

According to authors such as Taylor (1992) and Welford (1992), a proactive stance therefore requires total managerial commitment. It means incorporating environmental concerns into all the activities of the organisation, like product quality, employee relations and corporate image. Little (1991) adapted the traditional business value chain (Porter, 1985) to the environmental management in order to identify the various ways in which the internal performance drivers can contribute in the development of competitive environmental strategies (Figure 13.6). Similar attempts were made by James (1992, in Beaumont, Pederson and Whitaker, 1993). Taylor's research (1992) showed that leading companies are using environmental pressures to improve operational efficiency, heighten corporate image, develop new products and opportunities and thus, gain a competitive edge. This could mean a change in corporate culture, objectives, plans and even allocation of resources (Welford and Gouldson, 1993).

Kumar (1999, pp. 7-8) highlighted that environmental management needs to be addressed in a systematic way, dealing with the company as a whole rather than in a compartmentalised way. Corporate structures need to be flexible and everyone must identify and respond to the role they must play in improving environmental performance. When it comes to the incorporation of environmental considerations, cooperative strategies provide a way forward. To date, companies have been the dominant ideology in business, but cooperative strategies between businesses, also involving the public and regulatory agencies, can bring about benefits which are sustainable.

Hunt and Auster (1990) presented a complementary model, which is an empirically based environmental continuum model distinguishing five stages of environmental programme development (Table 13.1). Stages 1 and 2 ("beginner" and "firefighter") only devote minimal attention to environmental issues, while Stages 3, 4 and 5 ("concerned citizen," "pragmatist,"

Fig. 13.6
The Environmental Value Chain

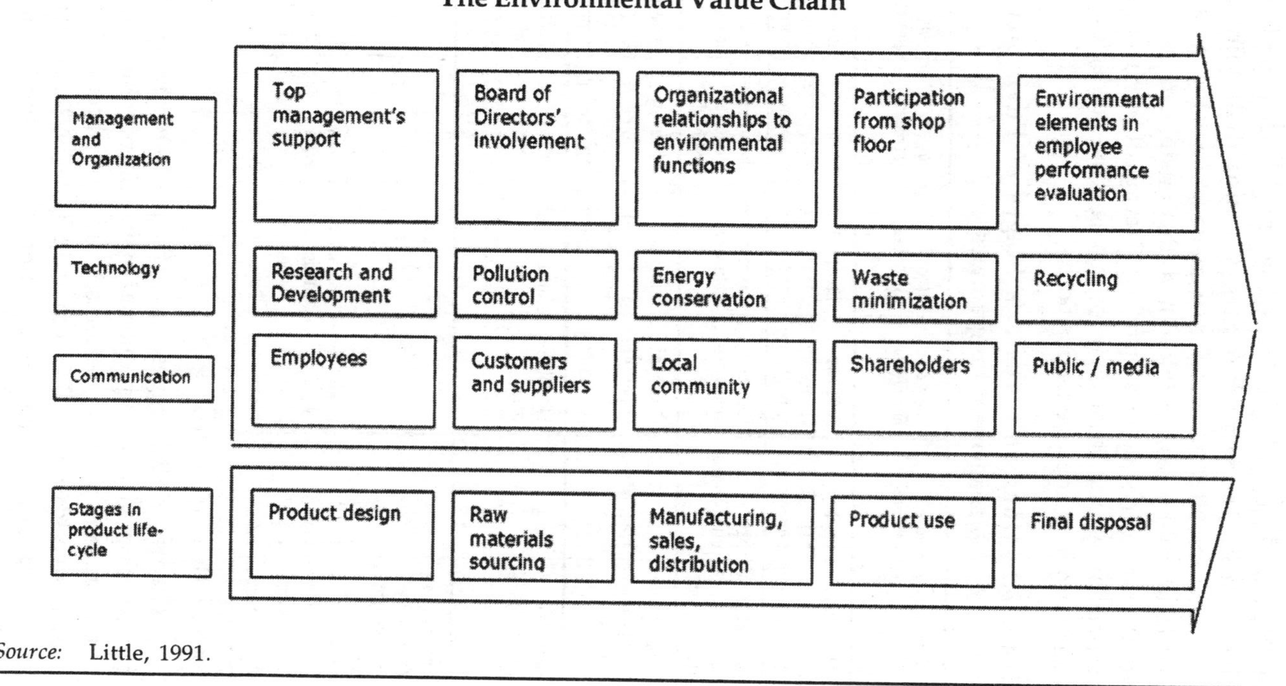

Source: Little, 1991.

and "proactivist") apply more aggressive policies regarding the environment. The number of Stage 5 ("proactivist") firms was very low; and all firms at lower stages could be doing more to be environmentally responsible. Thus, this model can indicate at what stage (or stages) a firm is in terms of environmental responsibility, and what types of management strategies it can use in order to improve its position.

Table 13.1: Hunt and Auster's Stages of Environmental Management Programmes

Criteria	*Stage 1: Beginner*	*Stage 2: Fire Fighter*	*Stage 3: Concerned Citizen*	*Stage 4: Pragmatist*	*Stage 5: Proactivist*
Mindset of Corporate Managers	Envir. Management unnecessary	Address Issue only as necessary	Envir. Management worthwhile	Envir. Management important	Envir. Management priority item
Support of top management	No involvement	Piecemeal involvement	Commitment in theory	Aware and moderately involved	Actively involved
Integration of Programme with Co.	Not integrated	Piecemeal basis only	Minimal interaction with other departments	Moderate integration with other departments	Actively involved with other departments
Reporting Structures	None	Exceptions only	Internal only	Internal; some external reporting	Formalised internal and external reporting
Environment Programme's Involvement with:					
Legal	None	Moderate	Moderate	Daily	Daily
PR	None	None	Moderate	High	Daily
Mfg./Prodn.	None	None	None	Moderate	Daily
Prod. Design	None	None	None	Minimal	Daily

Source: Hunt and Auster, 1990.

Gladwin (1993) suggested that the theory of strategic choice can be adopted to environmental management which, in other words, means an organisation's search for different types of competitive advantage. Bostrum and Poysti (1992) felt that there are a number of economic benefits from environmental considerations. A more effective use of raw materials in production results in diminishing costs for example, and a greener corporate image leads to an increase in market share. New market opportunities might also be created in the form of new products and technology. Some of the main constituents of competitive advantage are listed by Welford and Gouldson (1993) and can be seen in Figure 13.7.

Fig. 13.7

The Constituents of Competitive Advantage

Source: Welford and Gouldson, 1993.

Tracking the changes in the production to obtain better environmental results is important vis-à-vis the benefits. Bhattacharya (2004, p. 184) highlighted some examples to show how some multinationals do it (Table 13.2). It reveals that if certain innovative solutions could be adopted by slight modification of process design, alteration of raw materials, efficient technologies, improved infrastructure, etc., then immediate outcome may be observed in terms of lower operating costs, energy savings, increased workers' safety, better efficiency, excess raw material savings, improved product quality, better productivity and finally, better image. Thus, it may be stated that there is enough scope for a company to incorporate environmental issues in business practice and accordingly, to adopt different proactive strategies for the purpose of incorporation of environmental issues in business.

Table 13.2: Summary of Some Product Innovation and the Likely Ecological and Business Benefits

Sector/Industry	*Environmental Issues*	*Innovative Solutions*	*Innovative Offsets*
Pulp/ Paper	Dioxine released by bleaching with chlorine	Improved cooking and washing processes. Elimination of chlorine by using oxygen, ozone, peroxide for bleaching, closed loop processes (still problematic)	Lower operating costs through greater use of by-product energy source. 25% initial price premium for chlorine free paper.
Paint and Coatings	Volatile Organic Compounds (VOCs) in solvents	New paint formulations (low sclvent content paints, water borne paints). Improved application techniques, Powder or radiation cured coatings	Price premium for solvent-free paints, Improved coatings quality in some segments, worker safety benefits, higher coating transfer efficiency, Reduced coating costs through material saving.
Electronic manufacturing	Volatile Organic Compounds (VOCs) in cleaning agents	Semiaqueous terpene-based cleaning agents, Closed-loop systems. No clean soldering where possible.	Increase in cleaning quality and this in product quality, 30 to 80% reduction in cleaning costs, often for one-year payback periods, Elimination of an unnecessary production step

(Contd...)

Sector/Industry	*Environmental Issues*	*Innovative Solutions*	*Innovative Offsets*
Refrigerators	Chorofluorocarbon (CFC) used as refrigerants, Energy usage disposal	Alternative refrigerants (Propaneisobutane mix), thicker insulation, Better gaskets, improved compressors	10% better energy efficiency at same cost, 5% to 10% initial price premium for green refrigerator
Dry cell batteries	Cadmium mercury, lead, nickel, cobalt, zinc, and lithium releases in landfills or to the air (after incineration)	Rechargeable batteries of nickelhydride (for some applications), Rechargeable lithium batteries	Nearly twice as efficient at same cost, Higher energy efficiency expected to be price competitive in the near future
Printing inks	VOCs in petroleum inks	Water based inks and soy inks	Higher efficiency, brighter colours and better printability (depending on application)

Source: Bhattacharya, 2004.

Now, the next Chapter (14) discusses about various tools required for incorporation of environmental issues in business practice.

14

TOOLS FOR INCORPORATION OF ENVIRONMENTAL ISSUES IN BUSINESS PRACTICES

The tools that are applied for incorporation of environmental issues in business practice are Environmental Auditing, Life Cycle Assessment, Eco-Labelling, Environmental Management System, Pollution Prevention; etc. (Fava *et al.*, 1993; Cascio, Woodside and Mitchell, 1996). Issues dealing with an organisation's style of management include environmental management system, environmental auditing and environmental performance evaluation. Whereas, product evaluation consists of environmental aspects in product standards, eco-labelling and life cycle assessment.

Environmental Audit (EA) is a management tool comprising a systematic, documented, periodic and objective evaluation of performance of the organisation, management system and process designed to protect the environment with the aim of facilitating management control of practices which may have impact upon the environment and assessing compliance with the company-environment policies.

Life Cycle Assessment (LCA) is an evaluation of the environmental effects associated with any given activity from the initial gathering of raw material from the earth until the point at which all residuals are returned to the earth (Vigon et al., 1993). This evaluation includes all sidestream releases to the air, water and soil from the production of raw materials (including energy), the use of the product, and its final disposal, as well as from the processing of the product itself (Nash and Stoughton, 1994).

To increase consumer awareness and promote the use of eco-friendly products in the country, the Government of India has launched the eco-labelling scheme known as Scheme of Labelling of Environment Friendly Products (ECO-MARKS), 1991 (Jain and Kaur, 2004, pp. 183-184). The scheme was launched with view to provide an incentive for manufacturers and importers to reward genuine initiatives by companies to reduce adverse environmental impacts of their products; assist consumers to become environmentally responsible in their daily lives by providing information that would take account of environmental factors in their purchase decisions; encourage citizens to purchase products which have less harmful environmental impacts; improve the quality of the environment; and encourage the sustainable management of resources.

The introduction and operation of an **Environmental Management System (EMS)** makes for a continuous systematic improvement. An EMS follows the quality management approach, defining policy, specifying process controls, auditing performance and revising policy in the light of the assessment (Hutchinson and Hutchinson, 1996, pp. 86-88).

The ISO 14000 standards, formally adopted in 1996, establish benchmarks for environmental management performance and describe the measures that industry must take to conform to these standards. ISO's EMS model has five basic components: Commitment and environmental policy; Environmental management plan; Implementation; Measurements and evaluation; Continual review and improvement. ISO is currently developing a range of environmental standards in the form of the ISO 14000 series.

Many companies are now making **Pollution Prevention** a fundamental part of their operating strategy (Bishop, 2000, p. 278). The major elements involved in developing a pollution prevention programme include building support for pollution prevention throughout the company, organising the programme, setting goals and objectives, performing a preliminary assessment of pollution prevention opportunities, and identifying potential problems and solutions (US EPA, 1992).

Now, the next Chapter (15) highlights some cases that will show the benefits gained by some companies due to incorporation of environmental issues in their respective business practice.

15

CASES ILLUSTRATING APPLICATION OF ENVIRONMENTAL STRATEGY MODELS

In this section some cases are discussed that depict how corporate environmental philosophy brings about a change in the overall management percept of any firm leading finally, for a qualitative management change. For the sake of convenience, those success stories are presented here alphabetically.

Firms themselves often found, when they first introduced measures to tackle pollution, that they made big improvements in their environmental performance. Cairncross (1999, pp. 189-190) stated that some American companies go in for acronyms to underline the point: **3M** has a scheme called Pollution Prevention Pays, **Chevron** has SMART (Save Money and Reduce Toxics), Texaco has WOW (Wipe Out Waste) and **Dow Chemical** has WRAP (Waste Reduction Always Pays). Even, corporations such as **McDonald's, Wal-Mart, Procter & Gamble, Monsanto and Du Pont** acknowledge that the environment must be protected and enhanced for economic growth to take place, and have taken action towards that goal (Lodge and Rayport, 1991).

3M's Pollution Prevention Pays claims to have saved some £500 million since 1975 (Cairncross, 1999, pp. 189-190). A typical tactic was to eliminate solvents used to bind abrasive discs to the paper backing. At its South Wales plant, solvents were replaced by a system of hot melting, a process which required no major capital outlay and saved the company £150 000 per year into the bargain (Hopfenbeck, 1992; Aspengreen, 1994). 3M has as a goal for 1995 to reduce air and water emissions by 90 per cent and solid wastes 50 per cent from the levels of 1990. This will cut the inflation-adjusted cost per unit of most products by 10 per cent (Lozada and Mintu-Wimsatt, 2004, pp. 188-189).

Bharat Heavy Electricals Ltd. (BHEL) developed eco-friendly power generation technology, thus, putting India next only to the US, Germany and Japan in the world to have developed such technology (Eco Consumer, 2001).

BMW is using design for disassembly in a pilot project aimed at building cars so they can eventually be taken part and recycled more easily (Lozada and Mintu-Wimsatt, 2004, pp. 188-189).

Sawhney and Jose (2003, p. 131) explained that hotel chain in South India, which used nature conservation as a means of differentiating itself from conventional tourist hotels and achieved considerable success. The Casino model creates a unique value proposition by building hotels in harmony with the environment. Casino's eco-friendly structures allowed it to complete its projects at a fraction of the cost and time it would have taken to build a regular star hotel or holiday resort. Casino's properties are highly valued and bookings are closed several months in advance. With a fanatically loyal clientele (one client even willed that his ashes be scattered in the seas adjacent to one of its properties) the Casino hotel chain is now acknowledged to be one of the most innovative and profitable eco-hotels in Asia.

The Confederation of Indian Industries (CII) took the initiative to promote greenness among member firms in the construction industry. It organised the Green Building Congress in September, 2001 and evolved the concept of green building. A green building is one which is energy efficient, makes efficient use of recycled materials, maintains healthy indoor air quality and uses renewable energy to the extent possible (Jain and Kaur, 2004, p. 201).

Dow Chemical may replace, within two years, chlorinated solvents used for cleaning industrial equipment with less-polluting, water-based systems. All of these corporate attempts are not only meant to capitalise on the potential profitability and cost reduction associated with green-product development. It is also an opportunity to improve their bona fides with a populace that is demanding exemplary environmental behaviour from the corporate community (Coddington, 1993).

Du Pont's waste reduction policies are estimated to have created new virtual capacity and avoided investment costs in excess of US$ 1 billion (Sawhney and Jose, 2003, pp. 131-132). Du Pont decided to take a leadership role by committing to a complete phase out of CFCs much before other manufacturers.

Excel Industries engaged in the conversion of municipal waste into an organic fertiliser is an example of how innovations may be applied to convert waste to health. Sawhney and Jose (2003, pp. 131-132) mentioned that even as early as 1996, Excel created a market potentially worth about Rs. 500 crores (5 bn).

Henkel's phosphate-free detergents banned detergents that contained phosphates and blew a large hole in the French detergent market (Cairncross, 1999, p. 180).

Firms may employ green manufacturing processes and green production facilities, but neither produce innovative eco-products nor actively engage in green promotion. The multinational major **Hindustan Coca Cola Beverages Ltd.** is one such firm. It has adopted a clean environment policy by way of optimising use of water and energy at all of its forty-three plants and has cut down its costs by using such a policy (Jain and Kaur, 2004, p. 194).

Concept, taken by BMW, is also being implemented by **IBM** Germany to dismantle and recycle computer parts (Lozada and Mintu-Wimsatt, 2004, pp. 188-189).

In the quest to generate dynamic competitive advantages, many firms are also innovating by re-conceptualising their products and services. A classic example is the case of **Interface carpets** in the US. Considering the fact that customers value the functionality of the carpet more than the ownership of the carpet itself, Interface innovated a new business model. The company designed compostable and recyclable carpets, which were leased rather than sold to customers. The results on the company's bottom lines were dramatic. Since 1994, the stock price, profits and annual sales have increased by 70 per cent, 80 per cent and 77 per cent respectively. Simultaneously, waste and emissions per revenue dollar reduced by over 50 per cent and 30 per cent respectively (Sawhney and Jose, 2003, p. 132).

J.K Tyres constitutes an example of a proactive enviropreneur. On its own, it took the initiative to develop eco-friendly tyres and launched them on World Environment Day on June 5, 2002 in the country. The high performance tyres claim to be having low carbon black, reduced rolling resistance and other green features (Financial Express, 2002).

LG is another business firm which claims to have initiated a series of image oriented environmental activities including tree plantation programmes, environmental awareness campaigns, vehicular pollution check campaign and launch of a 'No Plastic Campaign' within the factory premises (The Times of India, 2001).

Maruti Udyog Limited is one such firm to have explicitly involved an environment policy. Its four fold environment policy aims at continually improving and maintaining the environmental performance of its activities, products and services; reducing/preventing pollution; minimising wastes and maximising resource efficiency; striving to work beyond legal regulatory requirements; and enhancing environment awareness and commitment of company employees and business associates (Jain and Kaur, 2004, p. 196).

McDonald's has made a $100 million commitment to its consumers for recycling purposes (Lozada and Mintu-Wimsatt, 2004, p. 187).

Monsanto created a positive image by stressing its concern for the environment through strict plant and material controls. It then lobbied for higher standards and became a *de facto* manager of regulations. With Monsanto effectively setting the environmental standards, its competitors found it difficult and more expensive to bridge the gap that had been created between Monsanto and themselves. In fact, the most productive companies today follow the Highest Common Denominator approach, i.e., producing everything to the world's toughest standards (Sawhney and Jose, 2003, p. 132). Monsanto is one company that is developing new competencies to retain its position and grow. It is shifting the technology base for its agriculture business from bulk chemicals to biotechnology. It is betting that the bioengineering of crops rather than the application of chemical pesticides or fertiliser represents a sustainable path to increased agricultural yields (Magretta, 1997).

Motorola is incorporating LCA into their decision-making procedures to incorporate environmental considerations into all of its product designs in order to meet customers' environmental demands. Motorola found that it can have the biggest pollution prevention impact by focusing on the concept development stage of product design. In an effort to make up for the lack of detailed data available at this stage for making environmental assessments, Motorola developed a matrix-based streamlined Life Cycle Assessment procedure for the concept development design stage. The company is beginning to use full-scale Life Cycle Assessments for the manufacturing stage (Hoffman, 1997).

In India, too, studies by the National Productivity Council have shown that there is considerable potential to reduce wastes and waste treatment costs. In particular, the experience of **Orchid Chemicals** and **Madras Refineries** in recycling and reusing water indicate the huge potential savings that exist (Sawhney and Jose, 2003, p. 131).

Procter & Gamble (P&G) has pledged to spend $20 million per year to develop a composting infrastructure (Lozada and Mintu-Wimsatt, 2004, p. 187). P&G has taken several prominent initiatives. Refills for Downy fabric softener are being sold in concentrate form. The customer buys a plastic bottle once, then adds concentrate (sold in a small cardboard box) and dilutes it with water. This procedure cuts down greatly on plastic packaging headed for landfills (Schiller, 1990). "Enviro-paks" are also being tested for Downy: with this system, the customer refills the plastic bottle with a collapsible plastic pouch, or "bag-in-box". 70 per cent less plastic is used with the Enviro-pak system (Stuller, 1990).

P&G has also experimented with recycled plastic containers for Liquid Tide and Spic and Span, and paperboard "milk cartons" for Downy (Nelson-Horchler, 1989) and has developed a detergent (Ariel Ultra concentrate), sold in Europe, that cuts down on phosphate pollutants, since less detergent need to be used with each wash (Rolfes, 1990). All of these activities are strongly supported with print and television ads, couponing and other promotional activities. Results so far have been mixed: early Downy concentrate sales were slow due to consumer resistance to the idea of diluting concentrate (Swazy, 1990) and P&G was criticised in Europe by environmental groups since animal testing was used in the development of Ariel detergent (Rolfes, 1990). Colgate-Palmolive and Lever (makers of Wisk detergent and Snuggle fabric softener) have also experimented with bag-in-box systems and concentrates (Kiley, 1990) and Church and Dwight is developing a non-phosphate detergent (Benedetto and Chandran, 2004, pp. 275-276).

Firm may seek to bring market new and innovative green products. Firms may focus on the production of highly environment-friendly products. The **Reva Electric Car,** manufactured by the Maini group in Bangalore is another example of an environmentally differentiated product that has found markets in Norway, Nepal, UK and Malta (Sawhney and Jose, 2003, pp. 131-132). It is engaged in the manufacture of innovative zero-pollution and cost-effective electric cars for city mobility (Jain and Kaur, 2004, pp. 193-194).

Shaw developed a variety of technical and training instruments to start innovations in quality improvement, customer service and environmental performance within the corporation and also shared product test results, used satellite and computer information systems, disseminated technical information on manufacturing and product quality etc. By working closely with both suppliers and customers and by providing technical and quality information, Shaw could leverage its own quality, service and environmental objectives throughout its supply, production and marketing chains (Bhattacharya, 2004, p. 93).

Every year each business unit of Sony's Environmental Conservation Committee in Japan deduces and monitors the Environmental Action Plan objectives. In Japan, it reduced the waste disposal per unit of sales by 30 per cent in four years, to 54 per cent (Bhattacharya, 2004, p. 186).

Between 1989 and 1991, **Texaco** reduced its output of dirty air and water and solid wastes by 40 per cent and its toxic emissions by 58 per cent (Walley and Whitehead, 1994). Often, such changes were accompanied by striking savings.

Thomson multimedia tracks the cost of material used in its TVs and its other consumer products, its compliance with environmental regulations and its consumption of water, energy and power from local to global. The company saved $2.8 million by using one less Kilowatt per employee hour worked in 1998 than 1997 (Gordon, 2001).

Wal-Mart encourages the purchase of environmentally friendly products and reports that the green labeling programme that they initiated in 1989 contributed to an overall 25 per cent increase in sales for the year (Lozada and Mintu-Wimsatt, 2004, p. 187).

Xerox, too, has capitalised on the environmental wave and captured price premium through its green line products with fully recyclable and reusable parts (Sawhney and Jose, 2003, p. 132).

Ciba-Geigy, Coca-Cola, ConAgra, Dwight-Church, Electrolux, S. C. Johnson, Kroeger, Mitsubishi, Norsk Hydro, Nippon Steel, Pacific Gas and Electric and Westinghouse are just a few of the companies that have experienced the benefits of a biocentric economic philosophy (Neace, 2004). Thus, this section highlighted some live pictures of different companies who were successful in their journey due to incorporation of environmental issues in their business practice.

Now, the next Chapter (16) critically reviews opportunities that may be gained by the company as well as problems that may be faced by companies due to incorporation of environmental issues in business practice.

16

CHALLENGES IN INCORPORATION OF ENVIRONMENTAL ISSUES IN BUSINESS STRATEGY

The conceptual issues of the incorporation of environmental issues in business strategy have already been described in the preceding section. Even the theoretical development in this area has been highlighted illustrating some models. We have also discussed various tools for such incorporation. Some success stories have also been mentioned that focussed the benefits gained by some companies due to incorporation of environmental issues in their respective business practice. However, some issues need to be addressed for implementation of the same. In this section, based on available literature, we are going to critically review those issues.

Unless consumers truly understand and genuinely feel concerned about environmental issues, not much success can be expected with respect to environmental protection and preservation efforts at the community level. There is an imperative need to make people fully cognisant of environmental problems and issues and the implications in their personal and community lives, and educating them to engage in eco-friendly behaviour. Simply releasing environment related advertisements and issuing press releases will not do the job.

Being a "good corporate citizen" also may be reflected in the organisation's ability to respond to the green business opportunities. Organisations whose policies and actions are consistent also reduce the factors that could result in a green backlash (Polonsky, 2004, p. 214). Well-established environmental policies are an important component of a total environmental management programme. Implementation of a strong environmental programme requires an integrated management process (Buzzelli, 1991).

Polonsky (2004, p. 215) stated that planning is another area where an organisational green strength can arise. A well-developed organisational planning process enables the firm to anticipate opportunities and threats. This is an important strength, for many environmental threats will not be "considered" unless there is a long-term planning process designed to examine changes in the business and scientific environment. A further strength may be that organisations have "environmentally aware" managers. These managers may be better able to consider the implications of green business claims than their unaware counterparts. This is not to imply that aware managers are a necessity, but these managers will ensure that decisions incorporate consideration of green activities. Aware managers also may be better able to ensure that environmental policies and programmes are accurately carried out.

Accordingly, an Environmental Agenda, as proposed by Benedetto and Chandran (2004, p. 288), is set forth in Table 16.1 as a guideline for firms adopting a proactive stance toward environmental responsibility. (*See Table on next page*)

It could be used by management to fix responsibilities and to coordinate actions across the firm's departments. The agenda is developed with the ultimate firm objective of manufacturing an environmentally safe product considering all life cycle stages, including use and disposition. Each department's contribution to this objective is spelled out in the agenda. The agenda states that it is the role of R&D to devote time and effort to the development of products that are non-carcinogenic, biodegradable, or will not break down into hazardous components in landfills. Manufacturing must consider the pollution caused by emissions from new and existing plants and develop ways to reduce noxious emissions. Sales and distribution should be responsible for teaching middle-men and/or end users about proper use and disposition of products and make certain that these recommendations are being practiced. Advertising and public affairs departments must plan news releases and other

Table 16.1: A Proposed Environmental Agenda

Area	*Action Plan*
Manufacturing	Reduce noxious emissions from plants. Consider environmental consequences of building new plants. Examine alternate manufacturing technologies with less harsh environmental consequences. Examine use of more environmentally sound raw materials.
R&D/Quality Control	R&D efforts aimed at products that are environmentally sound. Better testing methods for determining environmental consequences of new products.
Advertising and Public Affairs	Communicate environmentally sound activities by firm to consumers and other interested publics. Prepare news releases and public relations activities. Cultivate relationships with media. Advise consumers of product safety; instructions for use.
Transportation/ Shipping	Advise middlemen and retailers of proper use and disposition of product. Encourage middlemen and retailers to follow environmentally sound practices for storage, use and disposition of product. Enlist assistance of retailers in getting environmental messages across to consumer.
Legal Affairs	Follow up on all environmental claims. Keep in touch with all current laws and regulations on the product, including initiatives by the Environmental Protection Agency. Advise management on the appropriate stance to take.
Finance/ Accounting	Estimate net effects on costs of environmental programmes. Do studies on cost/price tradeoffs to determine likely consumer response to price increases on environmentally sound products. Estimate long-term financial impact of environmental policies.

Source: Benedetto and Chandran, 2004.

activities that communicate environmentally sound activities undertaken by the firm. The legal department must follow up on all environmental claims and keep up to date on all changes in applicable laws. Finance and accounting should estimate the net effects of environmental programmes of overall corporate costs and profits. Other roles and responsibilities are also outlined in the agenda in Table 16.1. Of course, the agenda requires that top management is sufficiently committed to saving the environment that they allot adequate funds to support these activities, some of which can be very expensive.

However, company may face different difficulties in implementing green issues in business practice:

Firstly, there is difficulty in establishing policies at the corporate level that address all the environmental issues. Even if an organisation is able to adopt a green policy, it is invariably expensive as it might involve modifying the entire business process. Notwithstanding the fact whether one is a leader or a follower, a higher risk is associated in the tapping of the green business and employing green business strategies as a competitive tool. Even a follower reacting to competitive pressures can make the same mistake as the leader has done. Moreover, there is uncertainty involved as the environmentally responsible action of today might turn out to be harmful in the future. A firm faces the risk of coming back to square one and starting over, once again, the entire greening process. According to Jain and Kaur (2004, p. 202), the other problem with greening business is that too many environmental claims make consumers confused over claims and terminology such as eco-safe, environment friendly, recycled, recyclable and biodegradable.

Jain and Kaur (2004, p. 202) also stated that a major factor inhibiting the wide scale application and role of greening business is the failure among business firms to fully understand and embrace the green business concept. Many a firm has resorted to green business practice merely as a tactic to promote its commercial interests. Based on the motive for going green and the postures business firms adopt, an interesting typology of half-hearted green business practice has come into the green business literature.

The corporate environmental policy or vision statement, though signed by the CEO, is almost exclusively a staff product bearing little direct connection to the views or commitments of senior executives and operating managements (The Economist Intelligence Unit, 1999).

Regardless of the prevailing rhetoric, line managers act as if they are not accountable for environmental performance; they believe it is the environmental staff that is responsible. Furthermore, corporate personnel and evaluation systems fail to disabuse them of this notion.

As a result, conscientious environmental staff members often feel compelled to manage from the corporate centre and end up involving themselves too deeply in line operating decisions, where they lack authority and the appropriate business perspective.

Environmental-management functions are generally well defined and are monitored for improvement attention continuously. However, they do not address critical business processes that cut across functional hierarchies and stages of the product life cycle. Again, the result for environmental management can be functional isolation and irrelevance (The Economist Intelligence Unit, 1999).

Environmental-performance reporting is typically limited to meeting regulatory information requirements. Rarely is it part of a communications programme designed to reach many stakeholders, including employees, customers, investors, insurers, neighbours and the general public.

It was, thus, explored that there are certain problems that need to be addressed in implementation stages. Strategies to be adopted to address those problems should be firm and industry specific. It may have some cost implication. Nevertheless, it is clear that benefits to be obtained far outweigh those costs.

In this Part (Part-III), it was attempted to explore the insights of different models, various tools that are advocated to incorporate environmental issues in business strategy as well as different success stories illustrating application of those models. In the next Part, we would focus on the empirical aspects of corporate environmental management in the belief that conceptual and theoretical discussions made in the foregoing sections regarding the methodological and substantive aspects of environmental proactiveness would help us lead the present study towards the right direction on adopting strategic decision on environmental proactiveness in case of the sample units.

17

REFERENCES

Aspengreen, A.H. (1994), 'Developing Environmental Opportunities in Industrial Products', in Taylor, B., Hutchinson, C., Pollack, S. and Tapper, R. (ed.), *Environmental Management Handbook*, Pitman, London, Quoted in Hutchinson, Andrew and Hutchinson, Frances (1996), *Environmental Business Management: Sustainable Development in the New Millennium*, McGraw-Hill Publishing Company, England, p. 67.

Beaumont, J. R., Pederson, L. M. and Whitaker, B. D. (1993), *Managing the Environment*, Butterworth-Heinemann Ltd., Oxford, Quoted in Welford, Richard (1996), *Corporate Environmental Management: Systems and Strategies*, Universities Press (India) Limited, Hyderabad, pp. 19-24.

Benedetto, C. Anthony di and Chandran, Rajan (2004), 'Behaviours of Environmentally Concerned Firms: An Agenda for Effective Strategic Development', in Polonsky, Michael Jay and Mintu-Wimsatt, Alma T. (2004) (ed.), *Environmental Marketing: Strategies, Practice, Theory and Research*, Jaico Publishing House, Mumbai.

Bhattacharya, Jayanta (2004), *Global Corporate Environmentalism*, Asian Books Private Limited, New Delhi.

Bishop, Paul L. (2000), *Pollution Prevention: Fundamentals and Practice*, McGraw-Hill International Editions, Singapore.

Bostrum, T. and Poysti, E. (1992), *Environmental Strategy in the Enterprise*, Helsinki School of Economics, Helsinki, Quoted in Welford, Richard (1996), *Corporate Environmental Management: Systems and Strategies*, Universities Press (India) Limited, Hyderabad, pp. 25-26.

Buzzelli, David T. (1991), 'Time to Structure Environmental Policy Strategy', *The Journal of Business Strategy*, March/April, Vol. 12, No. 2, pp. 17-20, Quoted in Polonsky, Michael Jay (2004), 'Cleaning Up Green Marketing Claims: A Practical Checklist', in Polonsky, Michael Jay and Mintu-Wimsatt, Alma T. (2004) (ed.), *Environmental Marketing: Strategies, Practice, Theory and Research*, Jaico Publishing House, Mumbai, p. 214.

Cairncross, Frances (1999), *Green, Inc.: Guide to Business and the Environment*, Universities Press (India) Limited, Hyderabad.

Cascio, J., Woodside, G. and Mitchell, P. (1996), *ISO 14000 Guide*, McGraw-Hill, New York, Quoted in Bishop, Paul L. (2000), *Pollution Prevention: Fundamentals and Practice*, McGraw Hill, Singapore, p. 340.

Coddington, Walter (1993), *Environmental Marketing*, McGraw-Hill, New York, p. 149, Quoted in Lozada, Hector R. and Mintu-Wimsatt, Alma T. (2004), 'Green-Based Innovation: Sustainable Development in Product Management', in Polonsky, Michael Jay and Mintu-Wimsatt, Alma T. (2004) (ed.), *Environmental Marketing: Strategies, Practice, Theory and Research*, Jaico Publishing House, Mumbai, pp. 182-189.

Eco Consumer (2001), CUTS-CSPAC, *Eco-friendly Practices could Result in Cost Saving*, 9(3): 9, Quoted in Jain, Sanjay K. and Kaur, Gurmeet (2004), 'Green Marketing: An Indian Perspective', *Decision*, Vol. 31, No. 2, July-December 2004, p. 196.

Fava, J. A., Consoli, F., Denison, R., Dickson, K., Mohin, T. and Vigon, B. (1993), *Guidelines for Life-Cycle Assessment: A Code of Practice*, Society of Environmental Toxicology and Chemistry, Pensacola, FL, Workshop Proceedings, Quoted in Bishop, Paul L. (2000), *Pollution Prevention: Fundamentals and Practice*, McGraw Hill, Singapore, p. 257.

Financial Express (2002), *The Green Brigade on an Overdrive,* June 9, Quoted in Jain, Sanjay K. and Kaur, Gurmeet (2004), 'Green Marketing: An Indian Perspective', *Decision,* Vol. 31, No. 2, July-December 2004, pp. 193-194.

Gladwin, T. (1993), 'The Meaning of Greening: A Plea for Organisational Theory', in Fischer, K. and Schot, J. (ed.), *Environmental Strategies for Industry,* Island Press, Washington DC, Quoted in Welford, Richard (1996), *Corporate Environmental Management: Systems and Strategies,* Universities Press (India) Limited, Hyderabad, pp. 25-26.

Gordon, P. J. (2001), *Lean and Green: Profit for Workplace and the Environment,* Bernett Koehler Publisher's Inc., San Francisco, p. 218, Quoted in Bhattacharya, Jayanta (2004), *Global Corporate Environmentalism,* Asian Books Private Limited, New Delhi, p. 186.

Hart, Stuart L. (2005), 'Beyond Greening: Strategies for a Sustainable World', in Starkey, Richard and Welford, Richard (2005) (ed.), *The Earthscan Reader in Business and Sustainable Development,* Earthscan, London, pp. 12-15.

Hillary, Ruth (2001), *The CBI Environmental Management Handbook: Challenges for Business,* Earthscan Publications Ltd., London and Sterling, VA.

Hoffman, W. F. (1997), 'Recent Advances in Design for Environment at Motorola', *Journal of Industrial Ecology,* 1 (1), pp. 131-140, Quoted in Bishop, Paul L. (2000), *Pollution Prevention: Fundamentals and Practice,* McGraw Hill, Singapore, p. 278.

Hopfenbeck, W. (1992), *The Green Management Revolution,* Prentice Hall, London, Quoted in Hutchinson, Andrew and Hutchinson, Frances (1996), *Environmental Business Management: Sustainable Development in the New Millennium,* McGraw-Hill Publishing Company, England, p. 67.

Hunt, Christopher B. and Auster, Ellen R. (1990), 'Proactive Environmental Management: Avoiding the Toxic Trap', *Sloan Management Review,* Winter, pp. 7-18, Quoted in Benedetto, C. Anthony di and Chandran, Rajan (2004), 'Behaviours of Environmentally Concerned Firms: An Agenda for Effective

Strategic Development', in Polonsky, Michael Jay and Mintu-Wimsatt, Alma T. (2004) (ed.), *Environmental Marketing: Strategies, Practice, Theory and Research*, Jaico Publishing House, Mumbai, pp. 271-273.

Hutchinson, C. (1992), 'Corporate Strategy and the Environment', *Long Range Planning*, 25 (4), pp. 9-21, Quoted in Welford, Richard (1996), *Corporate Environmental Management: Systems and Strategies*, Hyderabad: Universities Press (India) Limited, pp. 24-29.

Hutchinson, Andrew and Hutchinson, Frances (1996), *Environmental Business Management – Sustainable Development in the New Millennium*, McGraw-Hill Publishing Company, USA.

Irwin, A. and Hooper, P. D. (1992), 'Clean Technology, Successful Innovation and the Greening of Industry: A Case Study Analysis', *Business Strategy and the Environment*, 1(2), pp. 1-10, Quoted in Welford, Richard (1996), *Corporate Environmental Management: Systems and Strategies*, Universities Press (India) Limited, Hyderabad, pp. 28-30.

Jain, Sanjay K. and Kaur, Gurmeet (2004), 'Green Marketing: An Indian Perspective', *Decision*, Vol. 31, No. 2, July-December 2004.

James, P. (1992), *The Corporate Response*, in Charter, M (ed), *Greener Marketing*, Greenleaf Publishing, Sheffield, Quoted in Welford, Richard (1996), *Corporate Environmental Management: Systems and Strategies*, Universities Press (India) Limited, Hyderabad, pp. 23-24.

Kiley, David (1990), 'A Long, Silent Spring Awaits Wasteful Brands', *Adweek's Marketing Week*, April 16, pp. 2-3, Quoted in Benedetto, C. Anthony di and Chandran, Rajan (2004), 'Behaviours of Environmentally Concerned Firms: An Agenda for Effective Strategic Development', in Polonsky, Michael Jay and Mintu-Wimsatt, Alma T. (2004) (ed.), *Environmental Marketing: Strategies, Practice, Theory and Research*, Jaico Publishing House, Mumbai, pp. 275-276.

Kumar, Arun (1999), *Environmental Problems: Protection and Control*, Institute for Sustainable Development, Lucknow and Anmol Productions Pvt. Ltd., New Delhi.

Little, A.D. (1991), *Seizing Strategic Environmental Advantage*, Centre for Environmental Assurance, London, Quoted in Welford, Richard (1996), *Corporate Environmental Management: Systems and Strategies*, Universities Press (India) Limited, Hyderabad, pp. 23-24.

Lodge, George and Rayport, Jeffrey (1991), 'Knee-Deep and Rising: America's Recycling Crisis', *Harvard Business Review*, September-October, pp. 128-139, Quoted in Lozada, Hector R. and Mintu-Wimsatt, Alma T. (2004), 'Green-Based Innovation: Sustainable Development in Product Management', in Polonsky, Michael Jay and Mintu-Wimsatt, Alma T. (2004) (ed.), *Environmental Marketing: Strategies, Practice, Theory and Research*, Jaico Publishing House, Mumbai, p. 187.

Lozada, Hector R. and Mintu-Wimsatt, Alma T. (2004), 'Green-Based Innovation: Sustainable Development in Product Management', in Polonsky, Michael Jay and Mintu-Wimsatt, Alma T. (2004) (ed.), *Environmental Marketing: Strategies, Practice, Theory and Research*, Jaico Publishing House, Mumbai.

Magretta, J. (1997), 'Growth through Global Sustainability: An Interview with Monsanto's CEO Robert B Shapiro', *Harvard Business Review*, January-February, 1997, Quoted in Starkey, Richard and Welford, Richard (2005), *The Earthscan Reader in Business and Sustainable Development*, Earthscan, London, p. 15.

Nash, J. and Stoughton, M. D. (1994), 'Learning to Live with Life Cycle Assessment', *Environmental Science and Technology*, 28: 236-237, Quoted in Bishop, Paul L. (2000), *Pollution Prevention: Fundamentals and Practice*, McGraw Hill, Singapore, p. 252.

Neace, M. Bill (2004), 'Marketing's Linear-Hierarchical Underpinning and a Proposal for a Paradigm Shift in Values to Include the Environment', in Polonsky, Michael Jay and Mintu-Wimsatt, Alma T. (2004) (ed.), *Environmental Marketing: Strategies, Practice, Theory and Research*, Jaico Publishing House, Mumbai, p. 71.

Nelson-Horchler, Joani (1989), 'Old Packages Never Die ....', *Industry Week*, September 4, pp. 88-90, Quoted in Benedetto, C. Anthony di and Chandran, Rajan (2004), 'Behaviours of Environmentally Concerned Firms: An Agenda for Effective Strategic Development', in Polonsky, Michael Jay and Mintu-Wimsatt, Alma T. (2004) (ed.), *Environmental Marketing: Strategies, Practice, Theory and Research*, Jaico Publishing House, Mumbai, pp. 275-276.

Polonsky, Michael Jay (2004), 'Cleaning Up Green Marketing Claims: A Practical Checklist', in Polonsky, Michael Jay and Mintu-Wimsatt, Alma T. (2004) (ed.), *Environmental Marketing: Strategies, Practice, Theory and Research*, Jaico Publishing House, Mumbai.

Porter, M. E. (1985), *Competitive Advantage*, The Free Press, New York, Quoted in Welford, Richard (1996), *Corporate Environmental Management: Systems and Strategies*, Universities Press (India) Limited, Hyderabad, pp. 19-24.

Rolfes, Rebecca (1990), 'How Green is Your Market Basket?' *Across the Board*, January/February, pp. 49-51, Quoted in Benedetto, C. Anthony di and Chandran, Rajan (2004), 'Behaviours of Environmentally Concerned Firms: An Agenda for Effective Strategic Development', in Polonsky, Michael Jay and Mintu-Wimsatt, Alma T. (2004) (ed.), *Environmental Marketing: Strategies, Practice, Theory and Research*, Jaico Publishing House, Mumbai, pp. 275-276.

Sawhney, Aparna and Jose, P. D. (2003), 'The Greening of Business Strategy: From Compliance to Competitive Advantage', *IIMB Management Review*, September 2003.

Schiller, Zach (1990), 'P&G Tries Hauling Itself Out of America's Trash Heap', *Business Week*, April 23, p. 101, Quoted in Benedetto, C. Anthony di and Chandran, Rajan (2004), 'Behaviours of Environmentally Concerned Firms: An Agenda for Effective Strategic Development', in Polonsky, Michael Jay and Mintu-Wimsatt, Alma T. (2004) (ed.), *Environmental Marketing: Strategies, Practice, Theory and Research*, Jaico Publishing House, Mumbai, pp. 275-276.

Stuller, Jay (1990), 'The Policies of Packaging', *Across the Board,* January/February, pp. 41-48, Quoted in Benedetto, C. Anthony di and Chandran, Rajan (2004), 'Behaviours of Environmentally Concerned Firms: An Agenda for Effective Strategic Development', in Polonsky, Michael Jay and Mintu-Wimsatt, Alma T. (2004) (ed.), *Environmental Marketing: Strategies, Practice, Theory and Research,* Jaico Publishing House, Mumbai, pp. 275-276.

Swazy, Alecia (1990), 'For Consumers, Ecology Comes Second', *The Wall Street Journal,* March 13, B1, Quoted in Benedetto, C. Anthony di and Chandran, Rajan (2004), 'Behaviours of Environmentally Concerned Firms: An Agenda for Effective Strategic Development', in Polonsky, Michael Jay and Mintu-Wimsatt, Alma T. (2004) (ed.), *Environmental Marketing: Strategies, Practice, Theory and Research,* Jaico Publishing House, Mumbai, pp. 275-276.

Taylor, S. R. (1992), 'Green Management: The Next Competitive Weapon', *Futures,* Sept 1992, pp. 669-680, Quoted in Welford, Richard (1996), *Corporate Environmental Management: Systems and Strategies,* Universities Press (India) Limited, Hyderabad, pp. 23-24.

The Economist Intelligence Unit (1999), *Best Practices: Environment,* Universities Press (India) Limited, Hyderabad, p. 16.

The Times of India (2001), *World Environment Day,* June 5, Quoted in Jain, Sanjay K. and Kaur, Gurmeet (2004), 'Green Marketing: An Indian Perspective', *Decision,* Vol. 31, No. 2, July-December 2004, pp. 199-201.

U.S. EPA (1992), *Facility Pollution Prevention Guide,* EPA/600/R-92/088, U. S. EPA, Washington, DC, Quoted in Bishop, Paul L. (2000), *Pollution Prevention: Fundamentals and Practice,* McGraw Hill, Singapore, p. 330.

Vigon, B.W., Tolle D.A., Cornaby, B.W., Latham, H.C., Harrison, C.L., Boguski, T.L., Hunt, R.G. and Sellers, J.D. (1993), *Life-Cycle Assessment: Inventory Guidelines and Principles,* EPA/600/R-92/245, U.S. EPA, Cincinnati, OH, Quoted in Bishop, Paul L. (2000), *Pollution Prevention: Fundamentals and Practice,* McGraw Hill, Singapore, p. 252.

Walley, Noah and Whitehead, Bradley (1994), 'It's Not Easy Being Green', *Harvard Business Review*, May-June, Quoted in Cairncross, Frances (1999), *Green, Inc.: Guide to Business and the Environment*, Universities Press (India) Limited, Hyderabad, pp. 189-190.

Waterman, R., Peters, T. and Philips, J. (1980), 'Structure In Not Organization', *Business Horizons*, June, pp. 14-26, Quoted in Hutchinson, Andrew and Hutchinson, Frances (1996), *Environmental Business Management: Sustainable Development in the New Millennium*, McGraw-Hill Publishing Company, England, pp. 111-113.

Welford, Richard (1996), *Corporate Environmental Management: Systems and Strategies*, Universities Press (India) Limited, Hyderabad, p. 19.

Welford, R.J. (1992), 'Linking Quality and the Environment', *Business Strategy and the Environment*, 1, 1, Quoted in Welford, Richard (1996), *Corporate Environmental Management: Systems and Strategies*, Universities Press (India) Limited, Hyderabad, pp. 23-24.

Welford, R.J. and Gouldson, A.P. (1993), *Environmental Management & Business Strategy*, Pitman Publishing, London, Quoted in Welford, Richard (1996), *Corporate Environmental Management: Systems and Strategies*, Universities Press (India) Limited, Hyderabad, pp. 23-26.

PART–IV

18

ENVIRONMENTAL PERFORMANCE ANALYSIS

There are four reasons why every organisation should take environmental factors into account in its management processes. Those four reasons are ethical, economical, legal and commercial. From ethical point of view, as human beings we have a duty to look after the world in which we live and to hand it on to our children in good shape. From economic point of view, conserving resources and not generating waste products or wasting energy means we save on cost. From legal point of view, more and more governments are passing laws to control how we interact with the environment. Therefore we need systems to make sure we stay within the law, otherwise we can be fined and damage our reputation. From commercial point of view, without evidence of an environmental management system, the number of customers prepared to trade will start to fall. On the other hand, by being able to demonstrate good environmental practice, new market opportunities may open up (Edwards, 2001).

Now, environmental regulations alone cannot solve the environmental problems. Implementation of regulations always remains as an issue. Gradually, awareness about environmental issues is increasing among policy makers and public in general. Therefore, environmental management is not only a compliance issue, but also it is a strategic business practice. There is wide scope of incorporation of environmental issues in business practice. Globally, green awareness, eco-friendly production, etc.

become buzz words, which indicate heightened industry awareness on environmental issues. It may be due to prolonged activities of environmental activists.

The focus of this work was on incorporation of environmental issues in business practice. In the present work, incorporation of environmental issues means whether business strategy and operational procedure incorporates environmental issues. To be more specific, it was considered that the first stage of addressing environmental issues in the business process would be making the operating units compliant with environmental regulations. Further, the process of compliance with environmental regulations would be incorporated in a holistic manner in process of the organisation. So the entire business process would have a focus towards environmental issues. Accordingly, we had chosen certain aspects of business process including certain strategic issues (e.g., corporate mission, compliance with environmental regulations, quality certification, etc.) that may reflect the level of incorporation of environmental issues in business practice. We tried to measure this level of integration by applying quantitative scores. We termed this as environmental proactiveness score. Further, it categorised the business units in a matrix for better classification of units on the basis of environmental performance and other suitable criteria. It also analysed the nature of variation in proactiveness among the sample units. Once this analysis would be in hand, it would be easier to draw a framework where incorporation of environmental issues would make a proactive stance towards sustainable corporate planning and strategic management. Further, it explored the unit specific determinants that may explain the variation in proactiveness among the sample units.

Accordingly, this Part (Part IV) presents empirical evidence about the present scenario of corporate environmental management and the level of incorporation of environmental issues in business practice of Indian Companies. The first and second Chapters (Chapter 19 and 20) of this Part analyse the empirical results relating to the general profile and also the extent of incorporation of environmental issues in business practice;

while in the third Chapter (Chapter 21), evaluative analyses are made based on preceding section to measure the environmental proactiveness of the industrial units and to analyse the nature of variation in proactiveness among the units. Further, Chapter 22 explores the unit specific determinants (if any) that may explain the variation in proactiveness among the sample units. The last Chapter (Chapter 23) concludes the major findings of the work.

19

GENERAL PROFILE OF INDUSTRIAL UNITS

In this Chapter, we highlighted some key general characteristics of the surveyed units that would reveal the basic profile of the units. It included tenure of establishment of the units (as on 2006), nature of ownership, annual production, capital investment, turnover, composition of manpower, etc. The Chapter starts with a description of methodology followed for selection of units for the purpose of environmental performance analysis of the industrial units. Exhibit 19.1 at a glance presents general profile of the industrial units at the end of the Chapter.

We got a list of grossly polluting units in West Bengal from the Annual Report of West Bengal Pollution Control Board (WBPCB), 2004-2005. It was reported in that Annual Report of WBPCB that there are total 332 numbers of grossly polluting units in West Bengal. Due to having some incomplete information in the list of grossly polluting units, the study concentrated on total 295 units (i.e., total 37 units are excluded for lack of information). Major concentrations (around 10% or more) of those units were seen in Howrah, Burdwan, Kolkata, 24 Pgs. (N), Hooghly and Medinipur districts. It was considered that units in these six districts may be sufficient to represent the units in West Bengal[1]. These six districts covered 250 (i.e. about 84.75%) number of total grossly polluting units in West Bengal. Survey was conducted among 25 per cent of those 250 units. Accordingly, total 63 number of grossly polluting units (18 units in Howrah, 12 in Burdwan, 11 in Kolkata, 8 in 24 Pgs. (N), 8 in Hooghly and 6 in Medinipur) were surveyed. The details are given in Table 19.1.

Table 19.1: Distribution of Grossly Polluting Units by District

Sl. No.	*District*	*Number of Grossly Polluting Units*	*Percentage of Grossly Polluting Units*	*25% of (3)*
(1)	(2)	(3)	(4)	(5)
1.	Howrah	71	24.07	18
2.	Burdwan	48	16.27	12
3.	Kolkata	45	15.25	11
4.	24 Pgs. (N)	31	10.51	8
5.	Hooghly	30	10.17	8
6.	Medinipur	25	8.47	6
	Total	**250**	**84.75**	**63**

Source: Annual Report of West Bengal Pollution Control Board, 2004-2005. Results Computed.

Based on the nature of sample units, we identified 5 major industry segments, namely, 'chemical'; 'ferrous metal'; 'food and beverage'; 'non-ferrous metal' and 'thermal power'. Rest of the sample units that did not fall under these 5 industry segments were clubbed under head 'others'. It was observed that 'others' industry segment included engineering unit, ceramic insulator, coal carbonization, cement industry, paint & dyes, pulp and paper, textile, etc.

The classification of sample units based on 6 industry segments chosen above is presented in Table 19.2.

As it was found that some of the grossly polluting units initially selected were closed, which was not mentioned in the List of the Grossly Polluting Units of WBPCB. Accordingly, we could concentrate only on 55 units instead of 63. Those 55 grossly polluting units were target units for our study i.e. around 87.30 per cent of total sample were finally selected for further analysis.

Table 19.2: Classification of Sample Units by Industry Segment

Sl. No.	*Industry Segments*	*No. of Units Surveyed*						
		24 Pgs. (N)	*Burdwan*	*Hooghly*	*Howrah*	*Kolkata*	*Medinipur*	*Total*
1.	Chemical	3	2	3	3	1	3	15
2.	Ferrous Metal	–	6	–	14	–	1	21
3.	Food & Beverage	–	–	1	–	3	–	4
4.	Non-Ferrous Metal	1	1	–	–	6	–	8
5.	Thermal Power	2	2	1	–	1	1	7
6.	Others	2	1	3	1	–	1	8
	Total	**8**	**12**	**8**	**18**	**11**	**6**	**63**

Source: Annual Report of West Bengal Pollution Control Board, 2004-2005. Results Computed.

Accordingly, Table 19.3 (*See on next page*) shows the list of those 55 target units by industry segment that exclude the units those had already been shut down. It reveals that among 55 surveyed units, the highest number of units (30.91%) were units of ferrous metal industry followed by units of chemical industry (21.82%). About 30 per cent surveyed units were units of non-ferrous metal industry and others. Out of all surveyed units, only 10.91 per cent were units of thermal power and the remaining 7.27 per cent were units of food and beverage industry. Analysis of surveyed units by district reflected that in Howrah, majority (76.93%) of the units were units of ferrous metal industry. Whereas, in Kolkata, majority (54.55%) of the units were units of non-ferrous metal industry.

The position of surveyed units based on tenure of establishment along with nature of ownership is depicted in Table 19.4. (*See on page 155*) It reveals that majority (90.91%) of the surveyed units was private and a small proportion of units were Government. Among the private units, a few (5.46% of total) were non-company (i.e. sole proprietorship, partnership, etc.) and rests (85.45%) were limited companies. It also presents that in some (41.81%) of the cases, the surveyed units had been established 31-50 years ago. Some (32.73%) units had been set up 11-30 years back. 9.09 per cent units had been established less than 10 years back. Rest 16.37 per cent units had been set up more than 50 years back.

The study also revealed that private units had been set up within last 70 years (as on 2006). Majority (78.72%) of them had been set up 11-50 years ago. In case of government units, 50 per cent of them had been established 31-50 years back.

The annual production capacity of each surveyed unit is presented in Table 19.5. (*See on page 156*) It should be pertinent to mention here that during collection of information from different units, the units of measurement of the production capacity were found to be in various forms. For the purpose of further analysis, we made certain conversion[2] to make those different units comparable.

Table 19.3: Classification of Surveyed Units by Industry Segment

Sl. No.	*Industry Segments*	*No. of Units Surveyed*													
		24 Pgs. (N)		*Burdwan*		*Hooghly*		*Howrah*		*Kolkata*		*Medinipur*		*Total*	
		No.	*%*	*No.*	*%*	*No.*	*%*	*No.*	*%*	*No.*	*%*	*No.*	*%*	*No.*	*%*
1.	Chemical	2	33.33	1	9.09	3	37.50	2	15.38	1	9.09	3	50.00	12	21.82
2.	Ferrous Metal	–	–	6	54.55	–	–	10	76.93	–	–	1	16.67	17	30.91
3.	Food & Beverage	–	–	–	–	1	12.50	–	–	3	27.27	–	–	4	7.27
4.	Non-Ferrous Metal	1	16.67	1	9.09	–	–	–	–	6	54.55	–	–	8	14.55
5.	Thermal Power	1	16.67	2	18.18	1	12.50	–	–	1	9.09	1	16.67	6	10.91
6.	Others	2	33.33	1	9.09	3	37.50	1	7.69	–	–	1	16.66	8	14.54
	Total	**6**	**10.91**	**11**	**20.00**	**8**	**14.54**	**13**	**23.64**	**11**	**20.00**	**6**	**10.91**	**55**	**100.00**

Source: Annual Report of West Bengal Pollution Control Board, 2004-2005. Results Computed.

Table 19.4: Tenure of Establishment of Surveyed Units

Sl. No.	Nature of Ownership	Tenure of Establishment (yrs.)													
		0-10		11-30		31-50		51-70		71-100		> 100		Total	
		No.	%	No.	%	No.	%	No.	%	No.	%	No.	%	No.	%
1.	Government	0	0	1	5.56	1	4.35	0	0	1	100.00	2	100.00	5	9.09
2.	Private	5	100.00	17	94.44	22	95.65	6	100.00	0	0	0	0	50	90.91
	Total	**5**	**9.09**	**18**	**32.73**	**23**	**41.81**	**6**	**10.91**	**1**	**1.82**	**2**	**3.64**	**55**	**100.00**

Source: Results computed.

Table 19.5: Analysis of Annual Production of Surveyed Units

Sl. No.	*Annual Production (MT/yr. or MU/yr.)*	*Industry Segments*												*Total*	
		Chemical		*Ferrous Metal*		*Food and Beverage*		*Non-Ferrous Metal*		*Thermal Power*		*Others*			
		No.	*%*	*No.*	*%*	*No.*	*%*	*No.*	*%*	*No.*	*%*	*No.*	*%*	*No.*	*%*
1.	< = 500	0	0	1	5.88	0	0	3	37.50	0	0	0	0	4	7.27
2.	500 – 1,000	3	25.00	4	23.54	0	0	4	50.00	2	33.33	2	25.00	15	27.28
3.	1,000 – 5,000	1	8.33	7	41.18	0	0	0	0	3	50.00	0	0	11	20.00
4.	5,000 – 10,000	0	0	0	0	0	0	0	0	1	16.67	0	0	1	1.82
5.	10,000 – 50,000	1	8.33	2	11.76	0	0	0	0	0	0	0	0	3	5.45
6.	50,000 – 1,00,000	0	0	2	11.76	4	100.00	1	12.50	0	0	4	50.00	11	20.00
7.	1,00,000 – 5,00,000	6	50.00	1	5.88	0	0	0	0	0	0	2	25.00	9	16.36
8.	> 5,00,000	1	8.34	0	0	0	0	0	0	0	0	0	0	1	1.82
	Total	**12**	**21.82**	**17**	**30.91**	**4**	**7.27**	**8**	**14.55**	**6**	**10.91**	**8**	**14.54**	**55**	**100.00**

Source: Results computed.

Accordingly, Table 19.5 presents that some (47.28%) of the surveyed units were having the annual production capacity of 500-5,000 MT. Out of all units of ferrous metal industry, 64.71 per cent were producing within this range. 20 per cent surveyed units were producing annually 50,000-1,00,000 MT, where the major contributors were units of food & beverage industry. 16.36 per cent units were producing annually 1,00,000-5,00,000 MT, where units of chemical industry (50%) played the lead role. It is worthwhile to mention here that units of thermal power were mainly producing 500-10,000 MU electricity annually.

On the basis of discussion with industrial experts during survey and previous literatures survey (Firth, 1979; Epstein and Young, 1998; HaBler and Reinhard, 2000), size of the surveyed units had been measured in terms of capital investment. It was estimated that if the capital investment is less than or equal to Rs. 1 crore, the unit will be designated as 'Very Small'. Accordingly, the unit will be designated as 'Small' for Rs. 1-10 crores capital investment; 'Medium' for Rs. 10-100 crores capital investment; 'Large' for Rs. 100-500 crores capital investment and 'Very large' for greater than Rs. 500 crores capital investment. The capital investment of the surveyed units is presented in Table 19.6. (*See on next page*) It reveals that in case of some (43.64%) of the surveyed units capital investment ranged between Rs. 100-500 crores i.e. out of all surveyed units, 43.64 per cent were 'large' units. Within this range, units of thermal power (83.33%) followed by units of chemical industry (41.66%) and units of ferrous metal industry (41.18%) were the major contributors. Out of all surveyed units, very few (5.45%) were 'very large' units. It should also be mentioned that significant number (21.82%) of surveyed units were 'small' followed by 'very small' units (20%). These included mainly units of non-ferrous metal industry followed by units of ferrous metal industry—out of all units of non-ferrous metal industry, 87.50 per cent and out of all units of ferrous metal industry, 58.82 per cent units fell under these two categories ('small' and 'very small').

Table 19.6: Analysis of Capital Investment of Surveyed Units

Sl. No.	Capital Investment (Rs. Crore)	Industry Segments													
		Chemical		Ferrous Metal		Food and Beverage		Non-Ferrous Metal		Thermal Power		Others		Total	
		No.	%	No.	%	No.	%	No.	%	No.	%	No.	%	No.	%
1.	< = 1	2	16.67	6	35.29	0	0	3	37.50	0	0	0	0	11	20.00
2.	1-10	2	16.67	4	23.53	2	50.00	4	50.00	0	0	0	0	12	21.82
3.	10-100	1	8.33	0	0	1	25.00	1	12.50	0	0	2	25.00	5	9.09
4.	100-500	5	41.66	7	41.18	1	25.00	0	0	5	83.33	6	75.00	24	43.64
5.	> 500	2	16.67	0	0	0	0	0	0	1	16.67	0	0	3	5.45
	Total	**12**	**21.82**	**17**	**30.91**	**4**	**7.27**	**8**	**14.55**	**6**	**10.91**	**8**	**14.54**	**55**	**100.00**

Source: Results computed.

The analysis of annual turnover of the surveyed units is presented in Table 19.7. (*See on page 160*) It reflects that some (34.55%) of the surveyed units were having annual turnover of Rs. 100-500 crores. Some (32.73%) units were having annual turnover in the range of Rs. 1-10 crores. This range was mainly executed by units of non-ferrous metal industry (62.50%) followed by units of ferrous metal industry (47.06%). It is worthwhile to mention here that some (21.82%) of the units were having annual turnover of more than Rs. 500 crores. On comparison with Table 19.6, it is pertinent to mention here that in case of 'very small' units, annual turnover was not satisfactory—only 1.93 times of capital investment. On the contrary, annual turnover of 'large' units was 5.89 times of capital investment and in case of 'very large' units it was 6.70 times of capital investment. In case of 'small' and 'medium' units, the value was moderate i.e. 3.46 and 4.69 times of capital investment respectively. It can be inferred that 'very large' and 'large' units were more efficient in use of capital in terms of capital turnover ratio compared to 'small' and 'very small' units.

Composition of manpower in surveyed units is reported in Table 19.8. (*See on page 161*) It reveals that out of the total manpower strength in the surveyed units, some (50.02%) were permanent employees, rests (49.98%) were contractual workers. Out of permanent employees, some (33.03%) were managerial staff members and rests (66.97%) were non-managerial level staff members. It was also found that number of permanent employees was more in units of chemical industry, units of food and beverage industry and thermal power units as compared to contractual workers. On the contrary, it is worthwhile to mention here that the number of contractual workers was remarkably higher in case of units of non-ferrous metal industry followed by units of ferrous metal industry as compared to permanent staff members. The study also revealed that number of non-managerial staff members was comparatively higher in all industry segments except units of non-ferrous metal industry. However, on an average, number of non-managerial staff members (66.97%) was almost twice as compared to managerial staff members (33.03%).

Table 19.7: Analysis of Annual Turnover of Surveyed Units

Sl. No.	Turnover (Rs. Crore)	*Industry Segments*													
		Chemical		*Ferrous Metal*		*Food and Beverage*		*Non-Ferrous Metal*		*Thermal Power*		*Others*		*Total*	
		No.	*%*	*No.*	*%*	*No.*	*%*	*No.*	*%*	*No.*	*%*	*No.*	*%*	*No.*	*%*
1.	< = 1	1	8.33	1	5.88	0	0	2	25.00	0	0	0	0	4	5.45
2.	1-10	3	25.00	8	47.06	1	25.00	5	62.50	0	0	0	0	17	32.73
3.	10-100	1	8.33	1	5.88	1	25.00	0	0	0	0	0	0	3	5.45
4.	100 – 500	5	41.67	4	23.53	1	25.00	1	12.50	1	16.67	7	87.50	19	34.55
5.	> 500	2	16.67	3	17.65	1	25.00	0	0	5	83.33	1	12.50	12	21.82
	Total	**12**	**21.82**	**17**	**30.91**	**4**	**7.27**	**8**	**14.55**	**6**	**10.91**	**8**	**14.54**	**55**	**100.00**

Source: Results computed.

Table 19.8: Composition of Manpower in Surveyed Units

Sl. No.	Industry Segments	Composition (%)			
		Permanent			Contractual
		Managerial	Non-managerial	Total	
1.	Chemical	31.10	68.90	60.80	39.20
2.	Ferrous Metal	26.15	73.85	47.06	52.94
3.	Food & Beverage	13.82	86.18	56.57	43.43
4.	Non-Ferrous Metal	59.28	40.72	39.55	60.45
5.	Thermal Power	13.85	86.15	51.02	48.98
6.	Others	48.30	51.70	46.61	53.39
	Total	**33.03**	**66.97**	**50.02**	**49.98**

Source: Results computed.

During the analysis, it was also found that in case of 61.82 per cent surveyed units total manpower strength was between 51 to 500. All units of food and beverage industry and majority (76.47%) of the units of ferrous metal industry fell in this category. In case of 16.36 per cent units, total manpower was less than 50. On the contrary, in case of 21.82 per cent units, total manpower was more than 500. It was observed that 36.36 per cent units were having permanent employees of 21-100. 52.94 per cent units of ferrous metal industry fell in this category. In case of 21.82 per cent units, the number of permanent employees varied between 201 and 500. Very few (9.09%) units were having permanent employees more than 1,000. The study also revealed that significant number (49.09%) of units was having management employees of less than 20. Some (41.82%) units had the management employees of 21-100 in number. Very few (9.09%) units were having more than 100 number of management employees. In case of 32.73 per cent units, number of contractual workers ranged between 101-500. 27.27 per cent units were having the number of contractual workers within the range of 21-50. In case of a few (16.36%) units, the number of contractual workers was more than 500.

EXHIBIT 19.1

General Profile of Industrial Units—At A Glance

- Majority (90.91%) of the surveyed units was private and a small proportion of units were Government. Among the private units, a few (5.46% of total) were non-company (i.e. sole proprietorship, partnership, etc.) and rests (85.45%) were limited companies.
- In majority (90.91%) of the cases, the surveyed units had been established more than 10 years back. Only 9.09 per cent units had been established less than 10 years back.
- Some (47.28%) of the surveyed units were having the annual production capacity of 500-5,000 MT. 20 per cent surveyed units were producing annually 50,000-1,00,000 MT. 16.36 per cent units were producing annually 1,00,000-5,00,000 MT. Units of thermal power were mainly producing 500-10,000 MU electricity annually.
- Out of all surveyed units, 43.64 per cent were 'large' units (having capital investment of Rs. 100-500 crores), very few (5.45%) were 'very large' units (having capital investment of greater than Rs. 500 crores). Significant numbers (21.82%) of surveyed units were 'small' (having capital investment of Rs. 1-10 crores) followed by 'very small' (20%) units (having capital investment of less than or equal to Rs. 1 crore).
- Some (34.55%) of the surveyed units were having annual turnover of Rs. 100-500 crores. Some (32.73%) units were having annual turnover in the range of Rs. 1-10 crores.
- In case of 'very small' units annual turnover was not satisfactory-only 1.93 times of capital investment. On the contrary, annual turnover of 'very large' units was 6.70 times of capital investment on average.
- Out of the total manpower strength in the surveyed units, some (50.02%) were permanent employees. Out of permanent employees, some (33.03%) were managerial staff members.

On an average, number of non-managerial staff members (66.97%) was almost twice as compared to managerial staff members (33.03%).

- In case of 61.82 per cent surveyed units total manpower strength was between 51 to 500. In case of 16.36 per cent units, total manpower was less than 50.
- 36.36 per cent units were having permanent employees of 21-100. In case of 21.82 per cent units, the number of permanent employees varied between 201 and 500.
- Significant number (49.09%) of units was having management employees of less than 20. Some (41.82%) units had the management employees of 21-100 in number.

NOTES

1. West Bengal is a State (Province) in India. It is divided into 19 districts for administrative control.
2. Note: In case of soft drink manufacturer (food and beverage industry), production units were provided in the form of 'bottle/min'. For the purpose of analysis, one bottle was considered as 300 ml or 0.3 lt and 1 lt was considered as 1 kg. Therefore one bottle production equals 0.3 kg or 0.0003 MT. Similarly, in case of distillery (food & beverage industry), sometimes production units were given in the form of 'litre'. For the purpose of analysis, 1 lt was considered as 1 kg. Therefore one lt production equals 1 kg or 0.001 MT. In this case, sometimes production units were given in the form of 'case'. For the purpose of analysis, 1 case was considered as 24 bottles. In case of pharmaceutical (chemical industry), production units were given in the form of 'no. of tablets'. For the purpose of analysis, one tablet was considered as 5 gm. In case of units of thermal power, units of electricity were expressed in the form of 'Million Unit (MU)'. For the purpose of analysis, this unit had been considered as it is. 1 MU was considered as 10^3 Megawatt hr or 10^6 kilowatt hr.

20

ENVIRONMENTAL PORTFOLIO ANALYSIS

Environmental portfolio analysis includes assessing the extent of incorporation of different environmental issues into overall corporate strategy formulation and implementation at operational levels. It covers discussion of corporate environmental policy; role of environment department in the production units; status of environmental compliance in the areas of air quality, wastewater quality, solid and hazardous wastes, noise level, etc.; EMS certification; status of conducting environmental audit; environmental cost management; etc. In the following sections, status of the sample units regarding incorporation of those environmental issues in their business practice is discussed thoroughly.

Corporate Environment Policy

An environment policy forms the foundation of environmental management. It is expected that in case of any proactive industry, environmental policy is needed to control the environmental impact of the industrial activities and operation, which will enable it to comply with all applicable laws, rules and regulations; to prevent pollution; to ensure employee awareness and responsibility on environmental issues by providing training and participation programmes; to reduce waste generation and contamination of air, water and land; to reduce resources consumption to the minimum level required. Thus, the environmental policy forms the basis upon which the organisation sets its objectives and targets in the area of environmental management.

Table 20.1: **Distribution of Surveyed Units Having Environment Policy by Size**

Sl. No.	*Having Environment Policy*	*Size of Surveyed Units*											
		Very small		*Small*		*Medium*		*Large*		*Very Large*		*Total*	
		No.	*%*	*No.*	*%*	*No.*	*%*	*No.*	*%*	*No.*	*%*	*No.*	*%*
1.	Yes	1	9.09	1	8.33	3	60	21	87.50	2	66.67	28	50.91
2.	No	10	90.91	11	91.67	2	40	3	12.50	1	33.33	27	49.09
	Total	**11**	**20.00**	**12**	**21.82**	**5**	**9.09**	**24**	**43.64**	**3**	**5.45**	**55**	**100.00**

Source: Results computed.

The distribution of surveyed units having environment policy is reported in Table 20.1. It was found that about 50.91 per cent of the surveyed units had an environment policy, whereas the rest (49.09%) of the units did not have any environment policy (Figure 20.1). The study also highlighted that in case of surveyed units having environment policy, units of thermal power played the lead role, since majority (83.33%) of the units of thermal power had such a policy. The performance was medium for units of chemical industry and units of food and beverage industry followed by units of ferrous metal industry. Whereas very poor performance was exhibited by units of non-ferrous metal industry, majority (87.50%) of non-ferrous metal units was not having any environment policy.

Fig. 20.1

Distribution of Surveyed Units Having Environment Policy

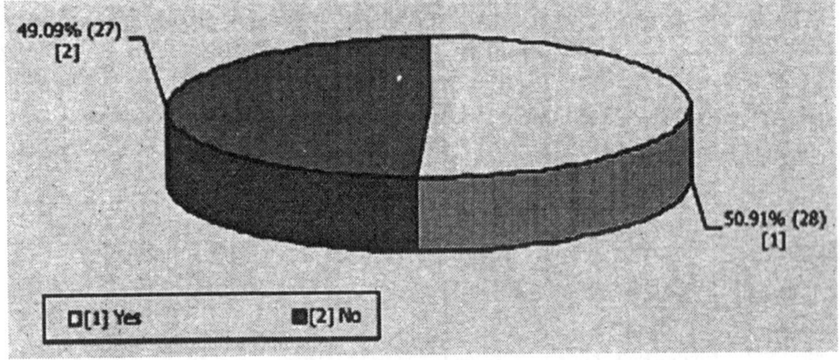

Source: Results computed.

The study also revealed that majority of 'large' (87.50%) units followed by 'very large' (66.67%) units had environment policy. Whereas performance was poor in case of 'very small' and 'small' units, where out of all 'very small' units, 90.91 per cent did not have any environmental policy. Similar incidence was reflected in case of 91.67 per cent 'small' units. Therefore, it can be inferred that 'large' and 'very large' units were more environmentally focussed to have environment policy compared to 'very small' and 'small' units.

The study also highlighted that out of 28 surveyed units having environment policy, in case of 67.86 per cent cases policy was formulated after 20 years of the establishment of the company. About 10 per cent surveyed units had formulated its environment policy within 4 years after their establishment. 14.28 per cent surveyed units had formulated their policy within 4-10 years after their establishment. Formulation of environment policy in case of rest 7.14 per cent was made within 10-20 years after their establishment.

Apart from formulation of policy, it is important to adopt such a policy. If any policy is not formally adopted, it will not be able to add any weightage. Formal adoption means the policy is signed by the management level. Such involvement and commitment is needed from the part of the top management level to make the unit environmentally proactive. Therefore, it is expected that the organization's environmental policy should be defined and documented by its top management within the context of the environmental policy of any broader corporate body of which it is a part, and with the endorsement of that body.

Fig. 20.2
Distribution of Surveyed Units Having Formal Adoption of Environment Policy

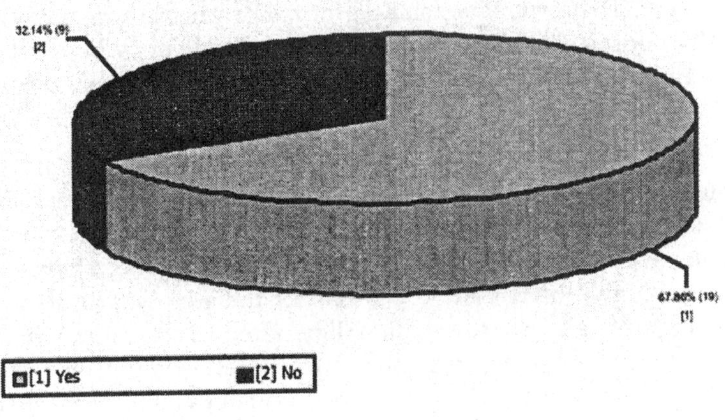

Source: Results computed.

Figure 20.2 reveals that out of 28 surveyed units having environment policy, 67.86 per cent had formally adopted their environment policy. Whereas rests 32.14 per cent had not formally adopted the policy. Performance was good in case of units of chemical, thermal power, food and beverage and non-ferrous metal industry segments. Units of ferrous metal industry showed very poor picture in this aspect, since out of all units of ferrous metal industry, 87.50 per cent of the units had not formally adopted their policy.

The study also highlighted that out of 19 surveyed units having formal adoption of environmental policy, in majority (63.15%) of the cases top management *viz.*, Managing Director, Vice President, Director, Asstt. Vice President, etc. signed the policy. In the rest (36.85%) of the cases, the signature during formal adoption of environment policy was done by middle management level employees, *viz.*, station manager, general manager, etc.

It is also expected that the environmental policy should be communicated to all persons who work for, or on behalf of, the organisation, including contractors working at an organisation's facility. The study revealed that 50 per cent of the surveyed units mentioned their environment policy in their mission statement/ preamble. In this aspect, units of certain industry segments *viz.*, chemical, food and beverage, non-ferrous metal and thermal power had shown remarkable performance. The performance was very poor in case of units of ferrous metal industry where out of all units of ferrous metal industry, none of them had mentioned the same.

It is expected that the environmental policy should be sufficiently clear to be able to be understood by internal and external interested parties, and should be periodically reviewed and revised to reflect changing conditions and information. The study highlighted that 50 per cent of the surveyed units had changed their environment policy, after it was found to be inadequate in some areas or to incorporate some progressive elements in the policy. In this area, units of chemical industry showed their high degree of environmental proactiveness followed by units of thermal power (80%). The result was unsatisfactory in case of certain industry segments *viz.*, ferrous metal, food and beverage and non-ferrous metal, where none of them felt to make any change of their existing environment policy.

The study also revealed that in case of 57.14 per cent units among the units that had changed their policy, environment policy had been changed after 2-5 years of the formulation of the policy. Here also units of chemical industry showed their high degree of awareness of environmental concern in their practice, as 5 units out of total 6 units had changed their policy within 5 years. 21.44 per cent of 'changed policy' units had changed the same after 8-10 years of the formulation of the policy and 14.28 per cen of 'changed policy' units had done the same after 5-8 years. The result was poor in case of 7.14 per cent units, where the environment policy had been changed after 10-12 years of its formulation.

Distribution of surveyed units having separate financial allocation for environment management is reported in Table 20.2. It was found that out of 28 surveyed units having environment policy, in 67.86 per cent cases, there was a separate financial allocation in the annual budget for fulfilling the objectives of the environment policy (Figure 20.3). In this aspect, certain industry

Fig. 20.3
Distribution of Surveyed Units Having Separate Financial Allocation for Environment Management

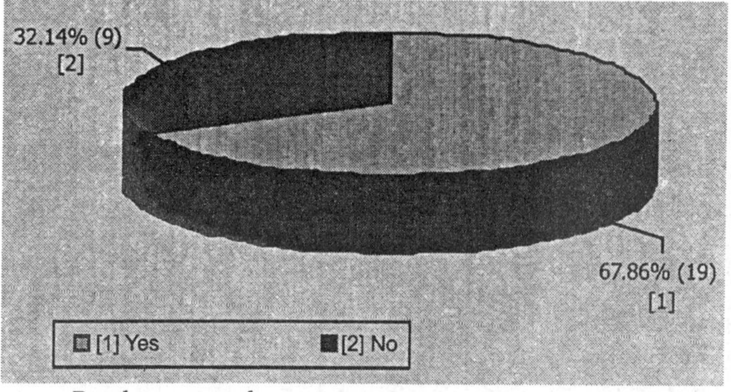

Source: Results computed.

segments viz., chemical, thermal power, food and beverage and non-ferrous metal showed good performance. On the contrary, units of ferrous metal industry showed a poor performance. It was observed that out of all units of ferrous metal industry, 87.50 per cent of the units did not have any separate financial allocation for the same.

Table 20.2: Distribution of Surveyed Units Having Separate Financial Allocation for Environment Management

Sl. No.	Separate Financial Allocation	Industry Segments													
		Chemical		Ferrous Metal		Food and Beverage		Non-Ferrous Metal		Thermal Power		Others		Total	
		No.	%	No.	%	No.	%	No.	%	No.	%	No.	%	No.	%
1.	Yes	6	100.00	1	12.50	2	100.00	1	100.00	5	100.00	4	66.67	19	67.86
2.	No	0	0	7	87.50	0	0	0	0	0	0	2	33.33	9	32.14
	Total	**6**	**21.43**	**8**	**28.57**	**2**	**7.14**	**1**	**3.57**	**5**	**17.86**	**6**	**21.43**	**28**	**100.00**

Source: Results computed.

The important findings in respect of having corporate environmental policy in the industrial units are reported in *Exhibit 20.1*.

EXHIBIT 20.1

Corporate Environment Policy of Industrial Units

- 50.91 per cent (28) of the surveyed units had an environment policy.
- Out of 28 surveyed units having environment policy, in case of 67.86 per cent cases policy was formulated after 20 years of the establishment of the company. About 10 per cent surveyed units had formulated its environment policy within 4 years after their establishment. 14.28 per cent surveyed units had formulated their policy within 4-10 years after their establishment.
- Out of 28 surveyed units having environment policy, 67.86 per cent (19) had formally adopted their environment policy.
- Out of 19 surveyed units having formal adoption of environmental policy, in majority (63.15%) of the cases top management signed the policy.
- 50 per cent of the surveyed units mentioned their environment policy in their mission statement/preamble.
- 50 per cent of the surveyed units had changed their environment policy, after it was found to be inadequate in some areas or to incorporate some progressive elements in the policy.
- In case of 57.14 per cent units among the units that had changed their policy, environment policy had been changed after 2-5 years of the formulation of the policy. 21.44 per cent of 'changed policy' units had changed the same after 8-10 years of the formulation of the policy. 14.28 per cent of 'changed policy' units had done the same after 5-8 years.
- Out of 28 surveyed units having environment policy, in 67.86 per cent cases, there was a separate financial allocation in the annual budget for fulfilling the objectives of the environment policy.

Role of Environment Department in the Production Units

During the collection of primary data and literature survey, it was observed that there is a remarkable role of environment department in any industry. A functional department may not be focussed to environmental issues as it is involved in day-to-day line activities. On the other hand, a separate staff department to address environmental issues may be more effective in proactive management of environmental concerns of the organisation. The environment department supervises the emission of air pollutants, generation of wastewater and solid and hazardous wastes, emanation of noise, etc. It coordinates the functions of all the other departments, specially production departments, so that the industry can meet the regulatory compliance. It instructs the other units for optimal utilisation of resources, cleaner production and pollution prevention.

Distribution of surveyed units having environment department is presented in Table 20.3. (*See on next page*) It was noted that majority of the surveyed units (61.82%) did not have any environment department. Only 38.18 per cent surveyed units had environment department (Figure 20.4). The analysis also

Fig. 20.4
Distribution of Surveyed Units Having Environment Department

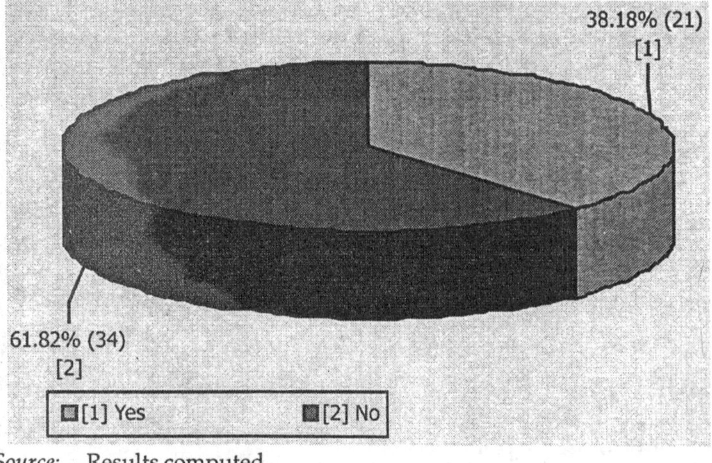

Source: Results computed.

Table 20.3: Distribution of Surveyed Units Having Environment Department

Sl. No.	*Having Environment Department*	*Industry Segments*													
		Chemical		*Ferrous Metal*		*Food and Beverage*		*Non-Ferrous Metal*		*Thermal Power*		*Others*		*Total*	
		No.	*%*	*No.*	*%*	*No.*	*%*	*No.*	*%*	*No.*	*%*	*No.*	*%*	*No.*	*%*
1.	Yes	6	50.00	1	5.88	3	75.00	1	12.50	6	100.00	4	50.00	21	38.18
2.	No	6	50.00	16	94.12	1	25.00	7	87.50	0	0	4	50.00	34	61.82
	Total	**12**	**21.82**	**17**	**30.91**	**4**	**7.27**	**8**	**14.55**	**6**	**10.91**	**8**	**14.54**	**55**	**100.00**

Source: Results computed.

revealed that all units of thermal power had an environment department. Result was poor in case of units of ferrous metal industry, where out of all units of ferrous metal industry only 5.88 per cent units had environment department.

The survey revealed that the environment department worked separately in case of 52.38 per cent units having such department. Whereas, in case of some (47.62%) of the units, environment department worked being clubbed with other departments. It was also found that in case of all of the units of thermal power, environment department functioned separately, whereas in case of 50 per cent units of chemical industry environment department worked separately and in case of the rests of the units of chemical industry, they worked being clubbed with other departments. In case of units of food and beverage industry and units of non-ferrous metal industry, environment department worked being clubbed with other departments.

As the appointment of a responsible senior manager is vital to drive environmental improvement and demonstrate organisational commitment, the profile of head/in-charge of environment department in surveyed units is presented in Table 20.4. (*See on next page*) In case of 23.81 per cent units having environment department, senior management level staff members, *viz.*, Managing Director (MD), etc. took the position of head/in-charge of the environment department (*See fig. 20.5 on page 176*). It is pertinent to mention here that no junior level staff members, *viz.*, Superintendent, Supervisor, Jr. Engineer, etc. occupied this position. They only played the supportive role of staff function, whereas line function was being controlled by middle management level staff members and during emergency situation, they took necessary advice and instruction from the senior management level staff members. As such, all of the surveyed units having environment department were seriously conscious of taking care of environmental matter in their business practice.

Table 20.4: Profile of Head/In-Charge of Environment Department in Surveyed Units

Sl. No.	*Head/ In-Charge of Environment Department*	*Industry Segments*													
		Chemical		*Ferrous Metal*		*Food and Beverage*		*Non-Ferrous Metal*		*Thermal Power*		*Others*		*Total*	
		No.	*%*	*No.*	*%*	*No.*	*%*	*No.*	*%*	*No.*	*%*	*No.*	*%*	*No.*	*%*
1.	Senior Management-level Staff	2	33.33	1	100.00	1	33.33	0	0	0	0	1	25.00	5	23.81
2.	Middle Management-level Staff	4	66.67	0	0	2	66.67	1	100.00	6	100.00	3	75.00	16	76.19
3.	Junior Management-level Staff	0	0	0	0	0	0	0	0	0	0	0	0	0	0
	Total	**6**	**28.57**	**1**	**4.76**	**3**	**14.29**	**1**	**4.76**	**6**	**28.57**	**4**	**19.05**	**21**	**100.00**

Source: Results computed.

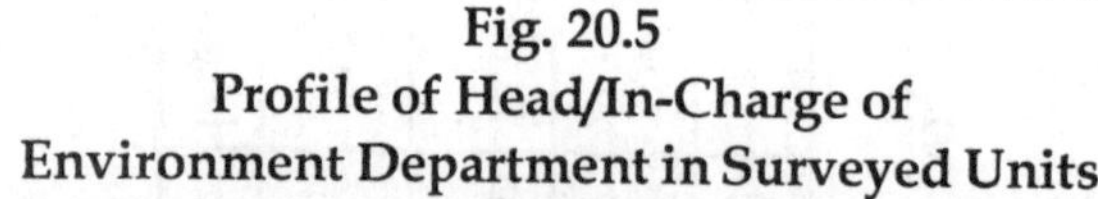

Fig. 20.5
Profile of Head/In-Charge of Environment Department in Surveyed Units

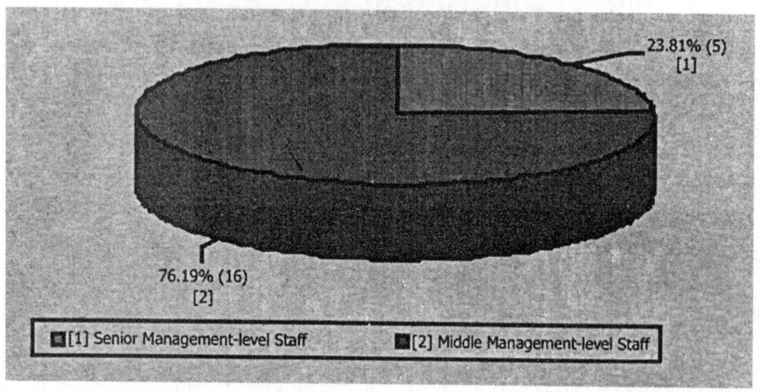

Source: Results computed.

The study also highlighted that head of the environment department was engineering graduate in case of majority (52.38%) of the surveyed units having environment department. Some (28.58%) of the head of the department had post graduate degree with environmental specialization. In a very few (9.52%) cases, head of the department was engineering graduate with environmental degree or diploma.

The study also indicated that in majority (80.95%) of the surveyed units having environment department, for day-to-day reporting, head of the environment department at unit level reported to the middle management level superiors, *viz.*, Operation Head, Safety Officer, Manager (Regulatory Affairs), Works Manager, General Manager, Head (HSE), Plant Head, Unit Head, Station Manager, etc. In a few cases (19.05%), head of the environment department reported to top management *viz.*, Chairman cum Managing Director (CMD), Director (Production), CEO, Executive Director Works, etc.

The important findings in respect of having environment department in the industrial units are reported in *Exhibit 20.2.*

EXHIBIT 20.2

Environment Department of Industrial Units

- Majority (61.82%) of the surveyed units did not have any environment department.
- The environment department worked separately in case of 52.38 per cent units having such department.
- In case of 23.81 per cent units having environment department, senior management level staff members took the position of head/in-charge of the environment department.
- Head of the environment department was engineering graduate in case of majority (52.38%) of the surveyed units having environment department. Some (28.58%) of the head of the department have post graduate degree with environmental specialisation.

Status of Environmental Compliance

Clause (Evaluation of compliance) of Environmental Management System ISO 14001: 2004 provides that consistent with its commitment to compliance, the organisation shall establish, implement and maintain a procedure(s) for periodically evaluating compliance with applicable legal requirements. The regulatory standard as per the Environment (Protection) Rules, 1986 has been presented in Exhibit 20.3.

EXHIBIT 20.3

The Environment (Protection) Rules, 1986 u/s 3, 3A, 3B states the standards for emission or discharge of environmental pollutants that has been specified in Schedules I to IV, VI and VII.

Schedule I, Rule 3

Sl. No.	Industry			Parameter	Standard
1.	All types of asbestos manufacturing units: (including all processes involving the use of asbestos)	Emissions		Pure asbestos material fibre/cc (Fibre of length more than 5 micrometer and diameter less than 3 micrometer with an aspect ratio of 3 or more	4
				Total dust, mg/Nm^3	2
2.	Beehive hard coke oven	Emissions[1]	(i) New unit	Particulate matter (corrected to 6% CO_2), mg/Nm^3	150
			(ii) Existing units	Particulate matter (corrected to 6% CO_2), mg/Nm^3	350
3.	Briquette industry (Coal)	Emissions[2]	(a) Units having capacity less than 10 tonnes	Particulate matter (corrected to 6% CO_2), mg/Nm^3	350
			(b) Units having capacity 10 tonnes or more	Particulate matter (corrected to 6% CO_2), mg/Nm^3	150
4.	Carbon black			Particulate matter emission, mg/Nm^1	150

(Contd...)

Sl. No.	Industry				Parameter	Standard
5.	Cement plants	Plant capacity[3]: 200 tonnes per day			Total dust (All sections), mg/Nm^3	400
		Greater than 200 tonnes per day			Total dust (All sections), mg/Nm^3	250
6.	Ceramic industry	Emissions[4]	A. Kilns	(a) Tunnel, Top Hat, Chamber	Particulate mater, mg/Nm^3	150
					Sulphur dioxide[5], mg/Nm^3	
				(b) Down-draft	Particulate matter, mg/Nm^3	1200
					Sulphur dioxide[5], mg/Nm^3	
				(c) Shuttle	Particulate matter, mg/Nm^3	150
					Sulphur dioxide[5], mg/Nm^3	
				(d) Vertical shaft kiln	Particulate matter, mg/Nm^3	250
					Sulphur dioxide[5], mg/Nm^3	
				(e) Tank furnace	Particulate matter, mg/Nm^3	150
					Sulphur dioxide[5], mg/Nm^3	
			B. Raw material handling processing and operations	(a) Dry raw materials handling and processing operations		
				(b) Basic raw materials and processing operations	Particulate matter[6], mg/Nm^3	
				(c) Other sources of air pollution generation	Particulate matter[6], mg/Nm^3	

(Contd...)

Sl. No.	Industry				Parameter	Standard
	C. Automatic spray unit	(a) Dryes	(i) Fuel fired dryers		Particulate matter, mg/Nm³	150
			(ii) For heat recovery dryers		Particulate matter[6], mg/Nm³	
		(b) Mechanical finishing operation			Particulate matter[6], mg/Nm³	
		(c) Lime/plaster of Paris manufacture	Capacity: More than 5 T/day		Particulate matter, mg/Nm³	500
			Upto 40 T/day		Particulate matter, mg/Nm³	150

(Contd...)

Sl. No.	Industry	Parameter	Standard
7.	Coke ovens (Concentrations in the effluents when discharged into inland surface waters)	pH	5.5-9.0
		BOD (3 days at 27°C), mg/1	30
		Suspended solids, mg/1	100
		Oil & grease, mg/1	10
8.	Copper, lead and zinc smelting	Particulate matter emission in concentrator, mg/Nm^3	150
		Emission of Oxides of sulphur in Smelter & Converter	Off-gases must be utilised for sulphuric acid manufacture. The limits of sulphur dioxide emission from stack shall not exceed 4 kg. per tonne of concentrated (one hundred per cent acid produced

(Contd...)

Sl. No.		*Industry*	*Parameter*		*Standard*
9.	Cotton textile industries (composite and processing)	Common	pH		5.5-9
			Suspended solid, mg/1		100
			BOD[7] (3 days at 27°C), mg/1		150
			Oil & grease, mg/1		10
10.	Edible oil & vanaspati industry[8]	Effluents	pH		6.5-8.5
			Suspended solids, mg/1		150
			Oil & grease, mg/1		20
			BOD (3 days at 27°C), mg/1		100
			COD, mg/1		200
		Wastewater discharge	Refinery/Vanaspati, m^3/tonne of product oil/Vanaspati)		2
11.	Electroplating		pH		6.0-9.0
			Oil & grease, mg/1		10
			Suspended solids, mg/1		100
12.	Fermentation industry (Distilleries, Maltries and Breweries)		pH		5.5-9.0
			Suspended solids, mg/1		100
			BOD (3 days at 27° C), mg/1	Disposal into inland surface water/river/stream	30
				Disposal on land or for irrigation	100

(Contd...)

Sl. No.		Industry			Parameter	Standard
13.	Food & Fruit processing industry[9]	Soft drinks	Effluents[10]	Fruit based/synthetic (more than 0.4 MT/day) bottles and tetrapack	pH	6.5-8.5
					Suspended solids, mg/1	100
					Oil and grease, mg/1	10
					BOD^5 20°C, mg/1	30
14.	Foundries	Emissions[10]: (a) Cupola capacity (melting rate)		Less than 3 MT/hr	Particulate matter, mg/Nm^3	450
				3 MT/hr and above	Particulate matter, mg/Nm^3	150
		(b) Arc furnaces Capacity: All sizes			Particulate matter, mg/Nm^3	150
		(c) Induction furnaces Capacity: All sizes			Particulate matter, mg/Nm^3	150
15.	Inorganic chemical industry (Wastewater discharge) Part 1 (metal compounds of Chromium, Manganese, Nickel, Lead and Mercury)	Effluents			pH	6.0-8.5
					Oil and grease, mg/1	10
					Suspended solids, mg/1	30
16.	Integrated iron and steel plants	I. Emissions	(a) Coke oven		Particulate matter, mg/Nm^3	50
			(b) Refractory material plant		Particulate matter, mg/Nm^3	150
		II. Effluents	(a) Coke oven Byproduct plant		pH	6.0-8.5
					Suspended solids, mg/1	100
					BOD (3 days at 27°C), mg/1	30
					COD, mg/1	250
					Oil and grease, mg/1	10
			(b) Other plants such as sintering plant, blast furnace, steel melting and rolling mill		pH	6.0-9.0
					Suspended solids, mg/1	100
					Oil and grease, mg/1	10

(Contd...)

Sl. No.	Industry		Parameter		Standard
17.	Iron Steel (Integrated)		Particulate matter emission	Sintering plant, mg/Nm^3	150
				Steel making, mg/Nm^3	
				During normal operations, mg/Nm^3	150
				During oxygen lancing, mg/Nm^3	400
				Rolling mill, mg/Nm^3	150
				Carbon monoxide from coke oven, kg. per tonne of coke produced	3
18.	Large pulp & paper	Emissions	Particulate matter[11], mg/Nm^3		250
		Effluents[12]	pH		7.0-8.5
			BOD_5 at 20°C, mg/1		30
			COD, mg/1		350
			Suspended Solids, mg/1		50

(Contd...)

Sl. No.		Industry	Parameter	Standard
19.	Natural rubber industry	Discharged into inland surface waters	pH	6.0-9.0
			BOD, mg/1	50
			COD, mg/1	250
			Oil & grease, mg/1	10
			Suspended solids, mg/1	100
		Disposal on land for irrigation	pH	6.0-8.0
			BOD, mg/1	100
			COD, mg/1	250
			Oil & grease, mg/1	10
			Suspended solid, mg/1	200
20.	Organic chemicals manufacturing industry	Efflurnts[13]	pH	6.5-8.5
			BOD (3 days at 27°C), mg/1	100
			Oil & grease, mg/1	10
21.	Plan industry (wastewater discharge)	Effluents	pH	6.0-8.5
			Suspended solids, mg/1	100
			BOD_5 20°C, mg/1	50
			Oil and grease, mg/1	10
22.	Pesticide industry	Effluents[14]	pH	6.5-8.5
			Oil and grease, mg/1	10
			BOD (3 days at 27°C), mg/1	100
			Suspended solids, mg/1	100

(Contd...)

Sl. No.		Industry	Parameter	Standard
23.	Petrochemicals (Basic and intermediates)	Effluents	pH	6.5-8.5
			BOD (3 days at 27°C), mg/1 (State Boards may prescribe the BOD value of 30 mg/1 if the recipient system so demands) COD, mg/1	50 250
			Total suspended solids, mg/1	1000
24.	Pharmaceutical manufacturing and formulation industry	Effluents[15]	pH	5.5-9.0
			Oil and grease, mg/1	10
			Total suspended solids, mg/1	100
			BOD (3 days at 27°C), mg/1	30
25.	Synthetic rubber (Concentrations in the effluents when discharged into inland surface waters)		pH	5.5-9.0
			BOD (3 days at 27°C), mg/1	50
			Chemical Oxygen Demand, mg/1	250
			Oil & grease, mg/1	10

(Contd...)

Sl. No.		Industry	Parameter	Standard
26.	Thermal power plants	Particulate matter emissions[16], mg/Nm³	Generation capacity 210 MW or more	150
			Generation capacity less than 210 MW	350
		Condenser cooling waters (once through cooling system	pH	6.5-8.5
		Boiler blowdowns	Suspended solids, mg/1	100
			Oil & grease, mg/1	20
		Ash-pond effluent	pH	6.5-8.5
			Suspended solids, mg/1	100
			Oil & grease, mg/1	20

Source: Mohanty (1997, pp. 27-69).

Note: See Notes 1 to 16 at the end of the chapter.

Schedule III, Rule 3

Ambient Noise Quality Standards in Respect of Noise

Area Code	*Category of Area*	*Limits in dB(A), Leq*	
		Day Time	*Night Time*
(A)	Industrial area	75	70
(B)	Commercial area	65	55
(C)	Residential area	55	45
(D)	Silence zone	50	40

Source: Mohanty (1997, p. 70).

Day time is reckoned in between 6 am and 10 pm.

Night time is reckoned in between 10 pm and 6 am.

Silence zone is defined as areas upto 100 m around such premises as hospitals, educational institutions and courts. The silence zones are to be declared by the Competent Authority. Use of vehicular horns, loudspeakers and bursting of crackers shall be banned in these zones.

Mixed categories of areas should be declared as one of the four above-mentioned categories by the Competent Authority and the corresponding standards shall apply. (*See Schedule Tables on pages 190-194*).

We collected information related to the ambient air quality status in and around the surveyed units. The values of different ambient air quality parameters *viz.*, suspended particulate matter (SPM), respirable particulate matter (RPM), CO, SOx and NOx were considered in the unit of μg/Nm³ and for further analysis, the study also dealt with the variation in percentage from regulatory standard[18] in case of each parameter. It was found that except one, in case of all of the remaining 54 surveyed units, SPM, RPM, CO, SOx and NOx levels were within the permissible limit. In case of only one unit of chemical industry, the RPM value exceeded the regulatory standard. The detailed statistical analysis of ambient air quality status in and around the surveyed units is presented in the following section (Table 20.5).

Table 20.5: Summary Statistics of Ambient Air Quality in and around the Surveyed Units

Sl. No.	*Ambient Air Quality Parameters*	*Concentration*			
		Min ($\mu g/Nm^3$)	*Max ($\mu g/Nm^3$)*	*Mean ($\mu g/Nm^3$)*	*Std. Dev.*
1.	SPM	113.00	330.00	188.91	38.05
2.	RPM	55.37	178.20	90.37	21.95
3.	CO	119.00	2000.00	723.32	431.02
4.	SOx	7.77	85.00	22.82	18.05
5.	NOx	11.80	79.90	36.79	16.78

Source: Results computed.

Schedule VI, Rule 3A

General Standards for discharge of environmental pollutants Part A Effluents

Sl. No.	*Parameter*	*Standards*			
		Inland surface water	*Public sewers*	*Land for irrigation*	*Marine coastal areas*
1.	Suspended solids, mg/l, Max	100	600	200	(a) For process wastewater-100 (b) For cooling water effluent 10 per cent above total suspended matter of influent
2.	pH value	5.5-9.0	5.5-9.0	5.5-9.0	5.5-9.0
3.	Oil and grease, mg/l, Max	10	20	10	20
4.	Biochemical oxygen demand (5 days at 20°C) [mg/l, Max]	30	350	100	100
5.	Chemical oxygen demand, mg/l, Max	250	-	-	250

Source: Mohanty (1997, pp. 77-78).

Part B

Waste Water Generation Standards

Sl. No.	Industry			Quantum
1.	Integrated Iron & Steel			16 (m^3/tonne) of finished steel
2.	Pulp & paper industries	Larger pulp & paper	Pulp & paper	175 (m^3/tonne) of paper produced
			Viscose staple fibre	150 (m^3/tonne) of paper produced
		Small pulp & paper	Viscose filament yarn	500 (m^3/tonne) of paper produced
			(i) Agro-residue based	150 (m^3/tonne) of paper produced
			(ii) Waste paper based	50 (m^3/tonne) of paper produced
3.	Fermentation industry	(a) Maltry		3.5 (m^3/tonne) of grain produced
		(b) Brewery		0.25 M^3/KL of beer produced
		(c) Distillery		12 M^3/KL of alcohol produced
4.	Textile industries: Man-made fibre	(i) Nylon & Polyster		120 (m^3/tonne) of fibre produced
		(ii) Viscose rayon		150 (m^3/tonne) of product
5.	Natural rubber processing industry			4 (m^3/tonne) of rubber

Source: Mohanty (1997, p. 80).

Part D
General Emission Standards

Concentration Based Standards		
Sl. No.	*Parameter*	*Standard Concentration not to exceed (in mg/Nm^3)*
1.	Particulate matter (PM)	150
2.	Carbon monoxide	1% max (v/v)

Source: Mohanty (1997, p. 81)

Schedule VII, Rule (3B)

National Ambient Air Quality Standard (NAAQS)

Pollutant	*Concentration in Ambient Air*				
	Time Weighted Average	*Industrial Area*	*Residential, rural and other area*	*Sensitive area*	*Method of measurement*
Sulphur dioxide (SO_2)	Annual average*	80 μg/m³	60 μg/m³	15 μg/m³	Improved West and Gaeke method
	24 hours**	120 μg/m³	80 μg/m³	30 μg/m³	Ultraviolet Fluorescence
Oxides of nitrogen as NO_2	Annual average*	80 μg/m³	60 μg/m³	15 μg/m³	Jacab and Hochheiser modified (Na-Arsenite) method
	24 hours**	120 μg/m³	80 μg/m³	30 μg/m³	Gas Phase Chemiluminescence
Suspended particulate matter (SPM)	Annual average*	360 μg/m³	140 μg/m³	70 μg/m³	High Volume Sampling
	24 hours**	500 μg/m³	200 μg/m³	100 μg/m³	Average flow rate not less than 1.1 m³/minute

(Contd...)

Pollutant	*Concentration in Ambient Air*				
	Time Weighted Average	*Industrial Area*	*Residential, rural and other area*	*Sensitive area*	*Method of measurement*
Respirable particulate matter (size less than 10 µm) (RPM)	Annual average*	120 µg/m³	60 µg/m³	50 µg/m³	Respirable particulate matter sampler
	24 hours**	150 µg/m³	100 µg/m³	75 µg/m³	
Carbon monoxide	8 hours**	5.0 mg/m³	2.0 mg/m³	1.0 mg/m³	Non disbersive, infrared spectroscopy
	1 hour	10.0 mg/m³	4.0 mg/m³	2.0 mg/m³	

Source: Mohanty (1997, pp. 86-87).

* Annual Arithmatic mean of minimum 104 measurements in a year taken twice a week 24 hourly at uniform interval.

** 24 hourly/8 hourly values shall be met 08 per cent of the time in a year, 2 per cent of the time, it may exceed but not on two consecutive days.

The study revealed that on an average, SPM level in ambient air was 188.91 µg/Nm^3 ranging between 113 µg/Nm^3 and 330 µg/Nm^3 with standard deviation of 38.05. Variation of SPM level from standard in ambient air quality was 62.22 per cent ranging between 34 per cent and 77.40 per cent with standard deviation of 7.61. RPM level in ambient air was 90.37 µg/Nm^3 ranging between 55.37 µg/Nm^3 and 178.20 µg/Nm^3 with standard deviation of 21.95. Variation of RPM level from standard in ambient air quality was 39.75 per cent ranging between -18.80 per cent and 63.09 per cent with standard deviation of 14.63. CO level in ambient air was 723.32 µg/Nm^3 ranging between 119 µg/Nm^3 and 2000 µg/Nm^3 with standard deviation of 431.02. Variation of CO level from standard in ambient air quality was 85.53 per cent ranging between 60 per cent and 97.62 per cent with standard deviation of 8.62. SOx level in ambient air was 22.82 µg/Nm^3 ranging between 7.77 µg/Nm^3 and 85 µg/Nm^3 with standard deviation of 18.05. Variation of SO_2 level from standard in ambient air quality was 80.98 per cent ranging between 29.17 per cent and 93.53 per cent with standard deviation of 15.05. NO_X level in ambient air was 36.79 µg/Nm^3 ranging between 11.80 µg/Nm^3 and 79.90 µg/Nm^3 with standard deviation of 16.78. Variation of NO_X level from standard in ambient air quality was 69.35 per cent ranging between 33.42 per cent and 90.17 per cent with standard deviation of 13.98.

The study dealt with total waste gas emission or the volumetric flow rate of flue gas. The record was taken in the unit of Nm^3/hr. The study also collected information regarding different air pollution parameters of stack emission. The values of different stack emission parameters viz., particulate matter, CO, SO_2 and NOx were considered in the unit of mg/Nm^3 and for further analysis the study also encountered the variation in percentage from regulatory standard[19] in case of each parameter. The study also measured the emission value of each parameter in the unit of kg per unit output. It was found that in case of one unit of chemical industry and 6 units of thermal power the emission of CO exceeded the permissible limit. The detailed statistical analysis of stack emission is presented in Table 20.6.

Table 20.6: Summary Statistics of Stack Emission of the Surveyed Units

Sl. No.	*Effluent Parameters*	*Emission Load per Unit (kg/MT)/(kg/MU)**					
		Chemical	*Ferrous Metal*	*Food & Beverage*	*Non-Ferrous Metal*	*Thermal Power*	*Others*
1.	PM	0.48	0.22	0.04	1.42	84.92	1.17
2.	CO	55.59	29.25	1.75	0.17	22862.59	97.61
3.	SO_2	1.38	0.43	NA	2.17	969.53	0.36
4.	NOx	0.23	0.26	NA	2.49	277.79	2.79

Source: Results computed.

In case of Thermal Power only.

The study also collected information regarding different parameters of treated effluent. The values of different effluent parameters *viz.*, total suspended solid (TSS), chemical oxygen demand (COD), biochemical oxygen demand (BOD), oil & grease and pH were considered in the unit of mg/l and for further analysis the study also dealt with the variation in percentage from regulatory standard[20] in case of each parameter. For future analysis, the study also measured the value of each parameter in the unit of mg per unit output. Status of wastewater parameters of surveyed units exceeding the regulatory compliance is presented in Table 20.7. (*See on next page*) In case of 10.91 per cent of surveyed units the TSS value exceeded the permissible limit. It was mostly found in case of 41.67 per cent units of chemical industry and 12.50 per cent units of non-ferrous metal industry. Similar incidence was found in case of 12.73 per cent of the surveyed units that crossed the regulatory standard of BOD value. It was mostly found in majority (75%) of units of food and beverage industry followed by some (16.67%) units of chemical industry and some (16.67%) units of thermal power. In case of 21.82 per cent of the surveyed units, pH value had crossed the regulatory standard that was mostly found in cases of 66.67 per cent units of chemical industry and some (33.33%) units of thermal power. The detailed statistical analysis of the treated effluent is presented in Table 20.8. (*See on page 199*)

We collected information related to the generation of solid wastes of the surveyed units. We dealt with the composition[21] of solid wastes, quantity of wastes generated and quantity recycled annually.

Status of recycling of solid wastes in surveyed units is presented in Table 20.9. (*See on page 200*) In case of majority (72.72%) of the surveyed units, 12-30 per cent solid wastes per unit were recycled annually out of total wastes generation. In a very few cases (12.73%), out of total generation of solid wastes, more than 40 per cent was being recycled. Recycling rate was high in case of units of chemical industry and units of ferrous metal industry, where 83.33 per cent units of chemical industry and 82.35 per cent units of ferrous metal industry recycled 12-25 per cent solid wastes of the total generation. It is remarkable to mention here that some (60%) units of thermal power recycled 40-50 per cent solid wastes out of total generation and 50 per cent units of

Table 20.7: Status of Wastewater Parameters of Surveyed Units Exceeding the Regulatory Compliance

Sl. No.	Wastewater Parameters	Industry Segments												Total	
		Chemical		*Ferrous Metal*		*Food and Beverage*		*Non-Ferrous Metal*		*Thermal Power*		*Others*			
		No.	*%*	*No.*	*%*	*No.*	*%*	*No.*	*%*	*No.*	*%*	*No.*	*%*	*No.*	*%*
1.	TSS	5	41.67	0	0	0	0	1	12.50	0	0	0	0	6	10.91
2.	BOD	2	16.67	0	0	3	75.00	0	0	1	16.67	1	12.50	7	12.73
3.	COD	0	0	0	0	0	0	0	0	0	0	0	0	0	0
4.	Oil & grease	0	0	0	0	0	0	0	0	0	0	0	0	0	0
5.	pH	8	66.67	0	0	0	0	1	12.50	2	33.33	1	12.50	12	21.82

Source: Results computed.

Table 20.8: Summary Statistics of Treated Effluent of the Surveyed Units

Sl. No.	*Effluent Parameters*	*Discharge Load per Unit (kg/MT)/(kg/MU)**					
		Chemical	*Ferrous Metal*	*Food and Beverage*	*Non-Ferrous Metal*	*Thermal Power*	*Others*
1.	TSS	15.66	3.27	0.89	8.07	82.78	4.32
2.	BOD	8.76	0.75	0.94	2.24	41.99	2.58
3.	COD	58.31	2.41	2.61	34.95	145.12	11.02
4.	Oil and Grease	1.11	0.11	0.06	0.39	7.01	0.24
5.	pH	8.04	4.65	6.58	6.52	7.84	6.15

Source: Results computed.

* in case of Thermal Power only.

food and beverage industry recycled 25-30 per cent solid wastes. On the contrary, recycling rate was poor in case of units of non-ferrous metal industry, where majority (55.55%) of the units recycled less than 12 per cent solid wastes. On an average, 21.75 per cent solid wastes per unit were recycled against generation per year ranging between 9.96 per cent and 65.47 per cent with standard deviation of 11.97.

Out of total quantity of solid wastes recycled, we also considered quantity and type of solid wastes recycled to the same unit and sold to the other units. The study found different uses[22] of the recycled solid wastes that were sold to the other units. For the purpose of analysis, the study also included amount of revenue generated annually due to selling of wastes. To avoid bias, the value was being matched with the market price of the respective item.

The status of solid wastes sold to the other units is presented in Table 20.10. (*See on page 201*) It is observed that in case of the majority (67.27%) of the surveyed units, 8-20 per cent of the solid wastes per unit were sold to the other units annually out of total wastes generation. In a very few cases (12.73%), out of total generation of solid wastes, more than 20 per cent was being sold. Recycling rate was high in case of units of chemical industry followed by units of ferrous metal industry.

Table 20.9: Quantity of Solid Wastes Recycled Against Generation in Surveyed Units

Sl. No.	*Solid Wastes Recycled Against Generation (%)*	*Industry Segments*													
		Chemical		*Ferrous Metal*		*Food and Beverage*		*Non-Ferrous Metal*		*Thermal Power*		*Others*		*Total*	
		No.	*%*	*No.*	*%*	*No.*	*%*	*No.*	*%*	*No.*	*%*	*No.*	*%*	*No.*	*%*
1.	< = 10	0	0	0	0	0	0	1	11.11	0	0	0	0	1	1.82
2.	10 – 12	0	0	2	11.76	0	0	4	44.44	0	0	0	0	6	10.91
3.	12 – 15	3	25.00	5	29.41	1	25.00	0	0	0	0	3	37.50	12	21.81
4.	15 – 20	2	16.67	5	29.41	1	25.00	2	22.23	0	0	1	12.50	11	20.00
5.	20 – 25	5	41.66	4	23.53	0	0	0	0	1	20.00	1	12.50	11	20.00
6.	25 – 30	0	0	1	5.89	2	50.00	0	0	1	20.00	2	25.00	6	10.91
7.	30 – 40	0	0	0	0	0	0	1	11.11	0	0	0	0	1	1.82
8.	40 – 50	2	16.67	0	0	0	0	0	0	3	60.00	0	0	5	9.09
9.	50 – 60	0	0	0	0	0	0	0	0	0	0	1	12.50	1	1.82
10.	> 60	0	0	0	0	0	0	1	11.11	0	0	0	0	1	1.82
	Total	**12**	**21.82**	**17**	**30.91**	**4**	**7.27**	**9**	**14.55**	**5**	**10.91**	**8**	**14.54**	**55**	**100.00**

Source: Results computed.

Table 20.10: Quantity of Solid Wastes Sold to Other Units against Generation in Surveyed Units

Sl. No.	Solid Wastes Sold Against Generation (%)	Industry Segments													
		Chemical		*Ferrous Metal*		*Food and Beverage*		*Non-Ferrous Metal*		*Thermal Power*		*Others*		*Total*	
		No.	%	No.	%	No.	%	No.	%	No.	%	No.	%	No.	%
1.	< = 6	0	0	0	0	0	0	0	0	1	16.67	1	12.50	2	3.64
2.	6 – 7	0	0	2	11.77	0	0	3	37.50	0	0	0	0	5	9.09
3.	7 – 8	0	0	2	11.77	0	0	1	12.50	0	0	1	12.50	4	7.27
4.	8 – 10	2	16.66	6	35.29	1	25.00	0	0	0	0	0	0	9	16.37
5.	10 – 12	3	25.00	2	11.76	1	25.00	2	25.00	0	0	2	25.00	10	18.18
6.	12 – 15	2	16.67	5	29.41	0	0	0	0	2	33.33	0	0	9	16.36
7.	15 – 20	3	25.00	0	0	2	50.00	1	12.50	0	0	3	37.50	9	16.36
8.	20 – 25	2	16.67	0	0	0	0	0	0	2	33.33	0	0	4	7.27
9.	25 – 30	0	0	0	0	0	0	0	0	1	16.67	1	12.50	2	3.64
10.	> 30	0	0	0	0	0	0	1	12.50	0	0	0	0	1	1.82
	Total	**12**	**21.82**	**17**	**30.91**	**4**	**7.27**	**8**	**14.55**	**6**	**10.91**	**8**	**14.54**	**55**	**100.00**

Source: Results computed.

Besides solid wastes, we collected information related to the generation of hazardous wastes of the surveyed units. We encountered the composition[23] of hazardous wastes, quantity of wastes generated, treated and recycled annually.

The study revealed that in case of majority (65.46%) of the surveyed units, 3.5-6.5 per cent hazardous wastes per unit were generated annually out of total wastes generation. In a very few cases (7.27%), out of total generation of wastes, more than 6.5 per cent were hazardous wastes. Generation of hazardous wastes was relatively higher in case of units of ferrous metal industry followed by units of chemical industry. Analysis found that 82.35 per cent ferrous metal units generated 4-6.5 per cent hazardous wastes and 66.67 per cent units of chemical industry generated 3.5-5.5 per cent hazardous wastes of the total generation of wastes.

Analysis of recycling of hazardous wastes (Table 20.11) revealed that in case of majority (78.18%) of the surveyed units, 10-20 per cent hazardous wastes per unit were recycled annually out of total generation of hazardous wastes. In a very few cases (18.18%), out of total generation of hazardous wastes, more than 20 per cent was being recycled. It is worthwhile to mention here that units of thermal power were showing satisfactory performance in this regard, as generation of hazardous wastes was very less and whatever hazardous wastes were being generated, recycling rate was high. Analysis found that 83.33 per cent units of thermal power recycled 20-32 per cent hazardous wastes.

Besides recycling of hazardous wastes, we have got information related to the disposal of hazardous wastes in case of the surveyed units. We dealt with the quantity of hazardous wastes stored/disposed without following required safety precaution.

Table 20.11: Quantity of Hazardous Wastes Recycled Against Generation in Surveyed Units

Sl. No.	*Hazardous Wastes Recycled Against Generation (%)*	*Industry Segments*													
		Chemical		*Ferrous Metal*		*Food and Beverage*		*Non-Ferrous Metal*		*Thermal Power*		*Others*		*Total*	
		No.	*%*	*No.*	*%*	*No.*	*%*	*No.*	*%*	*No.*	*%*	*No.*	*%*	*No.*	*%*
1.	< = 8	0	0	0	0	0	0	0	0	0	0	1	12.50	1	1.82
2.	8 – 10	0	0	1	5.88	0	0	0	0	0	0	0	0	1	1.82
3.	10 – 12	0	0	6	35.29	1	25.00	2	25.00	0	0	0	0	·9	16.36
4.	12 – 14	1	8.33	5	29.41	1	25.00	4	50.00	0	0	1	12.50	12	21.82
5.	14 – 16	2	16.67	0	0	0	0	0	0	0	0	1	12.50	3	5.46
6.	16 – 18	2	16.66	1	5.88	2	50.00	1	12.50	1	16.67	2	25.00	9	16.36
7.	18 – 20	5	41.67	3	17.66	0	0	0	0	0	0	2	25.00	10	18.18
8.	20 – 30	0	0	1	5.88	0	0	0	0	2	33.33	0	0	3	5.45
9.	30 – 32	0	0	0	0	0	0	1	12.50	3	50.00	1	12.50	5	9.09
10.	> 32	2	16.67	0	0	0	0	0	0	0	0	0	0	2	3.64
	Total	**12**	**21.82**	**17**	**30.91**	**4**	**7.27**	**8**	**14.55**	**6**	**10.91**	**8**	**14.54**	**55**	**100.00**

Source: Results computed.

It was alarming incidence to mention here that in case of majority (58.18%) of the surveyed units, out of total hazardous wastes generated annually 65-86 per cent wastes per unit were stored/disposed off without following required safety precaution (*See Table 20.12 on next page*). Even in significant cases (41.82 per cent), out of total generation of hazardous wastes, more than 86 per cent were stored/disposed off. Analysis revealed that on an average, 82.62 per cent ranging between 65.16 per cent and 92.07 per cent with standard deviation of 6.33 hazardous wastes per unit were stored/disposed against generation per year without following required safety precaution. A summary of waste management statistics is presented in Table 20.13. (*See Table on page 206*).

Besides reviewing the status of air quality, effluent quality and wastes of the surveyed units, we collected information on noise level in and around the surveyed units. We also dealt with the variation of noise level from regulatory standard.

The study analysed that on an average, noise level was 86.67 dB(A) ranging between 68 dB(A) and 121.23 dB(A) with standard deviation of 10.15. Variation of noise level from standard[24] was -15.56 per cent ranging between -61.64 per cent and 9.33 per cent with standard deviation of 13.53. So it may be stated that in case most of the surveyed units, noise level had crossed the regulatory standard except in case of some (75%) units of non-ferrous metal industry.

It is expected that any corrective or preventive action taken to eliminate the causes of actual and potential non-conformances shall be appropriate to the magnitude of problems and commensurate with the environmental impact countered.

Here the study looked into the fact whether any kind of preventive measure has been taken by the surveyed units in case of air, water, land and noise pollution. It also revealed the implementation status of the precautionary measure, if it is taken. Because if the implementation status of the preventive measure is satisfactory, then that unit may be considered as environmentally proactive one.

Table 20.12: **Quantity of Hazardous Wastes Stored/Disposed Off (Without Following Required Safety Precaution) Against Generation in Surveyed Units**

Sl. No.	*Storage/ Disposal of Hazardous Wastes Against Generation (%)*	*Industry Segments*													
		Chemical		*Ferrous Metal*		*Food and Beverage*		*Non-Ferrous Metal*		*Thermal Power*		*Others*		*Total*	
		No.	*%*	*No.*	*%*	*No.*	*%*	*No.*	*%*	*No.*	*%*	*No.*	*%*	*No.*	*%*
1.	< = 65	0	0	0	0	0	0	0	0	0	0	0	0	0	0
2.	65-70	2	16.67	0	0	0	0	1	12.50	3	50.00	1	12.50	7	12.73
3.	70-80	0	0	1	5.88	0	0	0	0	2	33.33	0	0	3	5.45
4.	80-82	5	41.67	3	17.65	0	0	0	0	0	0	2	25.00	10	18.18
5.	82-84	2	16.66	1	5.88	2	50.00	1	12.50	1	16.67	2	25.00	9	16.37
6.	84-86	2	16.67	0	0	0	0	0	0	0	0	1	12.50	3	5.45
7.	86-88	1	8.33	5	29.42	1	25.00	4	50.00	0	0	1	12.50	12	21.82
8.	88-90	0	0	6	35.29	1	25.00	2	25.00	0	0	0	0	9	16.36
9.	90-95	0	0	1	5.88	0	0	0	0	0	0	1	12.50	2	3.64
10.	> 95	0	0	0	0	0	0	0	0	0	0	0	0	0	0
	Total	**12**	**21.82**	**17**	**30.91**	**4**	**7.27**	**8**	**14.55**	**6**	**10.91**	**8**	**14.54**	**55**	**100.00**

Source: Results computed.

Table 20.13: Summary Statistics of Waste Management of the Surveyed Units

Sl. No.	*Wastes*	*Quantity of Wastes (tonne per unit)*					
		Chemical	*Ferrous Metal*	*Food and Beverage*	*Non-Ferrous Metal*	*Thermal Power*	*Others*
	Solid Wastes:						
1.	Generation per year	1,704.91	373.47	874.12	115.66	40,176.36	1,249.66
2.	Recycled per year	556.00	80.94	184.95	62.31	11,169.91	340.73
3.	Recycled to the other Unit per year	316.60	42.69	129.32	34.60	6,095.30	219.57
4.	Revenue Generation per year (Rs in lakhs)	34.49	3.55	14.61	2.99	226.02	16.43
	Hazardous Wastes:						
5.	Generation per year	105.99	21.20	38.02	4.79	4.04	69.48
6.	Treated per year	29.08	4.30	6.79	1.33	1.03	14.43
7.	Recycled per year	27.45	3.87	6.02	1.27	0.97	13.09
8.	Stored/Disposed off without following required safety precaution	78.55	17.33	32.00	3.52	3.07	5.39

Source: Results computed.

The status of measure taken by the surveyed units in the area of air, water, land and noise pollution is presented in Table 20.14. In the area of air and water pollution, in the majority (87.27% and 61.82% respectively) of the cases, surveyed units had taken specific measure. In the area of land pollution, in about 50 per cent of the cases surveyed units had taken specific measure. On the contrary, in the area of noise pollution in majority (58.18%) of the cases, surveyed units had not taken any specific measure.

Table 20.14: Specific Measure Taken by the Surveyed Units in the Area of Air, Water, Land and Noise Pollution

Sl. No.	*Specific Measure*	*Environmental Pollution*							
		Air		*Water*		*Land*		*Noise*	
		No.	*%*	*No.*	*%*	*No.*	*%*	*No.*	*%*
1.	Yes	48	87.27	34	61.82	28	50.91	23	41.82
2.	No	7	12.73	21	38.18	27	49.09	32	58.18

Source: Results computed.

The implementation status of the environmental management system in the surveyed units in the area of air, water, land and noise pollution is presented in Table 20.15. (*See on next page*) It was found that out of 48 surveyed units that had taken specific measure in the area of air pollution, in majority (62.50%) of the cases implementation status was average. Out of 34 surveyed units that had taken specific measure in the area of water pollution, in 41.18 per cent of the cases implementation status was average and in a few (5.88%) cases, it was under implementation. Out of 28 surveyed units that had taken specific measure in the area of land pollution, in 42.86 per cent of the cases implementation status was average and in a few (7.14%) cases, it was under implementation. Out of 23 surveyed units that had taken specific measure in the area of noise pollution, in 13.04 per cent of the cases implementation status was average and in some (17.39%) cases, it was under implementation.

Table 20.15: Implementation Status of the Environmental Management System in the Surveyed Units in the Area of Air, Water, Land and Noise Pollution

Sl. No.	*Implementation Status*	*Environmental Pollution*							
		Air		*Water*		*Land*		*Noise*	
		No.	*%*	*No.*	*%*	*No.*	*%*	*No.*	*%*
1.	Under Implementation	0	0	2	5.88	2	7.14	4	17.39
2.	Average	30	62.50	14	41.18	12	42.86	3	13.04
3.	Not Satisfactory	0	0	0	0	0	0	0	0
4.	Satisfactory	18	37.50	18	52.94	14	50.00	16	69.57
	Total	**48**	**100.00**	**34**	**100.00**	**28**	**100.00**	**23**	**100.00**

Source: Results computed.

The important findings in respect of having regulatory compliance of the industrial units are reported in *Exhibit 20.4*.

EXHIBIT 20.4

Status of Regulatory Compliance of Industrial Units

- Regarding ambient air quality status in and around the surveyed units, except one, in case of all of the remaining 54 surveyed units SPM, RPM, CO, SOx and NOx levels were within the permissible limit. In case of only one unit of chemical industry, the RPM value exceeded the regulatory standard.
- Regarding total waste gas emission or the volumetric flow rate of flue gas, in case of one unit of chemical industry and 6 units of thermal power the emission of CO exceeded the permissible limit.
- In case of 10.91 per cent of surveyed units the TSS value exceeded the permissible limit.
- 12.73 per cent of the surveyed units crossed the regulatory standard of BOD value.

- In case of 21.82 per cent of the surveyed units, pH value had crossed the regulatory standard.
- In case of majority (72.72%) of the surveyed units, 12-30 per cent solid wastes per unit were recycled annually out of total wastes generation. On an average, 21.75 per cent solid wastes per unit were recycled against generation per year ranging between 9.96 per cent and 65.47 per cent with standard deviation of 11.97.
- In case of the majority (67.27%) of the surveyed units, 8-20 per cent of the solid wastes per unit were sold to the other units annually out of total wastes generation.
- In case of majority (65.46%) of the surveyed units, 3.5-6.5 per cent hazardous wastes per unit were generated annually out of total wastes generation.
- In case of majority (78.18%) of the surveyed units, 10-20 per cent hazardous wastes per unit were recycled annually out of total generation of hazardous wastes.
- In case of majority (58.18 per cent) of the surveyed units, out of total hazardous wastes generated annually 65-86 per cent wastes per unit were stored/disposed off without following required safety precaution. On an average, 82.62 per cent ranging between 65.16 per cent and 92.07 per cent with standard deviation of 6.33 hazardous wastes per unit were stored/disposed against generation per year without following required safety precaution.
- On an average, noise level was 86.67 dB(A) ranging between 68 dB(A) and 121.23 dB(A) with standard deviation of 10.15.
- In the area of air pollution in the majority (87.27%) of the cases surveyed units had taken specific measure.
- Out of 48 surveyed units that had taken specific measure in the area of air pollution, in majority (62.50%) of the cases implementation status was average.
- In the area of water pollution in the majority (61.82%) of the cases, surveyed units had taken specific measure.

- Out of 34 surveyed units that had taken specific measure in the area of water pollution, in 41.18 per cent of the cases implementation status was average.
- In the area of land pollution in about 50 per cent of the cases, surveyed units had taken specific measure.
- Out of 28 surveyed units that had taken specific measure in the area of land pollution, in 42.86 per cent of the cases implementation status was average.
- In the area of noise pollution in majority (58.18 per cent) of the cases, surveyed units had not taken any specific measure.
- Out of 23 surveyed units that had taken specific measure in the area of noise pollution, in 13.04 per cent of the cases implementation status was average.

EMS Certification

Environmental Management System (EMS) is an integrated, holistic and proactive approach that is required to be made and maintained to incorporate environmental issues in business practice at each and every step. It is expected that Environmental Management System can take a number of forms and vary in complexity, but all provide a framework to manage environmental issues and define key responsibilities.

In contrast to the prevailing command-and-control model, ISO 14000 challenges each organisation to take stock of its environmental aspects, establish its own objectives and targets, commit itself to effective and reliable processes and continual improvement, and bring all employees and managers into a system of shared and enlightened awareness and personal responsibility for the environmental performance of the organisation. Thus, ISO 14001 is a proactive environmental protection strategy in which regulatory compliance is but one of the elements of a more inclusive and all encompassing approach (Cascio, Woodside and Mitchell, 1996). It is well-known that EMS is an effective way to control environmental problems and manage the environment in the rapidly growing community. It is one of the excellent tools for sustainable development.

Figure 20.6 reveals that out of all 55 surveyed units, certification was obtained by 25 (45.45%) units. Out of 25 certified units, 18 units were certified under ISO 9001 only. 3 units were certified under ISO 14001 besides ISO 9001. 4 units were certified under OHSAS 18001 besides ISO 9001 and ISO 14001. The study also found that majority (71.43%) of the ISO 14001 certified units had the quality management system other than ISO 9001.

Fig. 20.6
Certification Status of the Surveyed Units

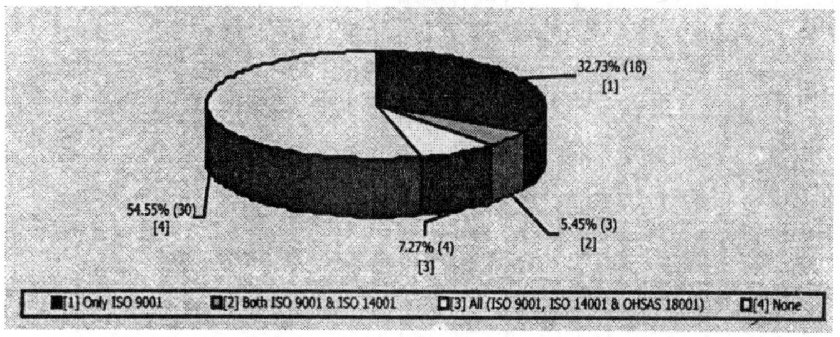

Source: Results computed.

The distribution of surveyed units having environment policy along with certification status is presented in Table 20.16. (*See on next page*) The status of certification of the surveyed units along with the classification by industry segment is presented in Table 20.17. (*See on page 213*) It was found from the analysis that all surveyed units having certification ISO 14001 and/or OHSAS 18001 had environment policy, whereas 66.67 per cent ISO 9001 certified units had environment policy. It is pertinent to mention here that majority (70%) of non-certified units did not have any environment policy.

It was also found that out of all ISO 14001 certified units in case of 57.14 per cent cases, both corporate office and production units were certified under ISO 14001. Whereas in case of the rest 42.86 per cent ISO 14001 certified units, only production units were certified under ISO 14001.

The study revealed that in case of 42.85 per cent units ISO 14001 certification was issued within 4-8 years after commissioning of the unit. In case of 14.29 per cent units, certification was issued within 10-12 years after commissioning of the unit. In case of remaining 42.86 per cent units, certification process was completed after 15 years.

Table 20.16: Distribution of Surveyed Units Having Environment Policy by Status of Certification

Sl. No.	*Having Environment Policy*	*Certification of Surveyed Units*									
		Only ISO 9001		*Both ISO 9001 & ISO 14001*		*All (ISO 9001, ISO 14001 and OHSAS 18001)*		*None*		*Total*	
		No.	*%*	*No.*	*%*	*No.*	*%*	*No.*	*%*	*No.*	*%*
1.	Yes	12	66.67	3	100.00	4	100.00	9	30.00	28	50.91
2.	No	6	33.33	0	0	0	0	21	70.00	27	49.09
	Total	**18**	**32.73**	**3**	**5.45**	**4**	**7.27**	**30**	**54.55**	**55**	**100.00**

Source: Results computed.

Table 20.17: Analysis of Certification Status of the Surveyed Units by Industry Segment

Sl. No.	*Certification*	*Industry Segments*													
		Chemical		*Ferrous Metal*		*Food and Beverage*		*Non-Ferrous Metal*		*Thermal Power*		*Others*		*Total*	
		No.	*%*	*No.*	*%*	*No.*	*%*	*No.*	*%*	*No.*	*%*	*No.*	*%*	*No.*	*%*
1.	Only ISO 9001	5	41.67	5	29.41	2	50.00	1	12.50	2	33.33	3	37.50	18	32.73
2.	Both ISO 9001 and ISO 14001	0	0	0	0	0	0	0	0	3	50.00	0	0	3	5.45
3.	All (ISO 9001, ISO 14001 and OHSAS 18001)	2	16.66	0	0	0	0	1	12.50	0	0	1	12.50	4	7.27
4.	None	5	41.67	12	70.59	2	50.00	6	75.00	1	16.67	4	50.00	30	54.55
	Total	**12**	**100.00**	**17**	**100.00**	**4**	**100.00**	**8**	**100.00**	**6**	**100.00**	**8**	**100.00**	**55**	**100.00**

Source: Results computed.

The study reflected that majority (57.14%) of the ISO 14001 certified units had got certification within 1-2 years after getting applied. Even some (42.86%) had got it within 1 year.

A major reason that many companies want to become registered is that their customers and shareholders are demanding it. Registration to ISO 14001 reassures customers that company has an environmental management system with the capability to provide products and/or services while minimising any negative effects on the environment.

Our study attempted to find out the various reasons for initiating ISO 14001 implementation. The major driving forces for such initiation are meeting compliance to all legal and statutory requirements; cost reduction by minimising waste and pollution; fulfillment of corporate/global policy; improved image of the company; improved working environment; increased competitiveness and trade; pressures of stakeholders (customers, financial institutions, foreign collaborators, etc.); social responsibility; and others (Cascio, Woodside and Mitchell, 1996). The importance of these driving forces for initiating ISO 14001 implementation as identified by the respondents is presented in Table 20.18. (*See on next page*) Majority (85.71%) of ISO 14001 certified units agreed that compliance with all legal and statutory requirement; cost reduction by minimizing waste and pollution; and improved image of the company were the 3 major driving forces for initiating ISO 14001 implementation (*See Fig. 20.7 on page 216*). Specially, ISO 14001 certified units of chemical, non-ferrous metal and thermal power industry segments had felt the necessity of having such certification.

The study also revealed that 42.86 per cent of ISO 14001 certified units felt that fulfillment of corporate/global policy and improved working environment were the two other driving forces for initiating ISO 14001 implementation. It is pertinent to mention here that ISO 14001 certified units of chemical industry indicated the importance of competitiveness for initiating ISO 14001 certification only. Only 14.29 per cent of ISO 14001 certified units commended that pressures of stakeholders was another driving force for initiating ISO 14001 implementation. It is remarkable to mention here that all ISO 14001 certified units undoubtedly stated that social responsibility was a major driving force for initiating ISO 14001 implementation.

Table 20.18: Importance for Initiating ISO 14001 Implementation in the Surveyed Units

Sl. No.	*Parameters*	*Industry Segment**				
		Chemical	*Non-Ferrous Metal*	*Thermal Power*	*Others*	*Overall*
1.	Compliance to All Legal and Statutory Requirements	100.00	100.00	100.00	None	85.71
2.	Cost Reduction by Minimising Waste and Pollution	100.00	100.00	100.00	None	85.71
3.	Fulfillment of Corporate/ Global Policy	100.00	100.00	None	None	42.86
4.	Improved Image of Company	100.00	100.00	100.00	None	85.71
5.	Improved Working Environment	100.00	100.00	None	None	42.86
6.	Increased Competitiveness and Trade Related Issues	100.00	None	None	None	28.57
7.	Pressures of Stakeholders	50.00	None	None	None	14.29
8.	Social Responsibility	100.00	100.00	100.00	100.00	100.00

Source: Results computed.

* Since units of remaining two industry segments (ferrous metal and food and beverage) were non-responsive regarding the driving forces for initiating ISO 14001 implementation because of not being certified under ISO 14001, therefore their responses were not encountered here. But the 'overall' column included all industry segments of units.

Fig. 20.7

Importance for Initiating ISO 14001 Implementation in Surveyed Units

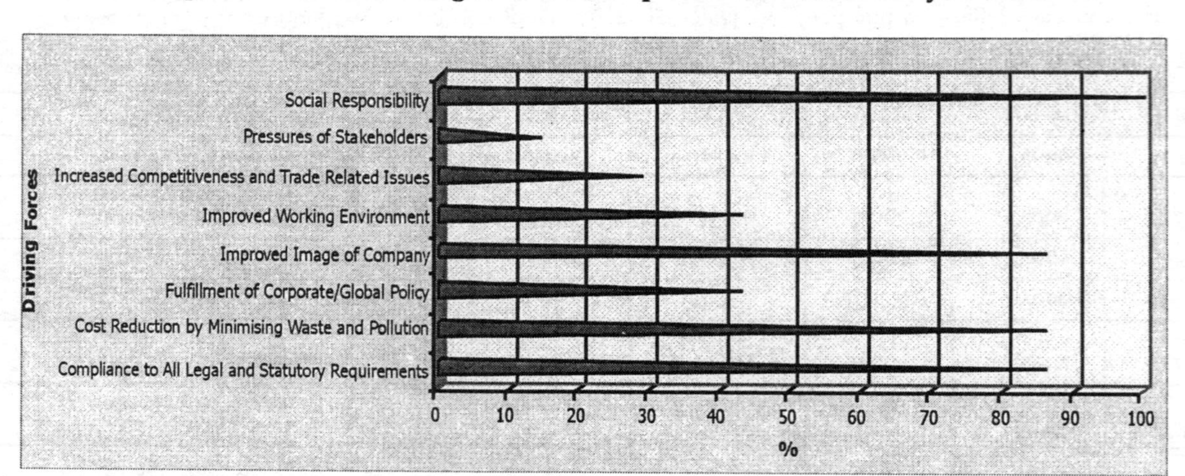

Source: Results computed.

It is desired that organisations that are already certified will have a system in place to incorporate the changes into their existing EMS. For such purpose, the role of management review committee is important.

It is expected that management must periodically review the environmental policy, objectives and the EMS to ensure they are still effective and relevant to the organization's needs in the light of changing circumstances. As mentioned under Clause 4.6 (Management review) of Environmental Management System ISO 14001: 2004, management shall perform periodic reviews of the EMS to ensure it remains effective and appropriate over time. Reviews shall include assessing opportunities for improvement and the need for changes to the environmental management system, including the environmental policy and environmental objectives and targets. The management review should cover the scope of the environmental management system, although not all elements of the environmental management system need to be reviewed at once and the review process may take place over a period of time.

Composition of the management review committee (MRC) for EMS in the surveyed units is presented in Table 20.19. (*See on next page*) It depicts that in majority (84%) of the ISO 14001 certified units EMS management review committee at the production-unit level was formed with the heads of all the operations department (*See fig. 20.8 on page 219*). In case of some (12%) units, MRC comprised of heads of all the operations department including staff members of environment department. In case of very few (4%) units, MRC was formed with staff members of all the departments. It is remarkable to mention here that units of only thermal power in majority (60%) of the cases formed management review committee involving not only heads of all the operations department, but also staff members of environment department.

The study revealed the fact that in case of majority (68%) of the ISO 14001 certified units, in-charge of the environment department chaired the EMS management review committee at the production unit level. In 20 per cent of the cases, production plant in-charge chaired the committee.

Table 20.19: Composition of the Management Review Committee for EMS in the Surveyed Units

Sl. No.	*Composition of the Management Review Committee*	*Industry Segments*													
		Chemical		*Ferrous Metal*		*Food and Beverage*		*Non-Ferrous Metal*		*Thermal Power*		*Others*		*Total*	
		No.	*%*	*No.*	*%*	*No.*	*%*	*No.*	*%*	*No.*	*%*	*No.*	*%*	*No.*	*%*
1.	Environment Department Staff only	0	0	0	0	0	0	0	0	0	0	0	0	0	0
2.	Heads of All the Operations Department	7	100.00	5	100.00	2	100.00	2	100.00	1	20.00	4	100.00	21	84.00
3.	Heads of All the Operations Department including Environment Department Staff	0	0	0	0	0	0	0	0	3	60.00	0	0	3	12.00
4.	Staff of All the Departments	0	0	0	0	0	0	0	0	1	20.00	0	0	1	4.00
	Total	**7**	**28.00**	**5**	**20.00**	**2**	**8.00**	**2**	**8.00**	**5**	**20.00**	**4**	**16.00**	**25**	**100.00**

Source: Results computed.

Fig. 20.8
Composition of the Management Review Committee for EMS in the Surveyed Units

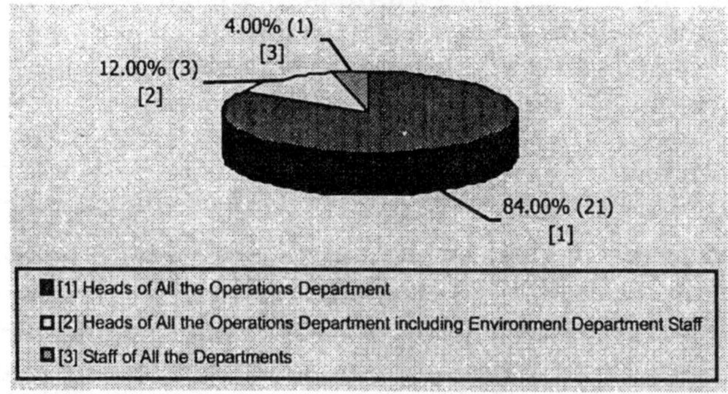

Source: Results computed.

The study also revealed that in case of majority (52%) of the ISO 14001 certified units, the EMS management review committee met twice in a year. In 24 per cent cases, meeting was arranged annually and in 20 per cent cases it varied between weekly to monthly based on the situation. In a very few (4%) cases, it was arranged only during a crisis period.

The study highlighted that majority (96.67%) of the non-ISO 14001 certified units had not set any targets towards obtaining EMS certification in future and majority (93.33%) of them did not have even adequate fund to implement the environmental management system.

The important findings in respect of having EMS certification of the industrial units are reported in *Exhibit 20.5.*

EXHIBIT 20.5

Status of EMS Certification of Industrial Units

- Out of all 55 surveyed units, certification was obtained by 25 (45.45%) units.
- Out of 25 certified units, 18 units were certified under ISO 9001 only. 3 units were certified under ISO 14001 besides ISO 9001. 4 units were certified under OHSAS 18001 besides ISO 9001 and ISO 14001.

(Contd...)

- Majority (71.43%) of the ISO 14001 certified units had the quality management system other than ISO 9001.
- In case of 42.85 per cent units ISO 14001 certification was issued within 4-8 years after commissioning of the unit. In case of 14.29 per cent units, certification was issued within 10-12 years after commissioning of the unit.
- Majority (57.14 per cent) of the ISO 14001 certified units had got certification within 1-2 years after getting applied.
- Majority (85.71%) of ISO 14001 certified units agreed that compliance with all legal and statutory requirement; cost reduction by minimising waste and pollution; and improved image of the company were the 3 major driving forces for initiating ISO 14001 implementation.
- 42.86 per cent of ISO 14001 certified units felt that fulfillment of corporate/global policy and improved working environment were the two other driving forces for initiating ISO 14001 implementation.
- Only 14.29 per cent of ISO 14001 certified units commended that pressures of stakeholders was another driving force for initiating ISO 14001 implementation.
- All ISO 14001 certified units undoubtedly stated that social responsibility was a major driving force for initiating ISO 14001 implementation.
- In majority (84%) of the ISO 14001 certified units EMS management review committee at the production-unit level was formed with the heads of all the operations department.
- In case of majority (68%) of the ISO 14001 certified units, in-charge of the environment department chaired the EMS management review committee at the production-unit level.
- In case of majority (52%) of the ISO 14001 certified units, the EMS management review committee met twice in a year.
- Majority (96.67%) of the non-ISO 14001 certified units had not set any targets towards obtaining EMS certification in future.

(Contd...)

- Majority (93.33%) of the non-ISO 14001 certified units did not have even adequate fund to implement the environmental management system.

Status of Conducting Environmental Audit

It is expected that the audit process is a key element in ensuring the Environmental Management System work and that policy and procedures are kept upto date. Clause (Internal audit) of Environmental Management System ISO 14001: 2004 provides that the company shall establish and maintain programme(s) and procedures for periodic environmental management system audits to be carried out. Internal environmental audits are carried out to determine that the EMS has been properly implemented and maintained and that it conforms to the requirements of the Standard.

Analysis of status of undertaking environmental audit (*See Table 20.20 on next page*) revealed that majority (60%) of the surveyed units did not undertake environmental audit. Remaining 40 per cent only undertook the audit (*See Fig. 20.9 on page 223*). Here units of thermal power played the lead role, as out of all units of thermal power, 83.33 per cent undertook environmental audit.

In case of the majority (59.09%) of the surveyed units, the environmental audit was undertaken both at company and production-unit level (*See Fig. 20.10 on page 223*). Analysis (*See Table 20.21 on page 224*) of level at which environmental audit was undertaken also revealed that all units of non-ferrous metal industry, majority (60%) of the units of chemical industry and majority (80%) of the units of ferrous metal industry usually fell under this category. Some (18.18%) of the units undertook environmental audit only at company level and some (22.73%) only at the production unit-level.

For an EMS that has been assessed, most assessors will accept that auditing once a year is adequate, unless the activity is particularly important or the last audit threw up problems which make it desirable to organise a repeat audit soon afterwards to check that what was wrong or incomplete has been corrected. It is expected that an audit schedule is prepared annually so that every topic is audited at least once a year; the frequency of audits depends on the importance of the topic and the outcome of previous audits.

Table 20.20: Status of Undertaking Environmental Audit in the Surveyed Units

Sl. No.	*Undertaking Environmental Audit*	*Industry Segments*													
		Chemical		*Ferrous Metal*		*Food and Beverage*		*Non-Ferrous Metal*		*Thermal Power*		*Others*		*Total*	
		No.	*%*	*No.*	*%*	*No.*	*%*	*No.*	*%*	*No.*	*%*	*No.*	*%*	*No.*	*%*
1.	Yes	5	41.67	5	29.41	2	50.00	1	12.50	5	83.33	4	50.00	22	40.00
2.	No	7	58.33	12	70.59	2	50.00	7	87.50	1	16.67	4	50.00	33	60.00
	Total	**12**	**21.82**	**17**	**30.91**	**4**	**7.27**	**8**	**14.55**	**6**	**10.91**	**8**	**14.54**	**55**	**100.00**

Source: Results computed.

Fig. 20.9
Status of Undertaking Environmental Adult in the Surveyed Units

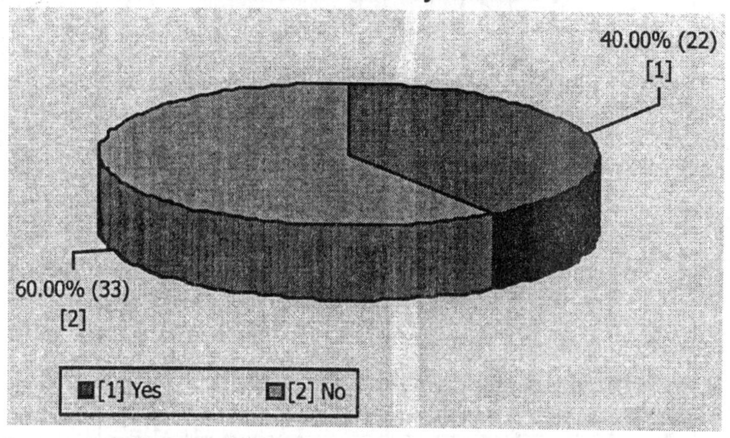

Source: Results computed.

Fig. 20.10
Level of Undertaking Environmental Audit in the Surveyed Units

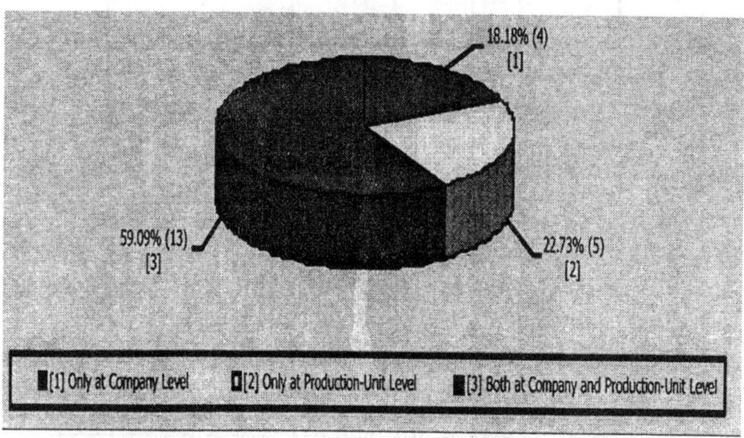

Sources: Results computed.

Table 20.21: Level of Undertaking Environmental Audit in the Surveyed Units

Sl. No.	Level at which Environmental Audit is Undertaken	Industry Segments													
		Chemical		Ferrous Metal		Food and Beverage		Non-Ferrous Metal		Thermal Power		Others		Total	
		No.	%	No.	%	No.	%	No.	%	No.	%	No.	%	No.	%
1.	Only at Company Level	0	0	0	0	0	0	0	0	4	80.00	0	0	4	18.18
2.	Only at Production-Unit Level	2	40.00	1	20.00	2	100.00	0	0	0	0	0	0	5	22.73
3.	Both at Company and Production-Unit Level	3	60.00	4	80.00	0	0	1	100.00	1	20.00	4	100.00	13	59.09
	Total	**5**	**22.73**	**5**	**22.73**	**2**	**9.09**	**1**	**4.54**	**5**	**22.73**	**4**	**18.18**	**22**	**100.00**

Source: Results computed.

Frequency of the environmental audit undertaken by the surveyed units is presented in Table 20.22. (*See on next page)* Only 38.89 per cent of the surveyed units undertook environmental audit annually (*See Fig. 20.11 on page 227*). Analysis revealed that all units of food and beverage industry, all units of thermal power and 40 per cent of the units of chemical industry undertook annual environmental audit. In 38.89 per cent cases, surveyed units carried out environmental audit twice per year.

Internal audits of an environmental management system can be performed by personnel from within the organisation or by external persons selected by the organisation, working on its behalf. In either case, the persons conducting the audit should be competent and in a position to do so impartially and objectively. Auditors are also required to be alert to the environmental impact of the activities they are auditing and to draw attention to any aspect which they feel is not adequately represented or controlled in the EMS.

Table 20.23 (*See on page 228*) shows that in case of majority (72.22%) of the surveyed units executing production unit-level environmental audit, production unit environment department undertook the audit (*See Fig. 20.12 on page 227*). All units of chemical industry, all units of non-ferrous metal industry, 60 per cent units of ferrous metal industry and 50 per cent units of food and beverage industry fell under this category. In a few (11.11%) cases, corporate environment department as well as outside agency undertook the audit. Such incidence was found in case of all units of thermal power and 20 per cent units of ferrous metal industry.

Analysis of status of external verification of environmental audit undertaken by the surveyed units showed that in 53.85 per cent cases environmental audit undertaken by internal departments was verified externally (*See Fig. 20.13 on page 229*). In case of all units of ferrous metal industry, all units of food and beverage industry and 20 per cent units of chemical industry, there was no verification. Whereas the environmental audit was verified by all units of non-ferrous metal industry and 80 per cent units of chemical industry. In other cases external verification was not prevalent in the units of thermal power and units of food and beverage industry.

Table 20.22: Frequency of Environmental Audit in the Surveyed Units

Sl. No.	*Frequency*	*Industry Segments*													
		Chemical		*Ferrous Metal*		*Food and Beverage*		*Non-Ferrous Metal*		*Thermal Power*		*Others*		*Total*	
		No.	*%*	*No.*	*%*	*No.*	*%*	*No.*	*%*	*No.*	*%*	*No.*	*%*	*No.*	*%*
1.	Monthly	0	0	0	0	0	0	0	0	0	0	1	25.00	1	5.56
2.	Quarterly	0	0	2	40.00	0	0	1	100.00	0	0	0	0	3	16.66
3.	Half-yearly	3	60.00	2	40.00	0	0	0	0	0	0	2	50.00	7	38.89
4.	Annually	2	40.00	1	20.00	2	100.00	0	0	1	100.00	1	25.00	7	38.89
	Total	**5**	**27.78**	**5**	**27.77**	**2**	**11.11**	**1**	**5.56**	**1**	**5.56**	**4**	**22.22**	**18**	**100.00**

Source: Results computed.

Fig. 20.11
Frequency of Environmental Audit in the Surveyed Units

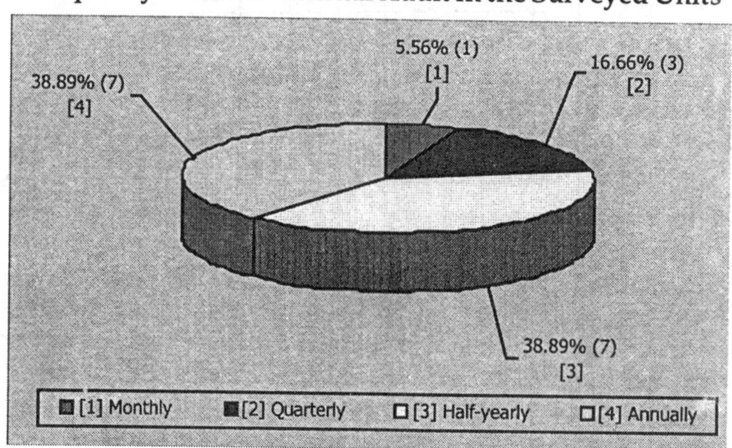

Source: Results computed.

Fig. 20.12
Persons Undertaking Environmental Audit in the Surveyed Units

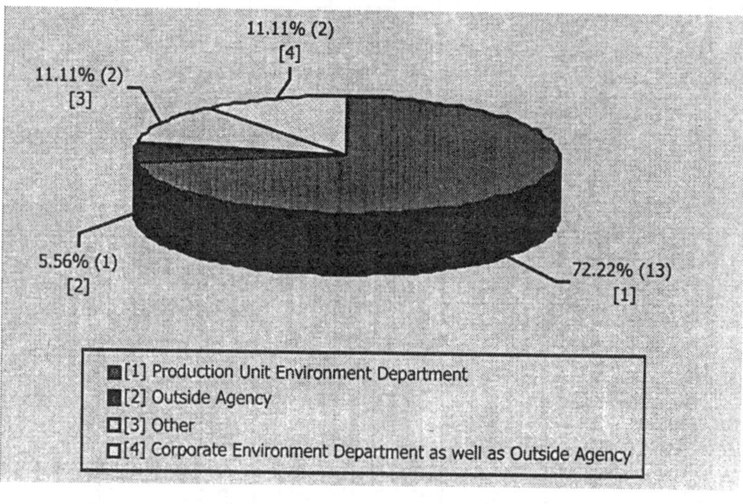

Source: Results computed.

Table 20.23: Person Undertaking Environmental Audit in the Surveyed Units

Sl. No.	*Person Undertaking Environmental Audit*	*Industry Segments*													
		Chemical		*Ferrous Metal*		*Food and Beverage*		*Non-Ferrous Metal*		*Thermal Power*		*Others*		*Total*	
		No.	%	*No.*	%	*No.*	%	*No.*	%	*No.*	%	*No.*	%	*No.*	%
1.	Production Unit Environment Department	5	100.00	3	60.00	1	50.00	1	100.00	0	0	3	75.00	13	72.22
2.	Outside Agency	0	0	0	0	0	0	0	0	0	0	1	25.00	1	5.56
3.	Other	0	0	1	20.00	1	50.00	0	0	0	0	0	0	2	11.11
4.	Corporate Environment Department as well as Outside Agency	0	0	1	20.00	0	0	0	0	1	100.00	0	0	2	11.11
	Total	**5**	**27.78**	**5**	**27.77**	**2**	**11.11**	**1**	**5.56**	**1**	**5.56**	**4**	**22.22**	**18**	**100.00**

Source: Results computed.

Fig. 20.13
External Verification of
Environmental Audit in the Surveyed Units

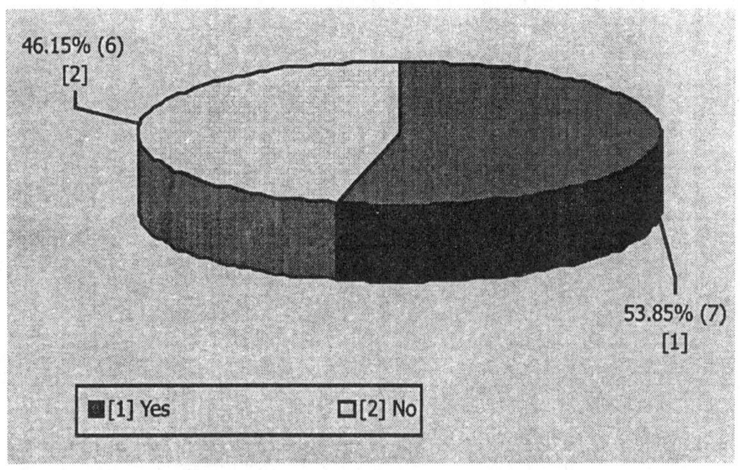

Status: Results computed.

The study revealed that there was no single surveyed unit where the reports of environmental audits were made available to the public.

Process adopted for environmental audit undertaken by the surveyed units is presented in Table 20.24. (*See on next page*) It was found that in majority (77.78%) of the surveyed units executing production unit-level environmental audit, the process adopted for environmental auditing was much more elaborate and comprehensive than PCB's guidelines (*See Fig. 20.14 on page 231*). Such instances were found in case of all units of food and beverage industry, non-ferrous metal industry, thermal power and 80 per cent of units of chemical industry. Whereas in remaining (22.22%) cases, the process was similar to that of Pollution Control Board's guidelines.

The important findings in respect of showing environmental audit performance of the industrial units are reported in *Exhibit 20.6.*

Table 20.24: Process Adopted for Environmental Audit in the Surveyed Units

Sl. No.	Process	Industry Segments													
		Chemical		Ferrous Metal		Food and Beverage		Non-Ferrous Metal		Thermal Power		Others		Total	
		No.	%	No.	%	No.	%	No.	%	No.	%	No.	%	No.	%
1.	Similar to the environmental statement as per Pollution Control Board's guidelines	1	20.00	3	60.00	0	0	0	0	0	0	0	0	4	22.22
2.	Much more elaborate and comprehensive than PCB's guidelines	4	80.00	2	40.00	2	100.00	1	100.00	1	100.00	4	100.00	14	77.78
	Total	**5**	**27.78**	**5**	**27.77**	**2**	**11.11**	**1**	**5.56**	**1**	**5.56**	**4**	**22.22**	**18**	**100.00**

Source: Results computed.

Fig. 20.14
Process Adopted for Environmental Audit in the Surveyed Units

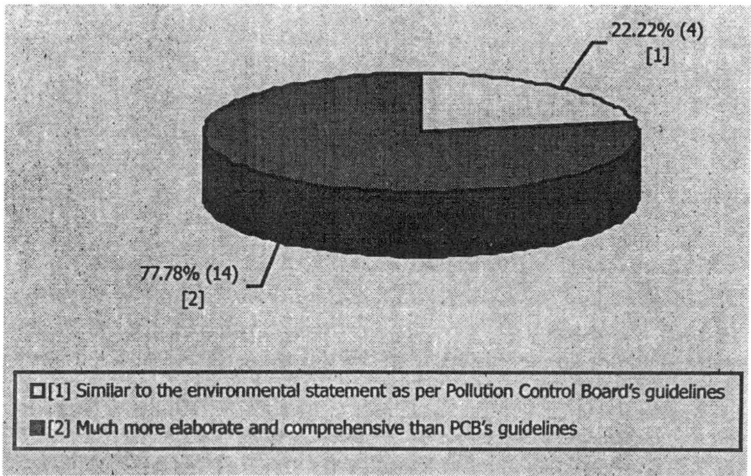

Source: Results computed.

EXHIBIT 20.6

Scenario of Environmental Audit Performance By Industrial Units

- Majority (60%) of the surveyed units did not undertake environmental audit.
- 38.89% of the surveyed units undertook environmental audit annually.
- In case of majority (72.22%) of the surveyed units executing production unit-level environmental audit, production unit environment department undertook the audit.
- In 53.85 per cent cases environmental audit undertaken by internal departments was verified externally.
- There was no single surveyed unit where the reports of environmental audits were made available to the public.

(Contd...)

- In majority (77.78%) of the surveyed units executing production unit-level environmental audit, the process adopted for environmental auditing was much more elaborate and comprehensive than PCB's guidelines.

Environmental Cost Management

Repetto and Austin (2001) demonstrated an approach for analysing and communicating the financial implications of the *environmental* exposure of a company. Accordingly, here, status of coverage of environmental management in the budget of the surveyed units is presented in Table 20.25. (*See on next page*) It was observed that in case of majority (72.73%) of the surveyed units, environmental improvement was covered in the company budget. Majority (91.67%) of the units of chemical industry, majority (75%) of the units of food and beverage industry, majority (70.59%) of the units of ferrous metal industry and all units of thermal power fell under this category. On the contrary, in case of 27.27 per cent units, environmental improvement was not covered in the company budget. 75 per cent units of non-ferrous metal industry showed such incidence.

Russo and Fouts (1997) stated that drawing on the resource-based view of the firm, environmental performance and economic performance are positively linked and that industry growth influences the relationship, with the returns to environmental performance higher in high-growth industries. Epstein and Young (1998) discussed the economic value added (EVA) performance measure and how its use can aid corporate environmental managers in promoting proactive environmental investments and in funding capital investments on environmental improvement, waste reduction and pollution control. Earnhart and Lizal (2006) examined the relationship between financial performance and environmental performance in a transition economy. They investigated whether successful financial performance begets or undermines good environmental performance. Several other studies (Thornton, Kagan and Gunningham, 2003; Zhu and Sarkis, 2004; Wagner, 2005) have been made to make a link between environmental and economic performance. Based on these

Table 20.25: Coverage of Environmental Improvement in the Budget of the Surveyed Units

Sl. No.	*Coverage of Environmental Improvement*	*Industry Segments*													
		Chemical		*Ferrous Metal*		*Food and Beverage*		*Non-Ferrous Metal*		*Thermal Power*		*Others*		*Total*	
		No.	*%*	*No.*	*%*	*No.*	*%*	*No.*	*%*	*No.*	*%*	*No.*	*%*	*No.*	*%*
1.	Yes	11	91.67	12	70.59	3	75.00	2	25.00	6	100.00	6	75.00	40	72.73
2.	No	1	8.33	5	29.41	1	25.00	6	75.00	0	0	2	25.00	15	27.27
	Total	**12**	**21.82**	**17**	**30.91**	**4**	**7.27**	**8**	**14.55**	**6**	**10.91**	**8**	**14.54**	**55**	**100.00**

Source: Results computed.

studies, here also we attempted to draw some financial implication due to consideration of environmental issues in business practice. We collected information related to budgetary allocation, investments made and costs incurred on environmental management, etc. Analysis of Annual budget for the study period (2005-2006) revealed that in case of majority of the surveyed units having separate financial allocation for environmental matters, 10-15 per cent of the total planned expenditure was separately allocated for fulfilling the objectives of environment policy. In case of some units, proportion of expenditure for the same was 5-10 per cent. The position was good for 21.05 per cent units, where 15-20 per cent of total planned expenditure was allocated for the purpose.

In case of majority (60%) of the surveyed units, covering environmental improvement in the company budget, adequate investments were being made to bring promising new green products to market (*See Table 20.26 on next page*). In this aspect, units of chemical industry (63.64%) played the lead role. All units of non-ferrous metal industry, units of thermal power and majority (66.67%) of the units of food and beverage industry were lagging behind in this aspect.

Status of developing accounting system to determine the full cost of Environment, Health and Safety (EHS) management in the surveyed units is presented in Table 20.27. (*See on page 236)* It indicates that majority (60%) of the surveyed units, covering environmental improvement in the company budget, developed accounting systems to determine the full cost of EHS management. In this aspect, majority (83.33%) of the units of thermal power, majority (72.73%) of the units of chemical industry and majority (66.67%) of the units of food and beverage industry played the lead role.

Table 20.26: Making Adequate Investments to Bring Green Products to Market by the Surveyed Units

Sl. No.	*Making Adequate Investments*	*Industry Segments*													
		Chemical		*Ferrous Metal*		*Food and Beverage*		*Non-Ferrous Metal*		*Thermal Power*		*Others*		*Total*	
		No.	*%*	*No.*	*%*	*No.*	*%*	*No.*	*%*	*No.*	*%*	*No.*	*%*	*No.*	*%*
1.	Yes	7	63.64	6	50.00	1	33.33	0	0	0	0	5	83.33	24	60.00
2.	No	4	36.36	6	50.00	2	66.67	2	100.00	6	100.00	1	16.67	16	40.00
	Total	**11**	**27.50**	**12**	**30.00**	**3**	**7.50**	**2**	**5.00**	**6**	**15.00**	**6**	**15.00**	**40**	**100.00**

Source: Results computed.

Table 20.27: Developing Accounting Systems to Determine Full Cost of EHS Management in the Surveyed Units

Sl. No.	*Developing Accounting Systems*	*Industry Segments*													
		Chemical		*Ferrous Metal*		*Food and Beverage*		*Non-Ferrous Metal*		*Thermal Power*		*Others*		*Total*	
		No.	*%*	*No.*	*%*	*No.*	*%*	*No.*	*%*	*No.*	*%*	*No.*	*%*	*No.*	*%*
1.	Yes	8	72.73	5	41.67	2	66.67	1	50.00	5	83.33	3	50.00	24	60.00
2.	No	3	27.27	7	58.33	1	33.33	1	50.00	1	16.67	3	50.00	16	40.00
	Total	**11**	**27.50**	**12**	**30.00**	**3**	**7.50**	**2**	**5.00**	**6**	**15.00**	**6**	**15.00**	**40**	**100.00**

Source: Results computed.

Burritt (1997) examined the process of cost allocation in the financial evaluation of environmental performance. Accordingly, we investigated the break up of costs incurred by the surveyed units for addressing environmental issues. Table 20.28 (*See on next page*) depicts the position of the surveyed units in this aspect. It was found that on an average units incurred 4.14 per cent of total costs for procurement of eco-friendly raw material with minimum figure of 3.03 per cent and maximum figure of 5.65 per cent. The picture was same in case of acquisition of new environmental pollution control equipment and waste treatment (Waste treatment includes treatment of solid wastes as well as hazardous wastes generated including treatment of wastewater in a unit). It was found that units incurred 3.22 per cent of total costs for modification of product with minimum figure of 2.62 per cent and maximum figure of 4 per cent. The cost involvement was same in case of modification and redesign of existing equipment and process; purchasing of new technologies; improvement of infrastructure; O&M improvement; etc. (*See Fig. 20.15 on page 240*). As any unit is less environmentally proactive, quantity of waste is more and waste disposal cost is also more. Analysis found that units incurred a major proportion of costs (13.35%) for disposal of waste where units of thermal power show the minimum figure of 8.53 per cent (on average) and maximum figure of 16.90 per cent (on average) was shown by units of ferrous metal industry.

Howes (1999) focussed on accounting for environmentally sustainable profits. Schaltegger and Wagner (2006) presented the logical corollary of how to measure sustainability performance, business competitiveness and economic success conceptually and empirically, before introducing a framework for the interaction of factors explaining the relationship of sustainability performance and competitiveness. Accordingly, here, break up of annual average cost saved by the surveyed units due to incorporation of environmental issues in the business practice is presented in Table 20.29. (*See on page 241*) It shows that out of total cost savings due to taking care of environmental issues, on an average units saved 10.23 per cent for reduction in consumption of resources with minimum figure of 9.92 per cent and maximum figure of 13.04 per cent. Minimisation of waste and pollution prevention was responsible for a similar cost saving.

Table 20.28: Annual Average Cost Incurred by the Surveyed Units for Addressing Environmental Issues

Sl. No.	*Particulars*	*Average Cost Incurred (%)*						
		Chemical	*Ferrous Metal*	*Food and Beverage*	*Non-Ferrous Metal*	*Thermal Power*	*Others*	*Total*
1.	Procurement of Eco-friendly Raw Material	4.37	3.03	3.80	5.12	5.65	4.30	4.14
2.	Acquisition of New Environmental Pollution Control Equipment	4.38	3.07	3.83	5.12	5.62	4.28	4.15
3.	Modification of Product	3.36	2.62	3.13	3.33	4.00	3.40	3.22
4.	Modification and Redesign of Existing Equipment and Process	3.41	2.65	3.11	3.35	3.95	3.33	3.22
5.	Waste Treatment	4.40	3.07	3.75	5.16	5.58	4.30	4.15
6.	Disposal of Waste	12.75	16.90	14.71	9.67	8.53	12.71	13.35
7.	Minor Hardware Installation	9.29	11.77	10.28	8.09	7.41	9.60	9.81
8.	Purchasing of New Technologies	3.40	2.64	3.14	3.32	3.99	3.35	3.23

(Contd...)

Sl. No.	Particulars	*Average Cost Incurred (%)*						
		Chemical	*Ferrous Metal*	*Food and Beverage*	*Non-Ferrous Metal*	*Thermal Power*	*Others*	*Total*
9.	Improvement of Infrastructure	3.43	2.63	3.16	3.39	4.00	3.39	3.25
10.	O & M Improvement	3.43	2.65	3.16	3.38	3.94	3.37	3.24
11.	Promotional Activities of Green Product in the Market	4.45	3.06	3.80	5.13	0	4.30	3.91
12.	Certification and Other Related Issues	16.52	10.15	10.98	17.72	21.15	15.18	15.61
13.	Cess and Permits	9.30	11.74	10.20	8.37	7.43	9.60	9.81
14.	Miscellaneous Purposes	23.52	29.94	26.57	18.90	22.29	23.96	25.33

Source: Results computed.

Fig. 20.15
Annual Average Cost (%) of Total Expenditure Incurred by the Surveyed Units for Addressing Environmental Issues

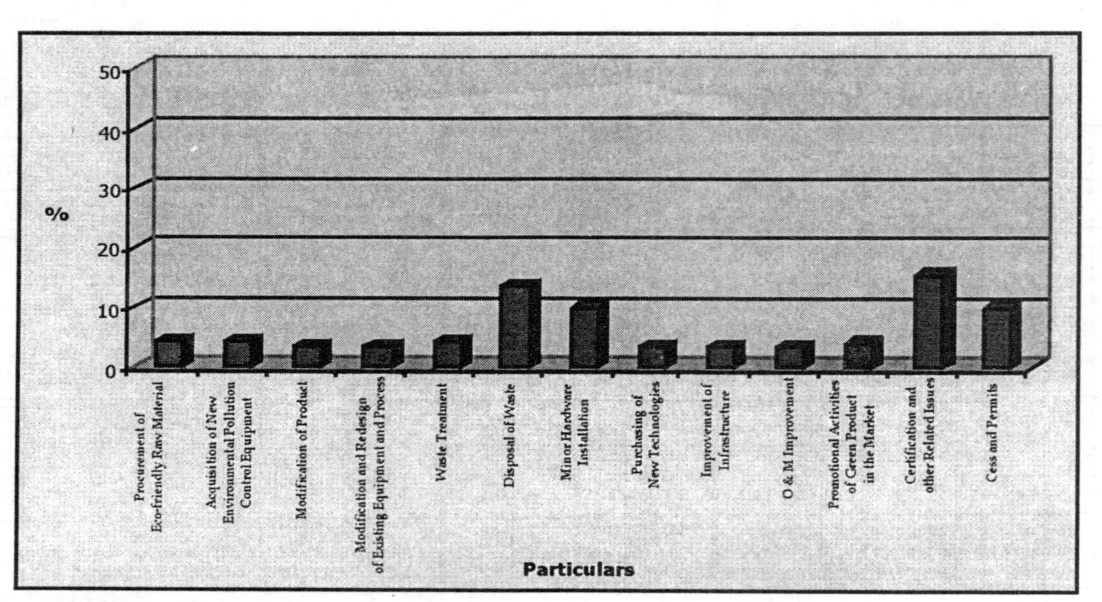

Source: Results computed.

Table 20.29: Annual Average Cost Saved by the Surveyed Units for Addressing Environmental Issues

Sl. No.	*Particulars*	*Average Cost Saved (%)*						
		Chemical	*Ferrous Metal*	*Food and Beverage*	*Non-Ferrous Metal*	*Thermal Power*	*Others*	*Total*
1.	Reduction in Consumption of Resources	10.47	8.23	9.92	11.79	13.04	10.61	10.23
2.	Minimisation of Waste and Pollution Prevention	10.50	8.24	9.93	11.66	13.08	10.64	10.24
3.	Substitution of Chemicals	1.92	1.28	1.59	2.43	2.75	1.93	1.85
4.	Fuel Savings	2.66	1.83	2.41	3.47	3.66	2.68	2.58
5.	Power Savings	2.65	1.85	2.39	3.42	3.69	2.68	2.59
6.	Lubricant Savings	2.66	1.85	2.41	3.47	3.68	2.69	2.59
7.	Wastewater Treatment	7.29	5.64	6.65	8.82	9.32	7.32	7.13
8.	Savings through Recycling	5.31	3.64	4.69	6.83	7.31	5.33	5.14
9.	Savings in Waste Disposal Costs	7.30	5.65	6.70	8.81	9.31	7.32	7.14
10.	Savings in Insurance Costs	2.65	1.82	2.42	3.47	3.66	2.67	2.58
11.	Miscellaneous Purposes	46.59	59.98	50.88	35.86	30.52	46.14	47.91

Source: Results computed.

The motto 'it pays to be green' may be proved through analysis of financial implication of environmental costs incurred. Table 20.30 (*See on next page*) depicts the benefit cost ratios. We found that in case of majority (60%) of the units the ratio of total cost savings and total costs incurred was upto 1.20. In case of the remaining 40 per cent units, the ratio was more than 1.20 (Figure 20.16). On an average, the ratio was more than 1 with minimum figure of 1.02, maximum figure of 1.44 and average figure of 1.16. In other words, a unit may expect to save to Rs. 1.16 against an expenditure of Rs. 1 on average. Thus, surveyed units had benefited financially through incurring costs to incorporate environmental issues in the business practice. In this aspect, thermal power was the best industry segment with the average figure of 1.26, whereas units of ferrous metal industry were the worst industry segment with the average figure of 1.08.

Fig. 20.16

Ratio of Total Cost Savings Against Total Costs Incurred by the Surveyed Units for Addressing Environmental Issues

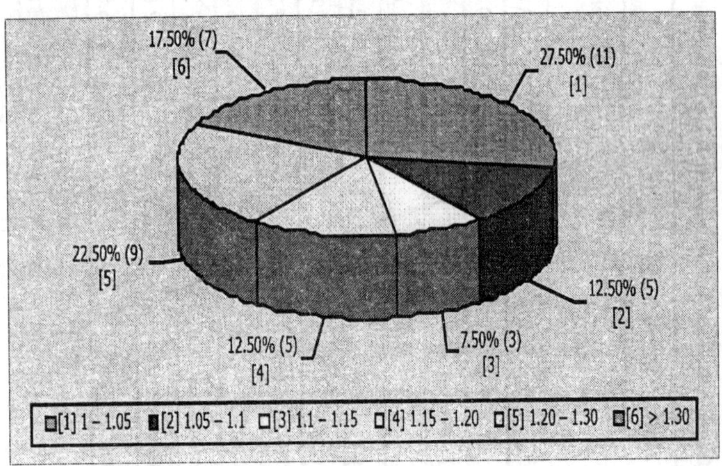

Source: Results computed.

Table 20.30: Ratio of Total Cost Savings against Total Costs Incurred by the Surveyed Units for Addressing Environmental Issues

Sl. No.	Total Cost Savings/ Total Costs Incurred	Industry Segments													
		Chemical		Ferrous Metal		Food and Beverage		Non-Ferrous Metal		Thermal Power		Others		Total	
		No.	%	No.	%	No.	%	No.	%	No.	%	No.	%	No.	%
1.	1-1.05	4	36.37	6	50.00	0	0	0	0	0	0	1	16.67	11	27.50
2.	1.05-1.1	0	0	2	16.67	1	33.33	1	50.00	0	0	1	16.67	5	12.50
3.	1.1-1.15	0	0	2	16.67	0	0	0	0	1	16.67	0	0	3	7.50
4.	1.15-1.20	0	0	1	8.33	2	66.67	0	0	1	16.67	1	16.67	5	12.50
5.	1.20-1.30	5	45.45	1	8.33	0	0	0	0	1	16.66	2	33.33	9	22.50
6.	> 1.30	2	18.18	0	0	0	0	1	50.00	3	50.00	1	16.66	7	17.50
	Total	11	27.50	12	30.00	3	7.50	2	5.00	6	15.00	6	15.00	40	100.00

Source: Results computed.

The important findings in respect of environmental cost management of the industrial units are reported in *Exhibit 20.7*.

EXHIBIT 20.7

Scenario of Environmental Cost Management By Industrial Units

- In case of majority (72.73%) of the surveyed units, environmental improvement was covered in the company budget.
- Analysis of annual budget for the study period (2005-2006) revealed that in case of majority of surveyed units having separate financial allocation for environmental matters, 10-15 per cent of the total planned expenditure was separately allocated for fulfilling the objectives of environment policy.
- In case of majority (60%) of the surveyed units, covering environmental improvement in the company budget, adequate investments were being made to bring promising new green products to market.
- Majority (60%) of the surveyed units, covering environmental improvement in the company budget, developed accounting systems to determine the full cost of EHS management.
- There were significant benefits appropriately expending on environmental issues. Such benefit cost ratio was more than 1 with minimum figure of 1.02, maximum figure of 1.44 and average figure of 1.16. In other words, a unit may expect to save to Rs. 1.16 against an expenditure of Re. 1 on average.

Therefore, it can be inferred from the analysis that all of the surveyed units reported that due to taking care of environmental issues in business practice, benefits exceeded costs. It is pertinent to mention here that the same inference was drawn by Chakrabarti and Mitra (2005) where they compared the costs incurred by the firms for installation of the device for controlling the air pollution generated from the production process with the benefit obtained from it. In our study, analysis also revealed that in case of all the ISO 14001 certified units, the ratio was greater than 1.30, whereas in case of the remaining units, the ratio was not so much satisfactory. Non-availability of proper fund to incorporate environmental issues and/or lack of commitment from top management and/or lack of taking initiative and/or lack of infrastructure, etc. might be responsible for poor cost-benefit ratios.

NOTES

1. For control of emissions and proper dispensation of pollutants the following guidelines shall be followed:
   (i) Units set up after the publication of this notification shall be treated as new units.
   (ii) A minimum stack height of 20 m shall be provided by each unit.
   (iii) Emissions from coke oven shall be channelised through a tunnel and finally emitted through a stack. Damper adjustment techniques shall be used to have optimum heat utilisation and also to control the emission of unburnt carbon particles and combustible flue gases.
   (iv) Wet scrubbing system or waste heat utilisation for power generation or byproduct recovery systems should be installed preferably to achieve the prescribed standards.
   (v) After four years from the date of this notification, all the existing units shall comply with the standards prescribed for the new units.
2. For control of emissions and proper dispersal of pollutants, the following guidelines shall be followed by the industry:
   (i) A minimum stack height of 20 m shall be provided.
   (ii) All ovens shall be modified to single chimney multi-oven systems.
   (iii) Emissions from coke oven shall be channelised through inbuilt draft stack. Optimum heat utilisation technique shall be used.
   (iv) In case of units having capacity 10 tonnes and above, wet scrubbing system shall be provided to control air pollution.
3. The Central and State Pollution Control Boards may fix stringent standards, not exceeding 250 mg/Nm^3 for smaller plants and 150 mg/Nm^3 for larger plants if the industry is located in an area which, in their opinion, requires more stringent standards.

   Where continuous monitoring integrators are provided on dust emission lines, the integrated average values over a period, to be fixed by the Central and State Boards but not exceeding 72 hours shall be considered instead of momentary dust emission values for conformity to standards.

4. Oxygen reference level for particulate matter concentration calculations far kilns mentioned at A(c) is 18 per cent and for those at A(b), and A(e) is 8 per cent.

5. The standard for sulphur dioxide in terms of stack height limits for kilns with various capacities of coal consumption shall be as indicated below:

Coal consumed per day	*Stack height*
Less than 8.5 mt	9 m
More than 8.5 to 21 mt	12 m
More than 21 to 42 mt	15 m
More than 42 to 64 mt	18 m
More than 64 to 104 mt	21 m
More than 104 to 105 mt	24 m
More than 105 to 126 mt	27 m
More than 126 mt	30 m or using formula H-14 $(Qg)^{0.3}$ (whichever is more)

In this notification, H-Physical height of the stack, Qg-Emission of sulphur dioxide in kg/hr., MT-Metric tonnes and m-meters.

6. All possible preventive measures should be taken to control pollution as far as practicable.

7. The special parameters to be stipulated by the Central Board in case of Union Territories and State Boards in case of States depending upon the dye used in the industry. Where the industry uses chrome dyes, sulphur dyes and/or phenolic compounds in the dyeing/printing
8. process, the limits on chromium of 2 mg/lt, sulphides of 2 mg/lt and phenolic compounds of 5 mg/lt, respectively shall be imposed.

Where the quality requirement of the recipient system so warrants, the limit of BOD should be lowered upto 30 according to the requirement by the State Boards for the States and the Central Board for the Union territories.

(i) The above standards shall be applicable to wastewater from processes and cooling.

(ii) BOD shall be made stringed upto 30 mg/l if the recipient fresh water body is source of drinking water supply.

(iii) The standards for boiler emissions shall be applicable as prescribed under Schedule I of these rules.

9. The emission from the boiler house shall conform to the standards already prescribed under the Environment (Protection) Act, 1986, vide Notification No. GSR 742 (E), dated 30-08-1990: Ref. [1991] 70 Comp. Cas. (St.)5.

10. To ascertain the category of 'unit fails' the average of daily productions and waste water discharge for the preceding 30 operating days from the date of sampling shall be considered.

11. It is essential that the stack is constructed over the cupola beyond the charging door and the emissions are directed through the stack which should be at least six times the diameter of the cupola.

    In respect of arc furnaces and induction furnaces, provision has to be made for collecting the fumes before discharging the emissions through the stack.

12. This standard of 250 mg/Nm^3 shall apply only for a period of 3 years with effect from the date on which the Environment (Protection) Second Amendment Rules, 1989, came into force. After three years the standard to be applicable is 15 mg/Nm^3.

13. The standards with respect to total waste water discharge for the large pulp and paper mills to be established from 1992, will meet the standards of 100 Cum/Ton of paper produced.

14. (i) No limit for COD is prescribed but it shall be monitored. If the COD in a treated effluent is persistently greater than 250 mg/l, such industrial units are required to identify chemicals causing the same. In case of these are found to be toxic as defined in Hazardous Chemicals Rules, 1989 in Part I of Schedule I, the State Boards in such cases may direct the industries to install tertiary treatment system stipulating time limit. This may be done on case-to-case basis.

    (ii) These standards are not applicable to small-scale detergent (formulating units).

15. Limits shall be complied with at the end of the treatment plant before any dilution.

    No limit for COD is prescribed. If the COD in a treated effluent is persistently more than 250 mg/l, such industrial units are required to identify the chemicals causing the same. In case, these are found to be toxic as defined in Schedule I of the Hazardous Chemicals Rules, 1989, the State Boards in such cases may direct the industries to install tertiary treatment, stipulating time limit. This may be done on a case-to-case basis.

16. State Board may prescribe limit for COD correlated with BOD limit.

State Board may prescribe limit for total dissolved solids depending upon uses of recipient water body.

Limits should be complied with at the terminal of the treatment unit before letting out of the factory boundary limits.

For the compliance of limits, analysis should be done in the composite sample collected every hour for a period of 8 hours.

17. Depending upon the requirement of local situation, such as protected area, the State Pollution Control Boards and other implementing agencies under the Environment (Protection) Act, 1986, may prescribe a limit of 150 mg/Nm^3, irrespective of generation capacity of the plant.

18. The regulatory standard of SPM in ambient air quality is 500 µg/Nm^3 for 24 hrs; in case of RPM, the value is 150 µg/Nm^3 for 24 hrs; in case of CO, the value is 5,000 µg/Nm^3 for 8 hrs; in case of SOx, the value is 120 µg/Nm^3 for 24 hrs; in case of NOx, the value is 120 µg/Nm^3 for 24 hrs (Mohanty, 1997, pp. 86-87).

19. The general emission standard of particulate matter in stack emission is usually 150 mg/Nm^3 except a few specific industries. For paper mill (large pulp and paper), it is 250 mg/Nm^3; for cement manufacturer, when plant capacity is 200 tonnes per day, it is 400 mg/Nm^3 and when plant capacity is greater than 200 tonnes per day, it is 250 mg/Nm^3; for power plant (when generation capacity less than 210 MW) and coke oven battery (existing units), it is 350 mg/Nm^3; for integrated iron & steel plant, during oxygen lancing, it is 400 mg/Nm^3 and at coke oven unit, it is 50 mg/Nm^3; for all types of asbestos manufacturing units (including all processes involving the use of asbestos), it is 2 mg/Nm^3; for foundries, when cupola capacity (melting rate) is less than 3 MT/hr, it is 450 mg/Nm^3; for ceramic unit, at down-draft of kiln unit, it is 1200 mg/Nm^3; at vertical shaft kiln unit, it is 250 mg/Nm^3; at automatic spray unit, when manufacturing capacity of lime/plaster of paris is more than 5 T/day, it is 500 mg/Nm^3, for coal carbonisation (units having capacity less than 10 tonnes), it is 350 mg/Nm^3. In case of CO, the general regulatory standard value is 1 per cent v/v. For the purpose of further analysis, it was required to convert this unit into a common measurable unit. In case of CO, 0.00001 per cent by volume equals 0.1 ppm. 1 ppm = 1,145 µg/Nm^3 and 1 mg = 1,000 µg. Therefore 1 per cent v/v equals 11,450 mg/Nm^3. It is pertinent to mention here that there is no prescribed limit by regulatory agency except a few cases in case of SO_2 and NOx emission through stacks. Accordingly, the study could not encounter the variation of SO_2 and NOx emission through stack from regulatory standard (Mohanty, 1997, pp. 81, 27-69).

20. The general regulatory standard of TSS in treated effluent is usually 100 mg/l (for inland surface water) except a few cases. For chemical

manufacturer (inorganic chemical industries), it is 30 mg/l; for vanaspati manufacturer, it is 150 mg/l; for petrochemicals (basics and intermediates), it is 1000 mg/l; for large pulp & paper, it is 50 mg/l; for natural rubber unit, it is 200 mg/l.

In case of BOD, the general regulatory standard value is usually 30 mg/l (for inland surface water) except a few cases. For petrochemicals (basics and intermediates) and paints industries, it is 50 mg/l (3 days at 27°C); for vanaspati manufacturer and pesticide industries, it is 100 mg/l (3 days at 27°C); for textile unit (cotton textile unit – composite & processing), it is 150 mg/l (3 days at 27°C); for rubber chemicals, in case synthetic rubber, it is 50 mg/l (3 days at 27°C); in case of natural rubber, during discharge into inland surface waters, it is 50 mg/l, during disposal on land for irrigation, it is 100 mg/l; for distilleries during disposal on land or for irrigation, it is 100 mg/l (3 days at 27°C); for organic chemicals manufacturing unit, it is 100 mg/l (3 days at 27°C).

In case of COD, the general regulatory standard value is usually 250 mg/l (for inland surface water) except a few cases. For vanaspati manufacturer, it is 200 mg/l; for paper mill (large pulp & paper), it is 350 mg/l.

In case of oil & grease, the general regulatory standard value is usually 10 mg/l (for inland surface water) except a few cases. For thermal power plant (at boiler blowdowns and ash-pond effluent) and vanaspati manufacturer, it is 20 mg/l.

In case of pH, the general regulatory standard value is usually 5.5-9.0 (for inland surface water) except a few specific cases. For thermal power plant (condenser cooling waters – once through cooling system and ash-pond effluent), petrochemicals, pesticide industry, soft drink industry, vanaspati manufacturer, organic chemicals manufacturing industry, it is 6.5-8.5; for electroplating, it is 6-9; for integrated iron & steel plant, at coke-oven byproduct unit, it is 6.0-8.5; at other plants such as sintering plant, blast furnace, steel melting and rolling mill, it is 6-9; for paint industry, chemical industry (inorganic chemical industry), it is 6.0-8.5; for large pulp & paper, it is 7.0-8.5 (Mohanty, 1997, pp. 77, 27-69).

21. Chemical industry usually generates scour, ETP sludge, process waste, viscous heavy tar, sewerage sludge, solvent, fly ash, spill, spent filter cake, organic by-product, metal complexes, oil impregnated coke, incinerator ash, etc.; Ferrous metal industry usually generates coal ash, grit, sand, slag, iron slag, carbon soot, clay, oil & scale bearing waste, pickling waste, burden fines, hydrochloric acid, sludge, tar, fly ash, blast furnace slag, refuse, trash, dust, timber, cyanide, debris, coal, coke, etc.; Food & beverage industry usually generates sludge,

grease, food waste, spent wash, fermentation washing, scour, chromium, process waste, viscous heavy tar, sewerage sludge, solvent, etc.; Non-ferrous metal industry usually generates metal sludge, process waste, dust, solvents, etc.; Thermal power plant usually generates fly ash, boiler slag, soot, ash, residue, slurry, bottom ash, water treatment sludge, sludge from metal cleaning wastes, etc.

22. Fly ash that is being generated from cement manufacturer, integrated iron and steel plant, paper mill, thermal power plants, pharmaceutical, asbestos cement pipes industry, is being used for manufacturing of Portland pozzolana cement; cement/silicate bonded fly ash/clay binding bricks and insulating bricks; clinker making. It is also used as raw material in OPC manufacture; also as structural fill for roads, construction on sites, land reclamation, etc.; as filler in mines, in bituminous concrete; as plasticiser; etc.

Blast furnace slag, that is being generally generated from integrated iron and steel plant, thermal power plants, is being used for manufacturing of slag cement, super sulphated cement, metallurgical cement, non-portland cement. It is also used in refractory and in ceramic as sital. It is used as a structural fill (air cooled stag); as aggregate in concrete; etc.

Ferro alloy and other metallurgical slag, that are being generated from asbestos cement pipe, cast iron foundry, cement manufacturer, integrated iron & steel plant, are being used as a structural fill. It is also used in making pozzolana metallurgical cement.

Lime sludge (paper and sugar sludges), that is being generated from chemical manufacturing plant, power plant & coke oven battery, vanaspati manufacturer, is being used as a sweetener for lime in cement manufacture. It is also used for manufacturing of lime pozzolana bricks/binders; for manufacturing of building lime and masonry cement. It is also used as a raw material for mini-cement plants. It is used for recycling in parent industry also.

23. Chemical industry usually generates lead, strong acids & bases, spent solvent, reactive wastes, refractory organics, volatile organic liquid, ETP Sludge, spent liquor, wash water, cyanide, solvent, metal waste, antibiotic waste, synthetic drug waste, organic acid, phenols, toxic chemicals, sulphide, fluoride, chromium, oil, slop oil, etc.; Ferrous metal industry usually generates strong acids & bases, sludges, cyanide wastes, oily waste, sluggy waste, slurry, phenol, silica, wastes containing toxic metal and emulsified oil, iron, tar sludge, sulphide, ammonia, benzene, xylene, toluene, napthalene, spent pickle liquor, lime, caustic wash, benzol acid sludge, etc.; Food & beverage industry usually generates dissolved organic, ETP Sludge, oil and grease, tar, cyanide, solvent, spent catalyst, rejected mobil/lub. oil, filter cake

etc.; Non-ferrous metal industry usually generates filter sludge, quench oil, spent salt bath, lead, silver, cyanide, chromic acid, soluble chromate, heavy melats (Cr^{6+}, Zn, Cd, Cu, Ni), solvent, mercury, selinium, strong acids and bases, lump lead slag, mercaptans, fumes and volatile metal, organic sulphide, etc.; Thermal power plant generates spent lubricant, spent clean-up-solvent, heavy metal (Cr, Zn, Fe, Mn, Ni), used oil, phenol, cyanide, thiocyanate, ammonia, solvent, etc.

24. The standard of noise level has been considered taking into consideration The Noise Pollution (Control & Regulation) Rules, 2000 where it is being stated that the ambient noise pollution standard in case of industrial area during day time (6:00 am-10:00 pm) is 75 dB(A) (Mohanty, 1997, p. 70).

21

EVALUATION OF ENVIRONMENTAL PROACTIVENESS

In this Chapter, before directly starting the technique adopted to evaluate the environmental performance for our sample units, let us have a glimpse of some of the related studies.

Epstein (1995) highlighted the measurement of corporate environmental performance as the best practices for costing and managing an Effective Environmental Strategy. Young (1996) stated that environmental performance measures can be seen as a step up from environmental management system and associated standards. He specifically differentiated between standards and measures by saying that EMS and standards only prove that an organisation is recognizing its environmental impact, not necessarily reducing it significantly. Whereas, measures can be used to monitor a company's progress (or lack of it) in reducing its environmental effect. Global Environmental Management Initiative (1998) made a survey of tools (metrics) for measuring environmental performance of 41 companies. The study revealed that metrics (tools) can measure the business value of environmental programmes or progress as well as the environmental performance of business operations. Ilinitch, Soderstrom and Thomas (1998) suggested a need for explicit environmental performance metrics in order to provide stakeholders with more reliable, consistent, and accurate information for comparing companies and making key strategic decisions and regulating information about company performance. Madsen (2003) stated that one of the best way of looking at the environment-competitiveness relationship is to compare a company's environmental performance with other units.

It was found from the survey that most of the units do not measure environmental performance to the fullest extent unless forced by legislation and for market pressures. The availability of environmental information has to be increased through legislation. Only when companies are compelled to disclose environmental information to stakeholders does industry respond positively to protecting the environment. Young (1996) argued that this response should be in the form of environmental performance measures, targets and hopefully improvements in environmental effects.

Selection of Environmental Performance Indicators for Assessing the Proactiveness

The term 'indicator' means, 'a thing that indicates'. Indicators are used to simplify the real world in research process. The demand for quick and operational measures in development work, has determined the use of indicators both at the macro and micro levels. The models generated by researchers and planners to depict real life situations are based on 'parameters', 'variables', 'units of analysis', 'factors', 'components', etc., and of the relationships between these. When the 'real life situations' are projects, a common denominators for the units of analysis is often 'indicators'.

In development studies, indicators are used for 2 main purposes:

(i) To differentiate central concepts – *e.g.* environmental proactiveness among the sample units in order to classify or rank them along the indicators;

(ii) To measure progress relating to interventions for social and economic change at the project and programme level.

In the field of environmental performance some authors used the term environmental performance indicators (EPIs), which Tyteca (1994) defined as tools that allow the analysis of the improvement (or deterioration) of a given firm's environmental performance.

Jacobs (1991) argued that as far as indicators of environmental performance are concerned, withdrawing the requirement that the environment should be measured in monetary terms is extremely helpful. European Green Table (1993) mentioned that 'environmental performance indicators are measures of company proficiency in protecting the environment'.

Ashford and Meima (1993), Fiksel (1994) and James (1994) explored the principal drivers of environmental performance. Welford and Gouldson (1993), in this context, also identified key environmental performance areas in organisations. Epstein (1995) identified ten indicators for corporations to measure their environmental performance. Global Environmental Management Initiative (1998) used a number of lagging indicators and a number of leading indicators. Even, to raise the profile of environmental issues among organisations in Northern Ireland and encourage improvement in environmental management and performance, the Northern Ireland Eighth Environmental Management Survey (2006) chose environmental policy, environmental audit, level of regulatory compliance, certification status, level of management bearing the responsibility to control environment department, employee awareness and training programme, etc. as prime environmental indicators. Thus, a considerable number of studies (Ilinitch, Soderstrom and Thomas, 1998; Dehua, Chan and Liyin, 2004; OECD, 2004; Takahashi and Nakamura, 2005; Huijbregts et. al., 2006; Ito, 2006; Sohal and Zutshi, 2006; Zutshi, 2006) have been undertaken to select the indicators for assessing the proactiveness.

Accordingly, the study concentrated on 6 primary indicators and some major sub-indicators that may lead the units towards environmental proactiveness. The primary 6 indicators are shown in *Exhibit 21.1*.

EXHIBIT 21.1

1. Having Environment Policy;
2. Having Environment Department;
3. Meeting Regulatory Compliance in the areas of
   - (A) Air Quality
   - (B) Effluent
   - (C) Generation of Solid and Hazardous Wastes
   - (D) Generation of Noise
4. EMS Certification;
5. Undertaking Environmental Audit;
6. Environmental Cost Management.

Measurement of Environmental Performance of Sample Units

Regarding quantification of environmental performance indicators, Davis (1994) stated that quantity measures give weight and usefulness to qualitative information such as environmental policies, but only as long as the qualitative message is clear. Fiksel (1994) expressed his opinion regarding such quantification in the same tune. In some studies, environmental performance indicators have been weighted on the basis of their relative importance to the environmental proactiveness. The weights used have either been determined by the researcher or taken from previous studies. While in some other studies, unweighted indicators have been used. In such an index, equal weight, i.e. 'one' has been assigned to each environmental performance indicator of the environmental proactiveness on the assumption that all environmental performance indicators are equally important to arrive at proactiveness score (for example, the Northern Ireland Eighth Environmental Management Survey, 2006). However, any weighted index may involve an element of subjectivity, but it may facilitate the true measurement of the score recognizing perceived importance of different primary indicators to overall environment management. It is most unlikely that each primary indicator has equal weightage in framing a real life environment policy.

Even, Rice (1993) produced a scorecard with a simple weighting scale for various categories of environmental performance areas. This produced later a ranking of companies. Business in the Environment and KPMG Peat Marwick (1992), Global Environmental Management Initiative (1998), Gupta and Goldar (2003), Wier *et al.* (2005) arguing in the same tune, put weightage of each performance level based on priority during the evaluation of environmental performance. Fiksel (1994) stated that there is no universal weighting scheme that will suit the needs of diverse organisations and each industry and/or company should develop a scheme that suits its business characteristics.

Accordingly, some score/weightage was attributed to each of the indicators mentioned above based on their importance towards environmental proactiveness for any unit, assuming total score/weightage being 1,000. Accordingly, Table 21.1 shows the importance given to each of the indicators.

Table 21.1: Importance of Primary Indicators

Sl. No.	*Primary Indicator*	*Score/Importance*
1.	Having Environment Policy	90
2.	Having Environment Department	90
3.	Meeting Regulatory Compliance	310
4.	EMS Certification	100
5.	Undertaking Environmental Audit	100
6.	Environmental Cost Management	310
	Total	**1,000**

Source: Results computed.

For awarding score to different environmental performance indicators, most researchers have followed a dichotomous procedure in which an environmental performance indicator has been awarded its assigned weight or score (i.e. 'one' in the case of unweighted index and a weighted score in the case of weighted index) if it was present (eg. Wehrmeyer *et al.*, 2002; Wagner, 2005; Schaltegger and Wagner, 2006). On the other hand, if the environmental performance indicator was not present, and it was found that the indicator was applicable to the concerned company, a score 'zero' has been awarded (eg. Ilinitch, Soderstrom and Thomas, 1998; Thornton, Kagan and Gunningham, 2003; Ito, 2006; The Northern Ireland Eighth Environmental Management Survey, 2006; Lu and Lo, 2007). However, a few researches have awarded score to environmental performance indicators on the basis of their merit of environmental proactiveness (Rice, 1993; Russo and Fouts, 1997; Gupta and Goldar, 2003; Dehua, Chan and Liyin, 2004; Zhu and Sarkis, 2004; Takahashi and Nakamura, 2005; Zutshi, 2006). Stating in the same tune, Business in the Environment and KPMG Peat Marwick (1992) depicted an example of the method of calculating weightings in the form of an index of emissions. In addition, it was stated that the weighting factor is subjective and will ultimately change over time due to the priorities of the decision maker.

However, considering nature of work, we were required to consider environmental management proactiveness of the surveyed units, which were diverse in nature regarding size, nature of product, quality of management, etc. Accordingly, in our study some score/weightage was also attributed to each of the sub-indicators under each indicator. Each of the sub-indicators was categorised into different scales based on responses obtained from surveyed units during collection of primary data. The interval of the scale was determined based on the nature of collected data. Again, some score/weightage was given to each interval of each sub-indicator. Though it was subjective, but it was considered unavoidable. The detailed scorecard that showed the proactiveness score value for each of the sub-indicators has been given in Exhibit 21.2 (*See on pages 258 to 274*) at the end of this Chapter. It is pertinent to mention here that after designing the scorecard, some revision was made based on discussion with the government officials as well as company executives working in the field of environment.

The study evaluated the score obtained of the surveyed units based on having corporate environment policy. Accordingly, the environmental performance score of the surveyed units considering the status of having corporate environment policy is reported in Table 21.2. (*See on page 275*)

EXHIBIT 21.2

Environment Management Proactiveness Scorecard

Sl. No.	*Parameter*		*Score*
1.	**Having Environment Policy**		
1.1	Time Taken (Yr.) for the Formulation of Environment Policy after Establishment of the Company	< = 1	30
		1-2	25
		2-4	22
		4-6	19
		6-10	16
		10-15	13
		15-20	10
		20-25	7
		25-30	4
		> 30	1
1.2	Mentioning Environment Policy in the Mission Statement/ Preamble	No	1
		Yes	30
1.3	Time Taken (Yr.) to Bring Change in Environment Policy after Its Formulation	< = 1	30
		1-2	25
		2-3	22
		3-5	19
		5-7	16
		7-8	13
		8-10	10
		10-12	7
		12-15	4
		> 15	1
2	**Having Environment Department**		
2.1	Head/In-Charge of Environment Department	Junior Management-level Staff	1
		Middle Management-level Staff	15
		Senior Management-level Staff	30

(Contd...)

Sl. No.	Parameter		Score
2.2	Qualification of the Head of Environment Department	Science Graduate	1
		Engineering Graduate Without Environmental Degree/Diploma	10
		General Management Graduate	20
		PG with Environmental Degree or Diploma	25
		Engineering Graduate with Environmental Degree or Diploma	30
2.3	Person to Whom the Head of the Environment Department Making Day-To-Day Report	Top Management	30
		Middle Management	15
		Bottom Management	1
3.	**Meeting Regulatory Compliance w.r.t.**		
	A) Air Quality		
3.1	Variation of SPM from Standard in Ambient Air Quality (%)	0-30	1
		30-40	2
		40-50	3
		50-55	4
		55-60	5
		60-62	6
		62-65	7
		65-70	8
		70-75	9
		> 75	10
3.2	Variation of RPM from Standard in Ambient Air Quality (%)	< = 0	1
		0-10	2
		10-20	3
		20-30	4
		30-40	5
		40-45	6
		45-48	7
		48-50	8
		50-60	9
		> 60	10

(Contd...)

Sl. No.	Parameter		Score
3.3	Variation of CO from Standard in Ambient Air Quality (%)	0-50	1
		50-60	2
		60-70	3
		70-80	4
		80-82	5
		82-84	6
		84-86	7
		86-90	8
		90-95	9
		>95	10
3.4	Variation of SO_2 from Standard in Ambient Air Quality (%)	0-30	1
		30-50	2
		50-70	3
		70-80	4
		80-82	5
		82-84	6
		84-86	7
		86-90	8
		90-92	9
		>92	10
3.5	Variation of NO_x from Standard in Ambient Air Quality (%)	0-40	1
		40-50	2
		50-60	3
		60-70	4
		70-72	5
		72-75	6
		75-80	7
		80-85	8
		85-90	9
		>90	10
3.6	Variation of PM Emission Through Stacks from Standard (%)	0-20	1
		20-40	2
		40-50	3
		50-60	4
		60-70	5
		70-75	6
		75-80	7
		80-85	8
		85-90	9
		>90	10

(Contd...)

Sl. No.	*Parameter*		*Score*
3.7	Variation of CO Emission Through Stacks from Standard (%)	< = 0	1
		0-10	2
		10-20	3
		20-40	4
		40-50	5
		50-55	6
		55-60	7
		60-70	8
		70-80	9
		> 80	10
3.8	Implementation Status in the Area of Control of Air Pollution	Under implementation	1
		Average	10
		Not Satisfactory	20
		Satisfactory	30
	B) Effluent		
3.9	Variation of TSS from Standard (%)	< = 0	1
		0-10	2
		10-30	3
		30-40	4
		40-45	5
		45-50	6
		50-55	7
		55-60	8
		60-65	9
		> 65	10
3.10	Variation of BOD from Standard (%)	< = (-50)	1
		(-50)-0	2
		0-10	3
		10-30	4
		30-50	5
		50-60	6
		60-70	7
		70-75	8
		75-80	9
		> 80	10

(Contd...)

Sl. No.	*Parameter*		*Score*
3.11	Variation of COD from Standard (%)	0-10	1
		10-20	2
		20-30	3
		30-50	4
		50-60	5
		60-70	6
		70-80	7
		80-84	8
		84-88	9
		> 88	10
3.12	Variation of O&G from Standard (%)	0-30	1
		30-40	2
		40-50	3
		50-60	4
		60-70	5
		70-75	6
		75-80	7
		80-85	8
		85-90	9
		> 90	10
3.13	Variation of pH from Standard (%)	< = (-20)	1
		(-20)-(-10)	2
		(-10)-(-5)	3
		(-5) - 0	4
		0-5	5
		5-10	6
		10-20	7
		20-30	8
		30-50	9
		> 50	10
3.14	Implementation Status in the Area of Control of Water Pollution	Under implementation	1
		Average	10
		Not Satisfactory	20
		Satisfactory	30

(Contd...)

Sl. No.	Parameter		Score
	C) Generation of Solid & Hazardous Wastes		
3.15	Quantity of Solid Wastes Recycled Against Generation (%)	< = 10	1
		10-12	2
		12-15	3
		15-20	4
		20-25	5
		25-30	6
		30-40	7
		40-50	8
		50-60	9
		> 60	10
3.16	Quantity of Solid Wastes Sold to Other Industries Against Generation (%)	< = 6	1
		6-7	2
		7-8	3
		8-10	4
		10-12	5
		12-15	6
		15-20	7
		20-25	8
		25-30	9
		> 30	10
3.17	Amount of Annual Revenue Generated due to Selling of Solid Wastes to Other Industries (Rs.)	< = 10,000	1
		10,000-40,000	3
		40,000-80,000	5
		80,000-1,00,000	7
		1,00,000-5,00,000	9
		5,00,000-10,00,000	11
		10,00,000-40,00,000	13
		40,00,000-80,00,000	15
		80,00,000-1,00,00,000	17
		> 1,00,00,000	20

(Contd...)

Sl. No.	*Parameter*		*Score*
3.18	Quantity of Hazardous Wastes Recycled Against Generation (%)	< = 8	1
		8-10	2
		10-12	3
		12-14	4
		14-16	5
		16-18	6
		18-20	7
		20-30	8
		30-32	9
		> 32	10
3.20	Quantity of Hazardous Wastes Stored/Disposed off [Without Following Required Safety Precautions] Against Generation (%)	< = 65	10
		65-70	9
		70-80	8
		80-82	7
		82-84	6
		84-86	5
		86-88	4
		88-90	3
		90-95	2
		> 95	1
3.21	Implementation Status in the Area of Control of Land Pollution	Under implementation	1
		Average	10
		Not Satisfactory	20
		Satisfactory	30
	D) Generation of Noise		
3.22	Variation of Noise Level from Standard (%)	< = (-40)	1
		(-40)-(-30)	2
		(-30)-(-20)	3
		(-20)-(-15)	4
		(-15)-(-10)	5
		(-10)-(-5)	6
		(-5)-0	7
		0-5	8
		5-8	9
		> 8	10

(Contd...)

Sl. No.	*Parameter*		*Score*
3.23	Implementation Status in the Area of Control of Noise Pollution	Under implementation	1
		Average	10
		Not Satisfactory	20
		Satisfactory	30
4.	**Certification**		
4.1	No. of Years after Which ISO 9001/9002 was Implemented after Commissioning of the Unit	< = 1	20
		1-2	17
		2-5	15
		5-10	13
		10-15	11
		15-20	9
		20-25	7
		25-30	5
		30-35	3
		> 35	1
4.2	No. of Years after Which ISO 14001 was Implemented after Commissioning of the Unit	< = 1	20
		1-2	17
		2-4	15
		4-6	13
		6-8	11
		8-10	9
		10-12	7
		12-15	5
		15-20	3
		> 20	1
4.3	Necessity of Number of Driving Forces for Initiating ISO14001 Implementation	All 9	20
		8	17
		7	15
		6	13
		5	11
		4	9
		3	7
		2	5
		1	3
		0	1

(Contd...)

Sl. No.	Parameter		Score
4.4	Composition of the Management Review Committee for EMS	Environment Department Staff Only	1
		Heads of All the Operations Department	10
		Heads of All the Operations Department including Environment Department Staff	15
		Staff of All the Departments	20
4.5	Frequency of Meeting of EMS Management Review Committee	Daily	20
		Weekly	16
		Monthly	12
		Biannually	8
		Annually	4
		Only During A Crisis	1
5	**Undertaking Environmental Audit**		
5.1	Status of Undertaking Environmental Audit	Only at Company Level	1
		Only at Production-Unit Level	10
		Both at Company and Production-Unit Level	20
5.2	Frequency of Environmental Audit (Production Unit-wise)	Monthly	20
		Quarterly	13
		Half-yearly	7
		Annually	1
5.3	Person Undertaking Environmental Audit (Production Unit-wise)	Production Unit Environment Department	1
		Outside Agency	10
		Production Unit Environment Department as well as Outside Agency	15
		Other	20

(Contd...)

Sl. No.	Parameter		Score
5.4	External Verification of Environmental Audit (Production Unit-wise)	No	1
		Yes	20
5.5	Process Adopted fo Environmental Audit	Similar to the environmental statement as per Pollution Control Board's guidelines	1
		Much more elaborate and comprehensive than PCB's guidelines	20
6	**Environmental Cost Management**		
6.1	Cost Incurred due to Procurement of Eco-friendly Raw Material (%)	< = 2	1
		2-2.5	2
		2.5-3	3
		3-4	4
		4-4.5	5
		4.5-5	6
		5-6	7
		6-7	8
		7-7.5	9
		> 7.5	10
6.2	Cost Incurred due to Acquisition of New Environmental Pollution Control Equipment (%)	< = 2	1
		2-2.5	2
		2.5-3	3
		3-4	4
		4-4.5	5
		4.5-5	6
		5-6	7
		6-7	8
		7-7.5	9
		> 7.5	10

(Contd...)

Sl. No.	Parameter		Score
6.3	Cost Incurred due to Modification of Product (%)	< = 2	1
		2-2.3	2
		2.3-2.5	3
		2.5-2.7	4
		2.7-3	5
		3-3.5	6
		3.5-3.7	7
		3.7-4	8
		4-4.5	9
		> 4.5	10
6.4	Cost Incurred due to Modification and Redesign of Existing Equipment and Process (%)	< = 2	1
		2-2.3	2
		2.3-2.5	3
		2.5-2.7	4
		2.7-3	5
		3-3.5	6
		3.5-3.7	7
		3.7-4	8
		4-4.5	9
		> 4.5	10
6.5	Cost Incurred due to Waste Treatment (%)	< = 2	1
		2-2.5	2
		2.5-3	3
		3-4	4
		4-4.5	5
		4.5-4.7	6
		4.7-5	7
		5-6	8
		6-7	9
		> 7	10

(Contd...)

Sl. No.	Parameter		Score
6.6	Cost Incurred due to Disposal of Waste (%)	< = 2	10
		2-4	9
		4-10	8
		10-11.5	7
		11.5-12	6
		12-13.5	5
		13.5-15	4
		15-18	3
		18-19.5	2
		> 19.5	1
6.7	Cost Incurred due to Minor Hardware Installation (%)	< = 2	1
		2-4	2
		4-6	3
		6-8	4
		8-8.5	5
		8.5-9	6
		9-10	7
		10-12	8
		12-13.5	9
		> 13.5	10
6.8	Cost Incurred due to Purchasing of New Technologies (%)	< = 2	1
		2-2.3	2
		2.3-2.5	3
		2.5-2.7	4
		2.7 – 3	5
		3-3.5	6
		3.5-3.7	7
		3.7-4	8
		4-4.5	9
		> 4.5	10

(Contd...)

Sl. No.	*Parameter*		*Score*
6.9	Cost Incurred due to Improvement of Infrastructure (%)	< = 2	1
		2-2.3	2
		2.3-2.5	3
		2.5-2.7	4
		2.7-3	5
		3-3.5	6
		3.5-3.7	7
		3.7-4	8
		4-4.5	9
		> 4.5	10
6.10	Cost Incurred due to O&M Improvement (%)	< = 2	1
		2-2.3	2
		2.3-2.5	3
		2.5-2.7	4
		2.7-3	5
		3-3.5	6
		3.5-3.7	7
		3.7-4	8
		4-4.5	9
		> 4.5	10
6.11	Cost Incurred due to Promotional Activities of Green Product in Market (%)	< = 2	1
		2-2.5	2
		2.5-3	3
		3-3.5	4
		3.5-4	5
		4-4.5	6
		4.5-4.7	7
		4.7-5	8
		5-7	9
		> 7	10

(Contd...)

Sl. No.	Parameter		Score
6.12	Cost Incurred due to Certification fees & Other Related Expenditure (%)	< = 5	1
		5-8	2
		8-10	3
		10-11	4
		11-11.5	5
		11.5-12	6
		12-20	7
		20-25	8
		25-28	9
		> 28	10
6.13	Cost Savings due to Reduction in Consumption of Resources (%)	< = 5	1
		5-6.5	2
		6.5-7	3
		7-8	4
		8-9	5
		9-11	6
		11-11.5	7
		11.5-12	8
		12-15.5	9
		> 15.5	10
6.14	Cost Savings due to Minimisation of Waste and Pollution Prevention (%)	< = 5	1
		5-6.5	2
		6.5-7	3
		7-8	4
		8-10	5
		10-11	6
		11-11.5	7
		11.5-12	8
		12-15.5	9
		> 15.5	10

(Contd...)

Sl. No.	*Parameter*		*Score*
6.15	Cost Savings due to Substitution of Chemical (%)	< = 1	1
		1-1.2	2
		1.2-1.4	3
		1.4-1.6	4
		1.6-1.8	5
		1.8-2	6
		2-3.5	7
		3.5-3.7	8
		3.7-3.9	9
		> 3.9	10
6.16	Cost Savings due to Fuel Savings (%)	< = 1.3	1
		1.3-1.5	2
		1.5-2	3
		2-2.5	4
		2.5-2.8	5
		2.8-3	6
		3-4	7
		4-4.5	8
		4.5-4.8	9
		> 4.8	10
6.17	Cost Savings due to Power Savings (%)	< = 1.3	1
		1.3-1.5	2
		1.5-1.7	3
		1.7-2	4
		2-2.5	5
		2.5-2.8	6
		2.8-3	7
		3-4.5	8
		4.5-4.8	9
		> 4.8	10

(Contd...)

Sl. No.	*Parameter*		*Score*
6.18	Cost Savings due to Lubricants Savings (%)	< = 1.3	1
		1.3-1.5	2
		1.5-2	3
		2-2.3	4
		2.3-2.5	5
		2.5-2.8	6
		2.8-3	7
		3-4.5	8
		4.5-4.8	9
		> 4.8	10
6.19	Cost Savings due to Wastewater Treatment (%)	< = 4	1
		4-4.5	2
		4.5-5	3
		5-5.5	4
		5.5-6	5
		6-7	6
		7-7.5	7
		7.5-8	8
		8-11.5	9
		> 11.5	10
6.20	Cost Savings due to Savings through Recycling (%)	< = 2	1
		2-2.5	2
		2.5-3	3
		3-4	4
		4-5	5
		5-5.5	6
		5.5-5.7	7
		5.7-6	8
		6-9.5	9
		> 9.5	10

(Contd...)

Sl. No.	Parameter		Score
6.21	Cost Savings due to Savings in Waste Disposal Costs (%)	< = 4	1
		4-4.5	2
		4.5-5	3
		5-6	4
		6-7	5
		7-7.5	6
		7.5-8	7
		8-11	8
		11-11.5	9
		> 11.5	10
6.22	Cost Savings due to Savings in Insurance Costs (%)	< = 1.3	1
		1.3-1.5	2
		1.5-1.8	3
		1.8-2	4
		2-2.5	5
		2.5-2.8	6
		2.8-3	7
		3-4.5	8
		4.5-4.8	9
		> 4.8	10
6.23	Ratio of Total Cost Savings Against Total Cost Incurred	1-1.05	1
		1.05-1.10	15
		1.10-1.15	30
		1.15-1.20	45
		1.20-1.30	60
		>1.30	90
	GRAND TOTAL		1,000

Table 21.2: Corporate Environment Policy: Performance Score of the Surveyed Units

Sl. No.	*Score (%)*	*Certification Status of the Surveyed Units*							
		ISO 14001		*ISO 9001*		*None*		*Total*	
		No.	*%*	*No.*	*%*	*No.*	*%*	*No.*	*%*
1.	0	0	0	6	33.33	21	70.00	27	49.09
2.	0-40	0	0	5	27.78	9	30.00	14	25.45
3.	40-50	1	14.28	1	5.56	0	0	2	3.64
4.	50-60	0	0	4	22.22	0	0	4	7.27
5.	60-70	3	42.86	2	11.11	0	0	5	9.09
6.	> 70	3	42.86	0	0	0	0	3	5.46
	Total	**7**	**12.72**	**18**	**32.73**	**30**	**54.55**	**55**	**100.00**

Source: Results computed.

The important findings in respect of the performance score on having corporate environment policy are reported in *Exhibit 21.3.*

EXHIBIT 21.3

- Out of 55 surveyed units, 27 units (49.09%) were not having any environment policy and consequently those units obtained nil score in this regard.
- Only 5.46 per cent units obtained greater than 70 per cent score, out of maximum achievable score, where all of them were ISO 14001 certified.
- Units that did not have any certification obtained less than 40 per cent score.
- Majority (85.72%) of the ISO 14001 certified units obtained more than 60 per cent score.

The environmental performance score of the surveyed units considering the status of having environment department is reported in Table 21.3.

Table 21.3: Environment Department: Performance Score of the Surveyed Units

Sl. No.	Score (%)	*Certification Status of the Surveyed Units*							
		ISO 14001		*ISO 9001*		*None*		*Total*	
		No.	*%*	*No.*	*%*	*No.*	*%*	*No.*	*%*
1.	0	0	0	7	38.89	27	90.00	34	61.82
2.	0-40	0	0	0	0	0	0	0	0
3.	40-50	3	42.86	3	16.67	1	3.34	7	12.73
4.	50-60	1	14.28	0	0	1	3.33	2	3.64
5.	60-70	2	28.57	5	27.78	1	3.33	8	14.55
6.	> 70	1	14.29	3	16.66	0	0	4	7.26
	Total	7	12.72	18	32.73	30	54.55	55	100.00

Source: Results computed.

The important findings in respect of the performance score on having environment department are reported in *Exhibit 21.4.*

EXHIBIT 21.4

- Out of 55 surveyed units, 34 units (61.82%) were not having any environment department and consequently those units obtained nil score in this area.
- 21 (38.18%) units obtained greater than 40 per cent score, out of maximum achievable score, where majority (85.71%) of them had some certification.
- Majority (90%) of the units that did not have any certification obtained zero score. In other words, units not having certification were also not having any environment department.
- ISO 14001 certified units had scored more than 40 per cent.

Compliance with regulatory norms is considered to be an important environment performance indicator. Accordingly, the environmental performance score of surveyed units considering the compliance status is reported in Table 21.4.

Table 21.4: Regulatory Compliance: Performance Score of the Surveyed Units

Sl. No.	*Score (%)*	*Certification Status of the Surveyed Units*							
		ISO 14001		*ISO 9001*		*None*		*Total*	
		No.	*%*	*No.*	*%*	*No.*	*%*	*No.*	*%*
1.	0	0	0	0	0	0	0	0	0
2.	0 – 40	0	0	0	0	0	0	0	0
3.	40-50	0	0	3	16.67	10	33.33	13	23.64
4.	50 – 60	0	0	5	27.78	19	63.33	24	43.64
5.	60 – 70	1	14.29	6	33.33	1	3.34	8	14.54
6.	> 70	6	85.71	4	22.22	0	0	10	18.18
	Total	**7**	**12.72**	**18**	**32.73**	**30**	**54.55**	**55**	**100.00**

Source: Results computed.

The important findings in respect of the performance score on meeting regulatory compliance are reported in *Exhibit 21.5.*

EXHIBIT 21.5

- Out of 55 surveyed units, 37 units (67.28%) obtained less than 60 per cent score.
- Only 18.18 per cent units obtained greater than 70 per cent score, out of maximum achievable score, where majority (60%) of them were ISO 14001 certified.
- Majority (96.66%) of the units that did not have any certification obtained less than 60 per cent score.
- Majority (85.71 per cent) of the ISO 14001 certified units obtained more than 70 per cent score.

The study evaluated the score value of the surveyed units based on having EMS certification as mentioned in the score sheet. Accordingly, the environmental performance score of the surveyed units considering the status of having EMS certification is reported in Table 21.5.

Table 21.5: EMS Certification: Performance Score of the Surveyed Units

Sl. No.	*Score (%)*	*Certification Status of the Surveyed Units*							
		ISO 14001		*ISO 9001*		*None*		*Total*	
		No.	*%*	*No.*	*%*	*No.*	*%*	*No.*	*%*
1.	0	0	0	0	0	30	100.00	30	54.55
2.	0-40	3	42.86	15	83.33	0	0	18	32.73
3.	40-50	1	14.29	2	11.11	0	0	3	5.45
4.	50-60	1	14.29	0	0	0	0	1	1.82
5.	60-70	2	28.56	1	5.56	0	0	3	5.45
6.	> 70	0	0	0	0	0	0	0	0
	Total	**7**	**12.72**	**18**	**32.73**	**30**	**54.55**	**55**	**100.00**

Source: Results computed.

The major findings in respect of the performance score on EMS certification may be summarised in Exhibit 21.6.

EXHIBIT 21.6

- Out of 55 surveyed units, 30 units (54.55%) were not having any EMS certification and consequently those units obtained nil score in this aspect.
- Only 12.72 per cent units obtained greater than 40 per cent score, out of maximum achievable score, where majority (57.14%) of them were ISO 14001 certified and the rests were ISO 9001 certified.

The environmental performance score of the surveyed units based on the status of undertaking environmental audit is presented in Table 21.6.

Table 21.6: Environmental Audit: Performance Score of the Surveyed Units

Sl. No.	*Score (%)*	*Certification Status of the Surveyed Units*							
		ISO 14001		*ISO 9001*		*None*		*Total*	
		No.	*%*	*No.*	*%*	*No.*	*%*	*No.*	*%*
1.	0	0	0	7	38.89	26	86.67	33	60.00
2.	0-40	0	0	2	11.11	1	3.33	3	5.45
3.	40-50	0	0	1	5.56	3	10.00	4	7.27
4.	50-60	4	57.14	3	16.67	0	0	7	12.73
5.	60-70	1	14.29	5	27.77	0	0	6	10.91
6.	> 70	2	28.57	0	0	0	0	2	3.64
	Total	**7**	**12.72**	**18**	**32.73**	**30**	**54.55**	**55**	**100.00**

Source: Results computed.

The important findings in respect of the performance score on environmental audit are reported in *Exhibit 21.7*.

EXHIBIT 21.7

- Out of 55 surveyed units, 33 units (60%) were not undertaking environmental audit and consequently those units obtained nil score in this area.
- Only 3.64 per cent units obtained greater than 70 per cent, out of maximum achievable score, where all of them were ISO 14001 certified.
- Units that did not have any certification scored less than 50 per cent.
- ISO 14001 certified units had obtained more than 50 per cent score.

The position of the surveyed units regarding environmental cost management was evaluated through scoring. Table 21.7 depicts the environmental performance score of the surveyed units considering the status of environmental cost management.

Table 21.7: Environmental Cost Management: Performance Score of the Surveyed Units

Sl. No.	Score (%)	Certification Status of the Surveyed Units							
		ISO 14001		ISO 9001		None		Total	
		No.	%	No.	%	No.	%	No.	%
1.	0	0	0	0	0	15	50.00	15	27.27
2.	0-40	0	0	2	11.11	15	50.00	17	30.91
3.	40-50	0	0	2	11.11	0	0	2	3.64
4.	50-60	0	0	5	27.78	0	0	5	9.09
5.	60-70	0	0	9	50.00	0	0	9	16.36
6.	>70	7	100.00	0	0	0	0	7	12.73
	Total	**7**	**12.72**	**18**	**32.73**	**30**	**54.55**	**55**	**100.00**

Source: Results computed.

The important findings in respect of the performance score on environmental cost management are reported in *Exhibit 21.8.*

EXHIBIT 21.8

- Out of 55 surveyed units, 15 units (27.27%) were not covering environmental improvement in their company budget and consequently those units obtained nil score in this aspect.
- Only 12.73 per cent units obtained greater than 70 per cent, out of maximum achievable score, and those units were ISO 14001 certified.
- Units that did not have any certification obtained less than 40 per cent score.
- Majority (88.89 per cent) of ISO 9001 certified units obtained score in the range of 40-70 per cent.
- ISO 14001 certified units obtained more than 70 per cent score.

Finally, the study evaluated the combined proactiveness score value of the surveyed units based on performance with respect to all of the six primary indicators. Accordingly, the overall environmental performance score of the surveyed units considering the status of all the six primary indicators is reported in Table 21.8.

Table 21.8: Overall Performance Score of the Surveyed Units

Sl. No.	*Score (%)*	*Certification Status of the Surveyed Units*							
		ISO 14001		*ISO 9001*		*None*		*Total*	
		No.	*%*	*No.*	*%*	*No.*	*%*	*No.*	*%*
1.	< 40	0	0	1	5.56	11	36.67	12	21.82
2.	40-50	0	0	3	16.67	8	26.67	11	20.00
3.	50-60	0	0	8	44.44	11	36.66	19	34.54
4.	60-70	0	0	6	33.33	0	0	6	10.91
5.	> 70	7	100.00	0	0	0	0	7	12.73
	Total	**7**	**12.72**	**18**	**32.73**	**30**	**54.55**	**55**	**100.00**

Source: Results computed.

An analysis of the combined performance score on overall environmental performance of the surveyed units is presented in *Exhibit 21.9.*

EXHIBIT 21.9

- Out of 55 surveyed units, 23 units (41.82%) obtained less than 50 per cent score, out of maximum achievable score.
- Out of these 23 units, 4 were ISO 9001 certified and the rests 19 did not have any certification.
- 25 (45.45%) units obtained 50-70 per cent score, out of which some (56%) were ISO 9001 certified and the rests did not have any certification.
- Out of all ISO 9001 certified units, majority (77.77%) obtained score in the range of 50-70 per cent.
- Units that were ISO 14001 certified had scored more than 70 per cent.

To reveal the picture of performance score of the surveyed units in more straight forward manner, we made the gradation of the surveyed units based on the combined proactiveness score of the surveyed units. The basis of gradation used by us is as follows:

Performance Score Obtained (%)	*Gradation of the Surveyed Units*
> 70	Excellent
60-70	Good
50-60	Moderate
40-50	Average
< = 40	Poor

Using the above-mentioned basis of gradation, we classified the units under different categories. Table 21.9 summarises the gradation of the surveyed units.

Table 21.9: Environmental Performance of the Surveyed Units Based on Gradation

Sl. No.	*Gradation*	*Certification Status of the Surveyed Units*							
		ISO 14001		*ISO 9001*		*None*		*Total*	
		No.	*%*	*No.*	*%*	*No.*	*%*	*No.*	*%*
1.	Excellent	7	100.00	0	0	0	0	7	12.73
2.	Good	0	0	6	33.33	0	0	6	10.91
3.	Moderate	0	0	8	44.44	11	36.67	19	34.54
4.	Average	0	0	3	16.67	8	26.66	11	20.00
5.	Poor	0	0	1	5.56	11	36.67	12	21.82
	Total	**7**	**12.72**	**18**	**32.73**	**30**	**54.55**	**55**	**100.00**

Source: Results computed.

An analysis of the environmental performance of the surveyed units based on gradation is presented in *Exhibit 21.10.*

EXHIBIT 21.10

- Out of 55 units, 12 (21.82%) were in 'poor' condition.
- Out of 12 'poor' units, majority (91.67%) of them did not have any certification.
- 11 (20%) units fell under 'Average'.
- Out of these 11 'Average' units, majority (72.73%) did not have any certification and only 3 were ISO 9001 certified.
- 19 (34.54%) units were in 'Moderate' condition.
- Out of 19 'Moderate' units, some (57.89%) did not have any certification and rests (42.11%) were ISO 9001 certified.
- 6 (10.91%) units were 'Good', all of which were ISO 9001 certified.
- All of the 7 (12.73%) ISO 14001 certified units were 'Excellent'.

The analysis of environmental performance of the surveyed units by industry is presented in Table 21.9, which depicts that in case of units of chemical industry, score value ranged between 27.76-82.60 per cent with a mean score of 53.60 per cent. In case of units of ferrous metal industry, score value ranged between 27.03-61.76 per cent with a mean score of 44.21 per cent. Food and beverage units scored between 46.27-56.89 per cent with a mean score of 52.36 per cent. It is worthwhile to mention here that there was no 'Excellent' ferrous metal and food and beverage unit. In case of units of non-ferrous metal industry, score value ranged between 36.72-76.40 per cent with a mean score of 53.76 per cent. Units of thermal power scored between 40.14-74.52 per cent with a mean score of 64.36 per cent. In case of units that were clubbed under others, score value ranged between 31.33-75.38 per cent with a mean score of 55.17 per cent. The statistics relating to environmental performance score by industry segment are presented in Table 21.10.

Table 21.10: Summary Statistics of Environmental Performance Score by Industry Segment

Sl. No.	*Industry Segments*	*Environmental Performance Score (%)*			
		Min (%)	*Max (%)*	*Mean (%)*	*Std. Dev.*
1.	Chemical	27.76	82.60	53.60	17.46
2.	Ferrous Metal	27.03	61.76	44.21	10.71
3.	Food & Beverage	46.27	56.89	52.36	4.43
4.	Non-Ferrous Metal	36.72	76.40	53.76	11.77
5.	Thermal Power	40.14	74.52	64.36	13.10
6.	Others	31.33	75.38	55.17	13.37
	Overall	27.03	82.06	52.03	13.89

Source: Results computed.

The analysis of environmental proactiveness of surveyed units by industry segment is reported in *Exhibit 21.11*.

EXHIBIT 21.11

- Highest mean score value was obtained by the units of thermal power.
- Poor performance was observed in case of ferrous metal industry.
- Medium performance was reflected in case of other industry segments.

The gradation of units on the basis of environmental performance score was further analysed to find out which type of units on the basis of size[1] performed better. The analysis of environmental performance of the surveyed units by size is presented in Table 20.10. Our analysis revealed that in case of very small units, score value ranged between 27.76-58.24 per cent with a mean score of 47.83 per cent. In case of small units, score value ranged between 29.27-55.29 per cent with a mean score of 43.98 per cent. It is worthwhile to mention here that there was no 'Excellent' very small and small unit. In case of medium units, score value ranged between 53.33-76.40 per cent with a mean score of 60.65 per cent. Large units scored between 27.03-75.38 per cent with a mean score of 53.07 per cent. In case of very large units, score value ranged between 68.57-82.60 per cent with a mean score of 77.02 per cent. The statistics relating to the environmental performance score by size are presented in Table 21.11.

Table 21.11: Summary Statistics of Environmental Performance Score by Size of the Units

Sl. No.	*Size of the Surveyed Units*	*Environmental Performance Score*			
		Min (%)	*Max (%)*	*Mean (%)*	*Std. Dev.*
1.	Very Small	27.76	58.24	47.83	10.06
2.	Small	29.27	55.29	43.98	9.07
3.	Medium	53.33	76.40	60.65	9.41
4.	Large	27.03	75.38	53.07	14.43
5.	Very Large	68.57	82.60	77.02	7.44

Source: Results computed.

The analysis of environmental proactiveness of surveyed units by size is presented in *Exhibit 21.12*.

EXHIBIT 21.12

- Highest mean score value was obtained by the very large units followed by medium units.
- Poor performance was observed in case of small units followed by very small units.
- Performance of large units is above average.

Development of Environmental Proactiveness Matrix

A two by two matrix is a useful tool for categorising things that can be reduced to two simple variables. Such matrix is one of the most well-known portfolio management decision making tools. In terms of business practice, such two by two matrix is termed as 'Portfolio Analysis', which was applied in case of the BCG Growth-Share Matrix (Kotler, 1998). It enables a rapid clustering (or separating) of information into four categories, which can be defined to suit the purpose of the exercise. It is particularly useful with groups as a way of visibly plotting out a common understanding or agreement of a subject.

In corporate environmental management, the aims of such a portfolio analysis are presented in *Exhibit 21.13*.

EXHIBIT 21.13

- To analyse the current business portfolio and decide which unit incorporates more or less environmental issues;
- To develop sustainable strategies for considering environmental issues more in the portfolio;
- To decide which units will no longer be sustained and which ones can be revived.

In several studies (Madsen and Ulhoi, 2001; Wehrmeyer *et al.*, 2002; OECD, 2004; Takahashi and Nakamura, 2005; Ito, 2006), the association between corporate size and environmental proactiveness has been tested. Even, most empirical studies (Henriques and Sadorsky, 1996; Bradford, 2000; Wehrmeyer *et al.*, 2002; OECD, 2004) have found significant and positive association between the corporate size and environmental proactiveness, suggesting that extent of environmental proactiveness increases with increase in size of firm. Moreover, size of the reporting company has been measured in one or more ways. In majority of those studies, corporate size has been measured in terms of total capital investment by Firth (1979); Epstein and Young (1998), HaBler and Reinhard (2000). Based on this, each surveyed unit was rated in terms of two major dimensions – 'Environmental Performance Score' and 'Size' [It is pertinent to mention here that based on capital investment, size of the surveyed units was determined].

The 'Size' on the vertical axis indicated size of the surveyed units i.e. either the unit is very large/large or it is very small/ small/medium. Accordingly, the vertical axis here, was categorized into two zones – 'large/ very large' and 'very small/ small/ medium'. As 'Size' was determined based on capital investment, therefore 'very small/ small/ medium' zone indicates the units having capital investment of 'less than or equal to Rs. 100 crores' and 'large/very large' zone indicates the units having capital investment of 'more than Rs. 100 crores'. Similarly, 'Environmental Performance Score', which was measured on the horizontal axis, referred to the overall performance score assigned to the surveyed units. Here the horizontal axis ranged from 0 per cent to 100 per cent. Environmental performance score above 50 per cent was considered high performance score. Further, 'Size' i.e. 'Capital investment' served here as a proxy for unit attractiveness, and 'Environmental Performance Score' served as a proxy for being environmentally proactive and gaining competitive advantage. The Environmental Proactiveness Matrix thus, mapped the business unit positions within these two important determinants of proactiveness.

Thus, Environmental Proactiveness Matrix is a portfolio planning model. In the Figure 21.1, the Environmental Proactivenes Matrix was divided into four cells, each indicated a different types of business practice based on the extent to which environmental issues are incorporated in the business practice. Those four cells are presented in *Exhibit 21.14*.

EXHIBIT 21.14

- ***Proactive:*** Units that obtained more than 50 per cent overall performance score and were of large/very large size were designated as 'Proactive' [Upper Right Cell of Figure 21.1].
- ***Performer:*** Units that obtained more than 50 per cent overall performance score, though were of very small/small/ medium size were designated as 'Performer' [Lower Right Cell of Figure 21.1].
- ***Underperformer:*** Units that were of large/very large size, but obtained less than or equal to 50 per cent overall performance score were designated as 'Underperformer' [Upper Left Cell of Figure 21.1].
- ***Laggards:*** Units that obtained less than or equal to 50 per cent overall performance score and were of very small/ small/medium size were designated as 'Laggards' [Lower Left Cell of Figure 21.1].

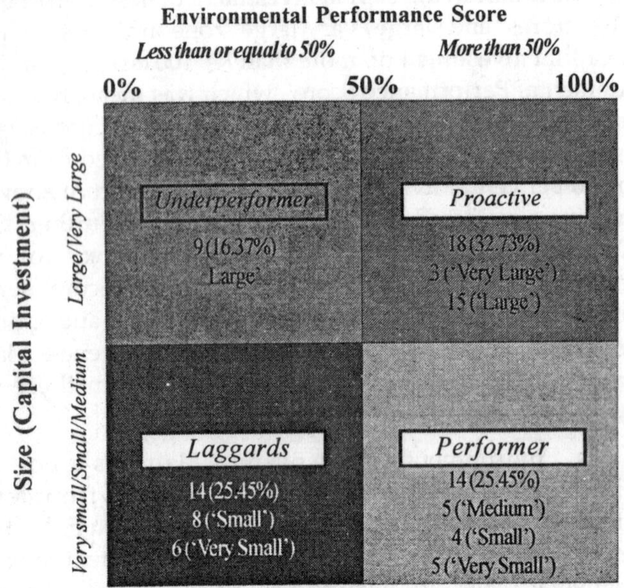

Source: Results computed.

Fig. 21.1
Environmental Proactiveness Matrix

The rationale of such classification was to give importance to performance score. We expected that size will also be a major determinant of a unit's proactiveness (We dealt with this issue further in the subsequent section). It is pertinent to mention here that size parameter has no role in scoring and any unit would not be necessarily having high score for its size. Regulations also do not discriminate between large scale and small scale units regarding pollution control requirements. Hence small units also need to be environmentally proactive and our attempt of this 2 x 2 matrix is aimed at identifying proactive and non-proactive groups in the same size class and also between different size classes.

After plotting all the 55 surveyed units in the Environmental Proactiveness Matrix, the study identified the portfolio of each of the surveyed units, which was tabulated in *Exhibit 21.15*.

EXHIBIT 21.15

Out of all surveyed units:

- 18 (32.73%) units were 'Proactive' in nature. All 'very large' units and 15 'large' units fell in this category.
- 14 (25.45%) units were 'Performer' in nature. All 'medium' units, 4 'small' units and 5 'very small' units fell in this category.
- 9 (16.37%) units were 'Underperformer' in nature. All of these 9 were 'large' units.
- 14 (25.45%) units were 'Laggards' in nature. 8 'small' units and 6 'very small' units fell in this category.

Thus, if we would analyse current business portfolio of our sample units based on Environmental Proactiveness Matrix, we find that all 'very large' units are 'Proactive' in nature. Out of 'large' units, 62.50 per cent are 'Proactive', whereas remaining (37.50%) are 'Underperformer'. All 'medium' units are 'Performer'. Out of 'small' units, only 33.33 per cent are 'Performer', whereas majority (66.67%) of them is 'Laggard'. Out of 'very small' units, 45.45 per cent are 'Performer' and remaining (54.55 per cent) are 'Laggard'.

Thus, from the perspective of strategic response to environmental issues, it was concluded that for 'Proactive' units, they are showing the best environmental performance and their business strategy is excellent; for 'Performer's, it is good. These two types of units can sustain for long time. Whereas, 'Underperformer's due to having high capital investment can properly allocate the fund for environmental issues and it will not be difficult to revive. But competition is tough for 'Laggard's – they are too minor to consider and they may face problem to achieve long-term sustainability.

Our analysis revealed the logic behind the poor performance score of 'Underperformer' though they were 'large/very large' units. Similarly, the study identified the problems with 'Laggards'. Some of the major lacuna that were identified are: sometimes they didn't have any environmental policy or if they had any environment policy, it took long time to formulate such a policy or they had not mentioned their environmental policy in the mission statement or they had not changed their environmental policy after its formulation; or they didn't have any environment department; or they didn't undertake any environmental audit or if they undertook environmental audit, it was done by only internal departments and not verified externally; or in the area of land/noise pollution they had not taken any preventive/precautionary measure or they recycled very insignificant amount of solid wastes and dumped their solid wastes instead of selling their wastes to the other units and as a result they didn't generate enough revenue or they disposed off their hazardous wastes without following required safety precaution; or they did not incur adequate cost for taking care of environmental issues and as a result they were not reaping benefits as desired.

However, the underlying idea of the Environmental Proactiveness Matrix is that the best strategy of environmental proactiveness is to dominate in environmental performance score along with the size of the unit. The thinking goes like this as presented in *Exhibit 21.16*.

EXHIBIT 21.16

1. Environmental proactiveness is greatest when the unit is large/very large i.e. capital investment is more than Rs. 100 crores (when only the vertical axis is considered).
2. A dominating environmental performance score gives the highest accumulated incorporation of environmental issues (when only the horizontal axis is considered).
3. High incorporation of environmental issues leads to lower environmental degradation.
4. Lower environmental degradation can either be used to lower risk and to reap benefit in terms of better image among customers and other stakeholders, better efficiency, or to increase dynamic competitive advantages.

In this context, such matrix can serve as a simple tool for viewing a corporate business portfolio at a glance and may serve as a starting point for discussing incorporation of environmental issues among strategic business units.

Table 21.12: Environmental Performance of the Surveyed Units by Industry Segment

Sl. No.	*Gradation*	*Industry Segments*													
		Chemical		*Ferrous Metal*		*Food and Beverage*		*Non-Ferrous Metal*		*Thermal Power*		*Others*		*Total*	
		No.	*%*	*No.*	*%*	*No.*	*%*	*No.*	*%*	*No.*	*%*	*No.*	*%*	*No.*	*%*
1.	Excellent	2	16.67	0	0	0	0	1	12.50	3	50.00	1	12.50	7	12.73
2.	Good	2	16.67	1	5.88	0	0	0	0	1	16.67	2	25.00	6	10.91
3.	Moderate	3	25.00	4	23.53	3	75.00	5	62.50	1	16.67	3	37.50	19	34.54
4.	Average	2	16.66	5	29.41	1	25.00	1	12.50	1	16.66	1	12.50	11	20.00
5.	Poor	3	25.00	7	41.18	0	0	1	12.50	0	0	1	12.50	12	21.82
	Total	**12**	**21.82**	**17**	**30.91**	**4**	**7.27**	**8**	**14.55**	**6**	**10.91**	**8**	**14.54**	**55**	**100.00**

Source: Results computed.

Table 21.13: Environmental Performance of the Surveyed Units by Size

Sl. No.	*Gradation*	*Size of Surveyed Units*											
		Very small		*Small*		*Medium*		*Large*		*Very Large*		*Total*	
		No.	*%*	*No.*	*%*	*No.*	*%*	*No.*	*%*	*No.*	*%*	*No.*	*%*
1.	Excellent	0	0	0	0	1	20.00	4	16.67	2	66.67	7	12.73
2.	Good	0	0	0	0	1	20.00	4	16.66	1	33.33	6	10.91
3.	Moderate	5	45.45	4	33.33	3	60.00	7	29.17	0	0	19	34.54
4.	Average	4	36.37	4	33.33	0	0	3	12.50	0	0	11	20.00
5.	Poor	2	18.18	4	33.34	0	0	6	25.00	0	0	12	21.82
	Total	11	20.00	12	21.82	5	9.09	24	43.64	3	5.45	55	100.00

Source: Results computed.

NOTE

1. We have used capital investment for classifying the units on the basis of size.

22

DETERMINANTS OF ENVIRONMENTAL PROACTIVENESS

In this Chapter, we have attempted to identify some unit specific determinants explaining the variations in the overall environmental performance score to see how far these unit specific determinants can explain the said variations.

Identification of Determinants of Environmental Performance Score

In respect of overall environmental performance score, the maximum score was 82.60 per cent and the minimum score was 27.03 per cent, with the mean and standard deviation of environmental performance score being 52.03 per cent and 13.89 per cent respectively. Now, it may be inferred that such a wide variation in the extent of environmental performance score was due to variation in incorporation of six environmental performance indicators in business practice of sample units.

But the inevitable question at this juncture is that: is there any unit specific determinants that play some role for such a wide variation in the extent of environmental performance score? i.e. are there any other unit specific determinants besides the environmental indicators?

Accordingly, in this Chapter an attempt was made to identify some unit specific determinants explaining the variations in the overall environmental performance score. The determinants are attributable to different unit characteristics, and we made an attempt to see how far these unit specific determinants can explain the said variations. The remainder of this Chapter deals with the selection of some unit specific determinants along with the formulation of hypotheses. This is followed by the description of model for empirical testing.

Taking cue from previous studies on environmental performance (Ashford and Meima, 1993; Welford and Gouldson, 1993; Fiksel, 1994; James, 1994; Henriques and Sadorsky, 1996; Bradford, 2000) and based on our sample survey, normally accepted norms, also the theoretical considerations and availability of data, some unit specific determinants had been selected as potential explanatory variables for explaining the variation in the environmental performance score among the selected units. Even, in a few studies, apart from theoretical considerations and empirical support, selection of unit specific determinants has also been guided by their applicability to the specific socio-economic and political environment on setting of the country under study (eg. Madsen and Ulhoi, 1996, 1997, 1999, 2001; Epstein and Young, 1998; Ilinitch, Soderstrom and Thomas, 1998; Wehrmeyer *et al.*, 2002; Madsen, 2003; OECD, 2004; Zhu and Sarkis, 2004; Takahashi and Nakamura, 2005; Earnhart and Lizal, 2006; Ito, 2006; Schaltegger and Wagner, 2006; Sohal and Zutshi, 2006; The Northern Ireland Eighth Environmental Management Survey, 2006; Zutshi, 2006; Lu and Lo, 2007). In addition to the above, our study also attempted to explore the importance of two unit specific determinants (i.e. age of the units and ratio of permanent workers out of total workers) on environmental performance score. These two are new variables since the idea of inclusion of these two were not taken into consideration in other studies reviewed earlier in the dissertation. The rationale for their inclusion has been discussed later in this Chapter. Based on all the issues mentioned above, the selected unit specific determinants are presented in *Exhibit 22.1*.

EXHIBIT 22.1

(i) Industry segment;

(ii) Nature of ownership of the units;

(iii) Total capital investment (size) of the units;

(iv) Total turnover of the units;

(v) Age of the units;

(vi) Ratio of permanent workers out of total workers.

To ascertain the quantitative and relative effect of these unit specific determinants, multiple regression equations were constructed and subsequently tested. All the possible variables that were believed to shape the environmental performance score were incorporated in the model. The rationale for the selection of the variables was discussed while explaining the model.

Model Specification for Evaluation of Environmental Performance Score

To examine the association between several unit specific determinants (independent variables) and the extent of environmental proactiveness (dependent variable), various statistical analyses had been made. In some studies the matched-pair statistical procedures had been used to test the difference between environmental performance scores of two country locations or two/more groups of sample firms. Some relied on ANOVA, Z-testing and chi-square testing, while student's t-test had been used by some others. Bivariate statistical analyses had also been used by some researchers. To make the examples more exhaustive and pertinent, Zhu and Sarkis (2004); Wagner (2005); Huijbregts *et al.* (2006) followed regression analysis, while Gupta and Goldar (2003) introduced the use of Ordinary Least Squares (OLS) regression to estimate a linear relationship between the market price and firm's environmental performance.

Accordingly, to examine whether the selected unit specific determinants can explain the variations in the extent of environmental performance score, multiple linear (OLS) regression analyses (Linear Enter model) had been made. Multiple regression analysis is a method for studying the effects and the magnitude of the effects of more than one independent variables on one dependent variable using ordinary least square method. It is an efficient and powerful hypothesis-testing and inference-making technique, since it helps to measure, with relative precision, the dependence of the dependent variable on the independent variables and thus, helps to explain the presumed phenomenon represented by the dependent variable (Kerlinger, 1973).

Accordingly, with the environmental performance score as the dependent variable and assuming a linear relationship, the following variables were identified as independent variables. The basis of selection of such variables was either the theoretical logic of exhibiting such relationship or some of the earlier studies considered them as a dependent variable. To be specific, the following was considered as independent variables:

- **Industry segment:** The industry segment indicates the nature of the industry viz., chemical or ferrous metal or food and beverage or nonferrous metal or thermal power (based on the major categorisation of industry segment) in which an unit belongs. Here, the industry segment was considered as an independent variable. It is likely that industry category/segment may have some influence on the incorporation of environmental issues of the business practice of the units of that industry segment. Almost all the studies (Wehrmeyer *et al.*, 2002; Takahashi and Nakamura, 2005) conducted on the subject also considered it as an independent variable. *We hypothesised that the extent of environmental performance score is associated significantly with industry segment viz., chemical, ferrous metal, food and beverage, non-ferrous metal and thermal power (Alternative hypotheses $H_1 1$, $H_1 2$, $H_1 3$, $H_1 4$, and $H_1 5$).* It is pertinent to mention here that to avoid dummy variables trap[1], one industry segment (here, 'miscellaneous') out of total six industry segments were not considered for further analysis.

  To test these hypotheses, dummy variable 'CHEMICAL' (chemical) was used, which took the value one, if industry segment was chemical, and 0 otherwise. Similarly, dummy variable 'FERROUSM' (ferrous metal) [which took the value one, if industry segment was ferrous metal, and 0 otherwise], 'FOODBEVE' (food and beverage) [which took the value one, if industry segment was food and beverage industry, and 0 otherwise], 'NONFERRO' (non-ferrous) [which took the value one, if industry segment was non-ferrous metal industry, and 0 otherwise], 'THERMALP' (thermal power) [which took the value one, if industry segment was thermal power, and 0 otherwise] were used.

- **Nature of ownership of the units:** The nature of ownership of the units indicated whether the unit was Government or not [i.e. otherwise it would be private sector]. It was expected that in case of government unit, the pattern of response in putting emphasis on environmental issues in business practice may be different as compared to that of private sector. It may be due to work culture and /or reluctant behaviour from the side of the bottom level staff members. Earnhart and Lizal (2006) assumed a negative association between the nature of ownership and the extent of environmental proactiveness. Going by this logic, the nature of ownership was considered as an independent variable. *We hypothesised that the extent of environmental performance score is associated negatively with Government ownership (Alternative hypothesis $H_1$6).*

  To test this hypothesis, a dummy variable 'NATUROWN' (Nature of Ownership of the Units) was used, which took the value one, if nature of ownership was government, and 0 otherwise (for private sector).

- **Total capital investment (size) of the units:** Size of the unit was considered to be an important variable that may explain the differences in proactiveness score. Several variables like turnover, capital investment, market capitalisation, manpower strength, etc. may serve as a proxy for the size. However, among those variables, two variables namely, capital investment and turnover are commonly used (Ito, 2006). Accordingly we used these two variables and to address multicollinearity we have modified the models as considered necessary.

As explained above, generally, we have used total capital investment for classification of units by size. Our analysis revealed that there are variations in the environmental performance score of units that are categorized on the basis of their size. It may be mentioned that 50 per cent of units under the 'large' and 'very large' categories fall under the 'underperformer' block, whereas 60.87 per cent of 'small' and 'very small' units fall under 'laggard' block. Thus, it was likely that there is a significant difference in environmental performance score due to the sizes of surveyed units. Further, a large number of studies (Henriques and Sadorsky, 1996; Bradford, 2000; Madsen and Ulhoi, 2001; Wehrmeyer *et al.*, 2002; OECD, 2004; Takahashi and Nakamura, 2005; Ito, 2006) conducted on the subject also considered the size as an independent variable. In a few studies size was considered based on total capital investment (Firth, 1979; Epstein and Young, 1998; HaBler and Reinhard, 2000). Secondly, in a different context, Buzbi (1975) pointed out that smaller firms may not possess the necessary resources for collecting and presenting an extensive array of information. As such, it was expected that the environmental performance score of smaller firms becomes poor. Epstein and Young (1998) also assumed a positive association between capital investment and the extent of environmental proactiveness. For the purpose of regression, total capital investments were measured at their book values. In order to avoid the problems caused by heteroscedasticity[2], natural logarithm of this variable was used to estimate its potential effect on the extent of environmental proactiveness. *We hypothesized that the extent of environmental performance score is associated positively with the company's capital investment (Alternative hypothesis $H_1 7$).*

- **Total turnover of the units:** As explained above, we have also used turnover as a proxy of size variable, as it was expected that there is high correlation between total capital investment and turnover (Stanga, 1976; Cooke, 1989; Ahmed and Nicholls, 1994; Raffournier, 1995; Marston and Robson, 1997; Papas, 2002), it was also logical to consider the effect of turnover of the unit on environmental performance score.

Moreover, based on the studies undertaken by OECD (2004), Schaltegger and Wagner (2006), it was assumed that there is a statistically significant positive relationship of environmental proactiveness and total turnover. As in the previous case, in order to avoid the problems caused by heteroscedasticity, natural logarithm of this variable was used to estimate its potential effect on the extent of environmental proactiveness and as such, *we hypothesized that the extent of environmental performance score is associated positively with the company's total turnover (Alternative hypothesis $H_1$8).*

- **Age of the units:** The age of the units indicated whether the unit is old or not. It is expected that in case of old unit, there may have some problems that hinder the responses of the units towards environmental issues. It may be due to lack of willingness to accept new concept and /or due to being rigid. Going by this logic, the age of the unit was considered as an independent variable and *we hypothesized that the extent of environmental performance score is associated negatively with the age of the units (Alternative hypothesis $H_1$9).*

  To test this hypothesis, a dummy variable 'AGE' (Age of the Units) was used, which took the value one, if the unit was set up more than 10 years back, and 0 otherwise (if the unit was set up within 10 years, as on 2006).

- **Ratio of permanent workers out of total workers:** Finally, ratio of permanent workers out of total workers was considered as an independent variable. It was expected that a unit having more proportion of permanent employees will be more proactive in their approach towards environmental issues. Such units having proper manpower planning and human resource strategy may have employees who are more committed towards organisational environmental performance. As such, *we hypothesised that the extent of environmental performance score is associated positively with the ratio of permanent workers out of total workers (Alternative hypotheses $H_1$10).*

Thus, in this study, environmental performance score (EPS) was considered as function of the ten independent or explanatory variables representing the selected unit specific determinants. In other words,

EPS = f (CHEMICAL, FERROUSM, FOODBEVE, NONFERRO, THERMALP, NATUROWN, LOGCAPIN, LOGTURNO, AGE, RATPERMW)

The values of EPS for each of the 55 sample units had been measured in terms of overall performance score taking into consideration of six indicators. In case of other independent variables *viz.*, industry segment like chemical, ferrous metal, food and beverage, nonferrous metal, thermal power; nature of ownership; and age, we handled only binary variables, not multichotomous ones i.e. out of all ten variables, seven were dummy variables. In particular, they were analysed by binary variables, i.e. 0 (no) or 1 (yes), using the Boolean logic as suggested by Green, Tull and Album (2000).

Thus, the model that had been considered for determination of relative role of each independent variable is presented in *Exhibit* 22.2.

EXHIBIT 22.2

$$EPS_i = \alpha + \beta_1 CHEMICAL + \beta_2 FERROUSM + \beta_3 FOODBEVE + \beta_4 NONFERRO + \beta_5 THERMALP + \beta_6 NATUROWN + + \beta_7 LOGCAPIN + \beta_8 LOGTURNO + \beta_9 AGE + \beta_{10} RATPERMW + e_i$$

---

where,

i = Index of unit (1, 2, ..., 55)

EPS = Environmental Performance Score

CHEMICAL = 1, if the industry segment is Chemical, or 0 otherwise

FERROUSM = 1, if the industry segment is Ferrous Metal, or 0 otherwise

FOODBEVE = 1, if the industry segment is Food and Beverage, or 0 otherwise

NONFERRO = 1, if the industry segment is Non-ferrous metal, or 0 otherwise

THERMALP = 1, if the industry segment is Thermal Power, or 0 otherwise

NATUROWN = 1, if nature of ownership is government, or 0 otherwise (for private sector)

LOGCAPIN = Natural log of book values of Total Capital Investment

LOGTURNO = Natural log of book values of Total Turnover

AGE = 1, if the unit is set up more than 10 years back, or 0 otherwise (if the unit is set up within 10 years, as on 2006)

RATPERMW = Ratio of Permanent Employees out of Total Workers

α = Constant

β = Parameters

e = Error term

Regression Analysis and Results

A multiple regression analysis using linear enter model was run for these variables through SPSS (version 10.0) statistical package. The prime observations is presented in *Exhibit* 22.3 on the basis of regression results:

EXHIBIT 22.3

- Values for the Model were found significant at 1 per cent level.
- 34 per cent environmental performance score was explained.
- Comparing observed values of t with the tabulated values of $|t|$, it was found that:
    - In a few cases the nature of industry segment had significant impact on the extent of variation in environmental performance score. The detail of the industry segment that showed significant impact are as under:

(Contd...)

  - Chemical industry (CHEMICAL) did not have significant influence on the extent of environmental performance score.
  - Ferrous metal industry (FERROUSM) did not have significant influence on the extent of environmental performance score.
  - Food and beverage Industry (FOODBEVE) did not have significant influence on the extent of environmental performance score.
  - Non-ferrous metal Industry (NONFERRO) had significant impact on the extent of environmental performance score at 1 per cent level of significance.
  - Thermal power plant (THERMALP) did not have significant influence on the extent of environmental performance score.

- Nature of ownership (NATUROWN) did not bear significant impact on the extent of environmental performance score. But it is pertinent to mention here that the regression coefficient was negative.
- Total Capital Investment (LOGCAPIN) had significant positive impact on the extent of environmental performance score at 5 per cent level of significance.
- Total Turnover (LOGTURNO) had significant positive impact on the extent of environmental performance score at 1 per cent level of significance.
- Age of the unit (AGE) did not bear significant impact on the extent of environmental performance score. But it is pertinent to mention here that the regression coefficient was negative.
- Ratio of Permanent Employees out of Total Workers (RATPERMW) did not have significant impact on the extent of environmental performance score.

Findings from the Results of Regression Analysis

From the results of multiple regression analysis, we found that among the industry segments, non-ferrous metal industry had significant impact on the extent of environmental performance score at 1 per cent level of significance. Whereas, other industry segments viz., chemical, ferrous metal, food and beverage, thermal power did not have significant influence on the extent of environmental performance score. Further, total turnover had significant positive impact on the extent of environmental performance score at 1 per cent level of significance and total capital investment had significant positive impact on the extent of environmental performance score at 5 per cent level of significance. On the contrary, ratio of permanent employees out of total workers did not have significant impact on the extent of environmental performance score. Also, nature of ownership and age of the unit did not bear significant impact on the extent of environmental performance score. But it is pertinent to mention here that in both of the cases the regression coefficients were negative. Hence, it may be stated that in case of government ownership or with the increase in age of the unit, environmental performance becomes poor. In the following paragraphs, the detail about the findings and causes are analysed.

Impact of Industry Segment

The nature of industry segment had significant impact on the extent of variation in environmental performance score in a few cases. Such significance varied based on nature. So far as industry segment like non-ferrous metal was concerned, the result indicated that it had significant impact on the extent of environmental performance score at 1 per cent level of significance i.e. non-ferrous metal industry was the major independent determinant of environmental performance score. It had been argued that the mean score value obtained by the surveyed units in case of units of non-ferrous metal industry was the second highest out of five industry segments. Since in our sample, majority (7 out of 8) of the units of non-ferrous metal industry were small/very small units, the emission of air pollutants, generation of effluents/solid and hazardous wastes, emanation of noise was also low. As a result, majority (62.5%) of the units of non-ferrous metal industry obtained moderate environmental performance score and majority (75%) of the units of non-ferrous metal industry were 'performer' to 'proactive'. It seems justifiable that because of having less emissions/ generations, companies were reaping benefits in terms of environmental performance score. It is worthwhile to mention here that majority (75%) of the units of non-ferrous metal industry neither had any environment policy, nor EMS certification, nor environment department, nor undertake environmental audit, nor cover environmental improvement in the company budget. For that purpose, during calculation of maximum achievable score, it did not at all cover the respective loop except the loop of meeting regulatory compliance. As a result, percentage of score attained out of maximum achievable score appeared to be high compared to others, where though it had covered each loop but due to having lack of proper facility, the respective score appeared to be too low as against maximum achievable score.

Industry segment like chemical, ferrous metal and food and beverage did not have significant influence on the extent of environmental performance score. In our analysis of environmental proactiveness of surveyed units by industry segment, majority of the units of certain industry segments *viz.*, chemical, ferrous metal and food and beverage showed poor to average performance and very few showed moderate performance. Actually these three industry segments generate vast quantity of wastewater and do not take proper mitigative measures. Even attempting to meet the compliance with regulatory requirements involves huge amount of cost that are more difficult for smaller companies to bear. Larger companies in the sample sometimes have been able to afford such cost because of their disproportionately greater financial strength.

So far as units of thermal power were concerned, the results indicated that they also did not have significant impact on the extent of environmental performance score. It had been argued that the mean score value obtained by the surveyed units in case of units of thermal power was the highest. It is pertinent to mention here that in our sample, all the units of the thermal power had separate environment department; out of 6 units of thermal power, 5 were ISO 9000/14001 certified; 5 undertook environmental audit; 5 had their own environmental policy; implementation status of various control measures in case of the majority of the units were satisfactory; even majority of the units separately allocated significant proportion of total planned expenditure for incorporating the environmental issues in business practice. Therefore, it seems probable that though the units were large/very large, yet the facilities/infrastructure were not so structured and systematic for which plants' images were not getting reflected in terms of environmental performance score.

Impact of Total Capital Investment (LOGCAPIN)

Total Capital Investment had significant positive impact on the extent of environmental performance score at 5 per cent level of significance i.e. it was the major independent determinant that affected significantly environmental performance score of the surveyed units. The result was very much consistent with some previous findings. Moreover, it seems arguable that because of having more capital investment, larger companies enjoy significant economies of scale in terms of generation of revenue and consequently, they afford to allocate significant proportion of total planned expenditure for incorporating the environmental issues in business practice.

Impact of Total Turnover (LOGTURNO)

Total Turnover had significant positive impact on the extent of environmental performance score at 1 per cent level of significance i.e. it was a significant independent determinant that affected environmental performance score. So far as total turnover was concerned, it led to the conclusion that the theoretical proposition that companies with high turnover will be more proactive was proved. Moreover, it was likely that companies with high turnover will have better competitive position that they can leverage for better investment in environmental issues.

Impact of Nature of Ownership (NATUROWN)

Nature of ownership did not bear significant impact on the extent of environmental performance score. But it is pertinent to mention here that the regression coefficient of nature of ownership became negative. This indicated that the theoretical proposition that in case of companies having government ownership, the environmental performance was poor compared to units in private sector. It was very logical from our findings that 52 per cent of the surveyed private sectors had environmental policy, whereas only 40 per cent of the surveyed government units had environmental policy. Even 42 per cent of the surveyed private units undertook environmental audit, whereas only 20 per cent of the surveyed government units undertook environmental audit. It seems that due to having poor work culture, lack of initiatives taken by employees, lack of commitment, etc., government units were exhibiting such poor performance. Nevertheless, the results of the model 2 and Model 3 suggest that the nature of ownership did not significantly explain the variation in the extent of environmental performance score.

Impact of Age of the unit (AGE)

Age of the unit did not bear significant impact on the extent of environmental performance score. It is pertinent to mention here that the regression coefficient of the age of the unit found to be negative. This indicated that the theoretical proposition that in case of companies that had been set up more than 10 years back, the environmental performance was poor. It seems that due to having rigid outlook, reluctance to accept new technology, lack of awareness, etc., old units were executing such poor performance. Nevertheless, the results suggest that the age of the unit did not significantly explain the variation in the extent of environmental performance score.

Impact of Ratio of Permanent Employees out of Total Workers (RATPERMW)

The association between the environmental performance score and the ratio of permanent employees out of total workers was not significant. The results suggested that such a ratio did not significantly explain the variation in the extent of the environmental performance score. It might be due to the multicollinearity problem its effect might not be reflected in the result, as it was usually found that in case of government units there is high inclination of the recruitment of employees as permanent worker.

The results of the multiple linear (OLS) regression analyses (Linear Enter model) showed that out of ten selected explanatory variables, only three variables namely, total turnover, total capital investment and industry segment like non-ferrous metal appeared to be significantly positive in explaining the variation in the extent of environmental performance score. The variables namely, industry segment *viz.*, chemical, ferrous metal, food and beverage, thermal power; nature of ownership; age of the unit; and ratio of permanent employees out of total workers were found to be statistically insignificant, suggesting that these variables could not significantly explain the variation in the extent of environmental performance score in our sample.

Going by the results of the multiple regression (OLS) analysis of 55 listed companies, it was possible to conclude that units with higher annual turnover or capital investment or units belonging to non-ferrous metal industry were more environmentally proactive than those units in industry segments like chemical, ferrous metal, food and beverage, thermal power generation.

In the next Chapter we would make concluding observations that would include our recommendation.

NOTES

1 If a qualitative variable has m categories, it is required to introduce only (m-1) dummy variables to avoid dummy variable trap, i.e. the situation of perfect collinearity or perfect multicollinearity, if there is more than one exact relationship among the variables. Accordingly, for each qualitative regressor the number of dummy variables introduced must be one less than the categories of that variable (Gujarati, 2006).

2 Heteroscedasticity, which means 'differing dispersion', may be a consequence of misspecifying the model mathematically. It happens

when the potential distribution of the disturbance term is different for different observations in the sample. It means that the probability of having an erratic value will be relatively high. There are two reasons to explain heteroscedasticity: the first concerns the variances of the regression coefficients. If there is no heteroscedasticity, and if the other regression model assumptions are satisfied, the OLS regression coefficients have the lowest variances of all the unbiased estimators that are linear functions of the observations of dependent variable. If heteroscedasticity is present, the OLS estimators are inefficient, because other estimators may be found that have smaller variances and are still unbiased. The second reason is that the estimators of the standard errors of the regression coefficients will be wrong. They are computed on the assumption that the distribution of the disturbance term is homoscedastic, which means 'same dispersion'. If this is not the case, they are biased, and as a consequence the t tests, and also the usual F tests, are invalid. It is quite likely that the standard errors will be underestimated, so the t statistics will be overestimated and the user will have a misleading impression of the precision of regression coefficients (Dougherty, 2007).

23

CONCLUSION

The findings of low level of environmental proactiveness of many sample units suggest that there exists scope for expansion of the extent of environmental proactiveness in different areas of corporate practices, particularly where low level of environmental performance score was observed. The regulators should design appropriate and effective enforcement mechanisms and properly activate them to ensure a higher level of environmental performance in corporate practices, so that unit level management can make informed judgments on the basis of such business practice. Since the present enforcement mechanism in India is viewed as unsatisfactory, a formal body may be set up with adequate administrative and/or quasi-judicial power to monitor and enforce environmental compliance in corporate practices.

Even in India the emission level norms set by the Pollution Control Board do not adequately discriminate between large and small units. They go generally by command and control system keeping the emission level under certain norms. However, the findings that very small and small size sample units show poor environmental performance score in comparison to very large, medium and large units raises a question regarding the relevance and justification of the blanket emission norms of all units irrespective of their size. Generally, for decision making purposes stakeholders require more information regarding larger companies in comparison to smaller companies. Moreover from the financial angle, larger companies can afford more resources for production and dissemination of information. The relevance and justification of applying entire environmental regulation, perhaps, depends primarily on two factors, namely information needs of the stakeholders and financial capabilities of the companies to produce and report information. On consideration of these two factors, along with other factors which the policy makers think appropriate, if it is found that a significant portion of existing requirements are not relevant for very small and small companies, separate provisions should be made for them. It may be suggested that the environmental regulations in India need to be more fine-tuned. It is a widely known fact that not only in environment and business, but also outside them that it is only reasonable and well thought laws that get higher compliance.

The research suggestion gains legitimacy from the fact that in advanced countries like United States, this factor has been given due consideration and the pollution laws have been formed in such a way that the control is done on area-wise rather than on individual units. Also the individual units are controlled on the basis of total quantum of pollutants in an emission created in a year rather than on the percentage of the pollutants in an emission. Some authorities feel that this is the most rational way to control pollution. It would however, be fair to point out that in India too the policy of giving exemptions and relaxations to small and medium sized enterprises have been recognised for complying with certain environmental standards. Even, the Supreme Court has also suggested that chemical industries should not be treated at par with the other industries, rather they should be treated separately. However, no separate set of environmental standards have yet been issued in place of exempted/relaxed ones. These lacunae should be removed. Under the present way of regulatory compliance many industries may become unviable because installation of sophisticated pollution control equipment is either technically not possible or commercially not viable in small and medium scale units. It will inhibit laudable economic enterprise as well as violate critical environmental constraints. As an alternative, the process of adaptive environmental management and policy design should be offered, which integrates environment with economic and social understanding at the very beginning of the design process in a sequence of steps during the design phase and after implementation.

Two basic difficulties had been identified with the present approach. First, the fundamental properties of any development or policy are set very early in the design stage. If problem arises because the original context is too narrow, any fundamental redesign is extremely difficult unless there is extraordinary pressure. Ultimately confrontation is generated as different groups identify clear conflicts with their own interests.

The second major problem with present protective and reactive response is that it makes the practice of environmental assessment arbitrary, inflexible and unfocussed. Each issue is often dealt with as if it were unique and as the environmental consequence would be separated from the economic ones. Deleterious social and economic impact can be induced through ecological forces that if recognized early, could at times be turned to human's benefit rather than simply suppressed and ignored.

It was also identified that the present environmental regulations have been found to be inadequate to ensure sustainable livelihoods in the developing countries due to poor and unreliable database; scarce skilled and technical expertise; weak understanding of local, provincial and national-ecological and economic dynamics; and ignorance of regional and global ecological and economic inter-linkages.

Though there is a plethora of legislation to prevent and control environmental pollution in the country, it is common knowledge that most of the laws are honored in breach rather than in practice. The best and easy solution would be awareness about the conservation of environment for the survival of mankind. Our work explored a few lacunae in environmental acts and policies.

As our study revealed that not only with respect to implementation, there are problems in the policy and planning level (*viz.*, having environmental policy, having separate environment department, undertaking environmental audit, allocating separately significant proportion of total planned expenditure for incorporating the environmental issues in business practice, EMS certification, role of top management, etc.), there are scope of rethinking at the corporate policy level i.e. at strategy formulation as well as unit level of strategy implementation.

Suggestions

Regarding enactment of laws, the law-making bodies would try to enforce it to the extent possible hence it is imperative for business units to make adequate arrangement so that adverse consequence for non-compliance is kept at minimum. Some industrialists may think that environmental pollution control is the anti-thesis of the industrial development. But, in reality, environmental pollution control and industrial development are complementary to each other and they are the two sides of the same coin. Therefore, the pseudo impression formed in the minds of the industrialists must be driven out first and they must be made to think that their efforts to keep the environment clean is not a statutory obligation imposed on them but it is a great service rendered by them to the human race not only for the present but also for the future. Unless the industrialists take the task of environmental pollution control very seriously, there is going to be a lull in the industrial development and danger to the human race. On the basis of our findings through exploratory and empirical research, we have drawn some suggestions targeting to policy level i.e. the regulatory agencies as well as unit level. The prime suggestions are as follows:

- There must be an integrated legislation framework at the central level and substantive laws at the state levels to address the specific needs of different ecosystems.
- There is an immediate need of capacity building and strengthening of infrastructure facilities of implementation agencies (regulatory agencies) to facilitate effective implementation of provisions of various environmental legislations.

- At the national level, each individual shall have appropriate access to information concerning the environment that is held by public authorities and the opportunity to participate in decision-making processes. States shall facilitate and encourage public awareness and participation by making information widely available.
- There is a need to incorporate provisions to force the corporate sector to disclose the facts about environmental activities and to provide for verification of the facts disclosed.
- It is needed to monitor regularly the environmental performance of the units from the side of regulatory agencies, whether the environmental parameters are within the permissible limit or not.
- As in case of environmental audit that is prepared by internal departments, verification is needed by some external agency, therefore from the side of regulatory agency, it is required to verify environmental audit periodically that is usually undertaken by the internal departments.
- It is needed to ask the units to submit the environmental statement annually to the Pollution Control Board. It is also necessary to verify those statements whether it is showing the truth or not and accordingly, proper action may be taken from the part of the Board.
- It is required to impose high tax to the companies that are exceeding regulatory compliance.
- It is needed to award the units who will be showing outstanding performance for taking care of environmental issues in the business practice.
- If the unit has lack of adequate fund to implement the environment management system, in that case proper grant may be allocated from the side of regulatory agency.
- If possible, some kind of training programme(s) may be organized from the side of regulatory agency to aware the employees about the environmental issues, in case the company doesn't have adequate fund to train them.

- Nature of industry segment and size of unit may be important to have norms and each industry segment may require different treatment both at policy and practice levels.
- To recognise environmental management as among the highest corporate priorities and as a key determinant to sustainable development, each unit needs to establish policies, programmes and practices for conducting operations in an environmentally sound manner. It is also required to integrate these policies, programmes and practices fully into each business as an essential element of management in all its functions.
- Each unit needs to continue to improve corporate policies, programmes and environmental performance, taking into account technical developments, scientific understanding, consumer needs and community expectations.
- Involvement of various stakeholders and creating appropriate environmental awareness among them are necessary to tackle the environmental issues effectively.
- Each unit needs to develop and provide products and services that have no undue environmental impact and are safe in their intended use, that are efficient in their consumption of energy and natural resources, and that can be recycled, reused, or disposed off safely.
- Each unit needs to develop, design and operate facilities and conduct activities taking into consideration the efficient use of energy and materials, the sustainable use of renewable resources, the minimisation of adverse environmental impact and wastes generation, and the safe and responsible disposal of residual wastes. It also needs to assess the requirement of installation of the pollution control equipments and effluent treatment plants. Concrete efforts are needed to measure the effluent flow and quantity of effluents discharged outside the premises.
- It is needed to have a full-fledged environment department in case of each unit, where the departmental head have

adequate knowledge to take decision in emergency condition and there may have proper delegation of authority so that a systematic organisation structure is to be maintained.

- It is desired to set environmental guidelines and standards that meet and where appropriate exceed current national and local statutory requirements, and where regulations do not exist provide in-house performance targets.
- It is needed to review and develop those guidelines and standards in the light of developments in technology and industrial practices and trends of legislation.
- For EMS, it is needed to conduct management review committee meeting regularly involving the stakeholders.
- A proactive stance requires total managerial commitment for incorporating environmental concerns into all the activities of the organisation, like product quality, employee relations and corporate image.
- Each unit needs to educate, train and motivate employees to conduct their activities in an environmentally responsible manner.
- Each unit needs to advise, and where relevant, educate customers, distributors and the public in the safe use, transport, storage and disposal of products provided; and to apply similar consideration to provision of services.
- Each unit requires to foster openness and dialogue with employees and public, anticipating and responding to their concerns about the potential hazards and impacts of operations, products, wastes or services, including those of trans-boundary or global significance.
- As a prerequisite all potential polluters must obtain consent to establish before initiating any action for setting up of new business/trade or going for expansion/modernisation. Whereas in case of a large unit, business house should submit Environmental Impact Assessment (EIA) and Environmental Management Plan (EMP) to the State/ Central Government for environmental clearance of the project.

- Each unit needs to take base line data regarding existing environmental status *viz.*, ambient air quality, meteorological data, surface and ground water quality, noise levels, terrestrial ecology to provide the reference for assessing the trend in the pollution level.
- Each unit needs to measure environmental performance; conduct regular environmental audits and periodically provide appropriate information to the board of directors, shareholders, employees, the authorities and the public. It also needs to prepare an Environmental Statement and submit to the Pollution Control Board.
- Each unit needs to develop and maintain, where significant hazards exist, emergency preparedness plans in conjunction with emergency services, relevant authorities and local community, recognising potential transboundary impacts.
- Each unit should mention their environment policy in their mission statement/preamble.
- It should be needed to communicate to the stakeholders regarding the financial implication of environmental costs incurred i.e. how much they are getting benefit financially through incurring costs to incorporate environmental issues in the business practice.
- Each unit should run after raising the turnover as companies with high turnover have better competitive position that they can leverage for better investment in environmental issues. It is possible through improving the competitive position of the unit concerned.

Generalisations of the findings of the study should be made after considering its context and scope. In the next section, we want to acknowledge certain scope of the further research, as these findings have important implications for future research. The concept of environmental proactiveness in business practice is broad in scope and several issues come within its purview. Hence, improvements and extensions of the present study can not be ruled out. There is need for continuing more exploratory and empirical research on different aspects of environmental proactiveness. Apart from the explanatory variables considered in the present work that was shown to impact environmental proactiveness, future research may analyze the impact of product positioning, cost savings, improvement in a product's value, community demands, employee satisfaction, customer conscience, multi-facility, change in sales, profitability, market scope (local or national/regional or global), head office (domestic/foreign), government incentive, decision making, new technology, sharing of ideas, competitiveness, financial ratios, market position or stock market valuation, return on sales, return on owners' capital employed, return on equity, etc. Future research may be made on sample units that are not grossly polluting units, but somehow polluting units. Future research may be conducted to identify the environmental proactiveness of small and medium companies in the Indian context in a more detailed way. Furthermore, in future, environmental management practices in industrial units for several years may be examined, after taking steps to standardise year wise data or reduce their asymmetries, instead of focusing on one-year data, as this could provide stronger and more relevant result. Future research may also pursue a comparative study of business practice and environment proactiveness of Indian companies and of that in developed countries, to see how far business practice and environment management practices in Indian companies are lagging behind the International level.

Summing Up

The present work has measured and reported various levels of environmental proactiveness, including the variability of both the extent of overall performance score and the extent of environmental performance by industry segment and size of the sample units. The study has observed that the average level of environmental proactiveness is moderate, though in some cases extent of such proactiveness is quite poor. The study has highlighted different areas of business practice where opportunity exists for improvement of environmental management practices. It has pointed out that the variation in the extent of such proactiveness is wide. The study has identified three variables, namely, total turnover, capital investment and one industry segment like non-ferrous metal, which have significantly explained the variation in environmental proactiveness. Based on the findings of present study, certain recommendations at policy level as well as unit level have been made.

It is expected that the findings of the present study along with recommendations at policy level and unit level may provide some assistance to the following groups of people: (a) corporate management who are in the top level to incorporate environmental issues into overall corporate strategy formulation and implementation at operational levels; (b) policy makers and the legislators who frame environmental regulatory policies and enact regulations; and (c) regulators who monitor and enforce such regulations. Our modest hope is that the study might thereby show up the areas where there is scope of improving the quality of environmental performance of the industrial units.

24

REFERENCES

Ahmed, K. and Nicholls, D. (1994), 'The Impact of Non-Financial Company Characteristics on Mandatory Disclosure Compliance in Developing Countries: The Case of Bangladesh', *International Journal of Accounting*, 29, pp. 62-77.

Ahuja, Ram (2003), *Research Methods*, Rawat Publications, New Delhi, pp. 193-194.

Ashford, N.A. and Meima, R. (1993), 'Designing the Sustainable Enterprise Summary Report', *The Greening of Industry Network*, Second International Research Conference, Cambridge, Massachusetts, Quoted in Welford, Richard (1996), *Corporate Environmental Management: Systems and Strategies*, Universities Press (India) Limited, Hyderabad, pp. 151-157.

Bhattacharyya, Dipak Kumar (2003), *Research Methodology*, Excel Books, New Delhi, p. 57.

Bradford, D. (2000), 'Motivating SMEs towards Improved Environmental Performance', *The IPTS Report, No. 41*, Institute for Prospective Technological Studies, Seville, pp. 25-29.

Burritt, Roger L. (1997), '*Corporate Environmental Performance* Indicators: Cost Allocation-Boon or Bane?' *Greener Management International*, Issue 17, p. 89.

Business in the Environment and KPMG Peat Marwick (1992), 'A Measure of Commitment—Guidelines for Measuring Environmental Performance', *Business in the Environment and KPMG Peat Marwick*, Quoted in Welford, Richard (1996), *Corporate Environmental Management: Systems and Strategies*, Universities Press (India) Limited, Hyderabad, p. 156.

Buzbi, S. L. (1975), 'Company Size, Listed Versus Unlisted Stocks, the Extent of Financial Disclosure', *Journal of Accounting Research*, 13(1), Spring, pp. 16-37.

Cascio, J., Woodside, G. and Mitchell, P. (1996), *ISO 14000 Guide: The New International Environmental Management Standards*, McGraw-Hill, USA, pp. 3-64.

Chakrabarti, Dr. Snigdha and Mitra, Dr. Nita (2005), 'A Report on Cost-Benefit Analysis of Air Pollution Control Technology—A Case Study of Secondary Lead Smelting Industry', West Bengal Pollution Control Board, Kolkata.

Cooke, T.E. (1989), 'Disclosure in the Corporate Annual Reports of Swedish Companies', *Accounting and Business Research*, 19(74), Spring, pp. 113-124.

Davis, J. (1994), *Greening Business: Managing for Sustainable Development*, Blackwell, Oxford, Quoted in Welford, Richard (1996), *Corporate Environmental Management: Systems and Strategies*, Universities Press (India) Limited, Hyderabad, p. 159.

Dehua, W., Chan, Edwin H.W. and Liyin, S. (2004), 'Scoring System for Measuring Contractor's *Environmental Performance*', *Journal of Construction Research, Vol. 5, Issue 1, pp. 139-147.*

Dougherty, Christopher (2007), *Introduction to Econometrics*, Oxford University Press, Oxford, 3rd ed., pp. 224-227.

Earnhart, Dietrich and Lizal, Lubomir (2006), 'Effects of Ownership and Financial *Performance* on *Corporate Environmental Performance*', *Journal of Comparative Economics, Vol. 34, Issue 1, pp. 111-129.*

Edwards, A. J. (2001), *ISO 14001 Environmental Certification Step by Step*, Butterworth-Heinemann, Oxford, pp. 1-2.

Epstein, Marc J. and Young, S. David (1998), 'Improving *Corporate Environmental Performance* through Economic Value Added', *Environmental Quality Management*, Vol. 7, Issue 4, pp. 1-7.

Epstein, Mark (1995), 'A Sound *Environmental* Policy Adds to Financial Success', *Corporate Board*, Vol. 16, Issue 95, p. 26.

European Green Table (1993), *Environmental Performance Indicators in Industry – Report 3: Draft Handbook*, August, Unpublished, Oslo, Quoted in Welford, Richard (1996), *Corporate Environmental Management: Systems and Strategies*, Universities Press (India) Limited, Hyderabad, p. 151.

Fiksel, J. (1994), 'Quality Metrics in Design for Environment', *Total Quality Environmental Management*, Winter, pp. 181-192, Quoted in Welford, Richard (1996), *Corporate Environmental Management: Systems and Strategies*, Universities Press (India) Limited, Hyderabad, pp. 151-159.

Firth, M. (1979), 'The Impact of Size, Stock Market Listing and Auditors on Voluntary Disclosure in Corporate Annual Reports', *Accounting and Business Research*, 9(36), Autumn, pp. 273-280.

Global Environmental Management Initiative (1998), *Measuring Environmental Performance: A Primer and Survey of Metrics In Use* [http://www. gemi. org/ MET_101.pdf, visited on 21st November 2006].

Green, Paul E., Tull, Donald S. and Albaum, Gerald (2000), *Research for Marketing Decisions*, Prentice-Hall of India Private Limited, New Delhi, 5th ed., p. 452.

Gujarati, Damodar N. (2006), *Basic Econometrics*, Tata McGraw-Hill Publishing Company Limited, New Delhi, 4th ed., p. 302.

Gun, A. M., Gupta, M. K. and Dasgupta, B. (2002), *Fundamentals of Statistics*, The World Press Private Limited, Kolkata, Volume II, pp. 591-592.

Gupta, Shreekant and Goldar, Bishwanath (2003), 'Do Stock Markets Penalise Environment-Unfriendly Behaviour?

Evidence from India', *Working Paper No. 116, Centre for Development Economics* [http://www.cseindia. org/programme/industry/pdf/stock_market.pdf, visited on 21st November 2006].

HaBler, Robert and Reinhard, Dirk (2000), '*Environmental*-Rating: An Indicator of *Corporate Environmental Performance', Greener Management International, Issue 29, p. 18.*

Henriques, I. and Sadorsky, P. (1996), 'The Determinants of an Environmentally Responsive Firm: An Empirical Approach', *Journal of Environmental Economics and Management*, 30, pp. 381-395.

Howes, Rupert (1999), 'Accounting for Environmentally Sustainable Profits', *Management Accounting: Magazine for Chartered Management Accountants*, Vol. 77, Issue 1, p. 32.

Huijbregts, Mark A. J., Rombouts, Linda J. A., Hellweg, S., Frischknecht, R., Hendriks, A. J., van de Meent, D., Ragas, Ad. M. J., Reijnders, L., Struijs, J. (2006), 'Is Cumulative Fossil Energy Demand a Useful Indicator for the *Environmental Performance* of Products?' *Environmental Science and Technology*, Vol. 40, Issue 3, pp. 641-648.

Ilinitch, Anne Y., Soderstrom, Naomi S. and Thomas, Tom E. (1998), 'Measuring *Corporate Environmental Performance', Journal of Accounting and Public Policy, Vol. 17, Issue 4/5, p. 383.*

Ito, Misako (2006), 'Environmental Consciousness Increases in Japanese Business', *Japanese Economy Division, Topic Report, JETRO Japan Economic Report* [http://www.jetro.go.jp/en/market/trend/special/pdf/jer0606-1e.pdf, visited on 21st November 2006].

Jacobs, M. (1991), *The Green Economy: Environment, Sustainable Development and the Politics of the Future Pluto Press*, London, Quoted in Welford, Richard (1996), *Corporate Environmental Management: Systems and Strategies*, Universities Press (India) Limited, Hyderabad, p. 151.

James, P. (1994), *Business Strategy and the Environment*, 3, 2, pp. 59-67, Quoted in Welford, Richard (1996), *Corporate Environmental Management: Systems and Strategies*, Universities Press (India) Limited, Hyderabad, p. 151.

Kaushik, K.P. (2007), 'Determinants of Retained Earnings in Highly Profitable Companies in India: A Comparative Study of Domestic and Multinational Companies', *The ICFAI Journal of Applied Finance*, The ICFAI University Press, Hyderabad, Vol. 13, No. 6, pp. 19-42.

Kerlinger, Fried N. (1973), *Foundations of Behavioral Research*, Holt Rinehart and Winston Inc., New York, p. 631.

Kothari, C. R. (2007), *Research Methodology—Methods and Techniques*, New Age International (P) Limited, Publishers, New Delhi, 2nd ed.

Kotler, Philip (1991), *Marketing Management: Analysis, Planning, Implementation and Control*, Prentice-Hall of India Private Limited, New Delhi, 9th ed., p. 39.

Lu, W. M. and Lo, S.F. (2007), 'A Benchmark-Learning Roadmap for Regional Sustainable Development in China', *Journal of the Operational Research Society*, Vol. 58, Issue 7, pp. 841-849.

Madsen, H. and Ulhoi, J.P. (1996), 'Environmental Management in Danish Manufacturing Companies: Attitudes and Actions', *Business Strategy and the Environment*, 5, pp. 22-29.

Madsen, H. and Ulhoi, J. P. (1999), 'Industry and the Environment: A Danish Perspective', *Industry and Environment*, 22, pp. 35-37.

Madsen, H. and Ulhoi, J.P. (2001), 'Integrating Environmental and Stakeholder Management', *Business Strategy and the Environment*, 10, pp. 77-88.

Madsen, Henning (2003), 'Have Trends in Corporate Environmental Management Influenced Companies' Competitiveness?' *Greener Management International* [http: //goliath.ecnext.com/ coms2/summary _0199-3498784_ITM, visited on 21st November 2006].

Madsen, Henning and Ulhoi, John P. (1996, 1997, 1999, 2001), *Analyses of Corporate Environmental Management: Methodological Aspects* [http://isi.cbs.nl/iama member/ CD2/pdf/574.PDF, visited on 21st November 2006].

Madsen, H., Sinding, K. and Ulhoi, J. P. (1997), 'Sustainability and Corporate Environmental Focus: An Analysis of Danish Small and Medium Sized Companies', *Managerial and Decision Economics*, 18, pp. 443-453.

Marston, C. L. and Robson, P. (1997), 'Financial Reporting in India: Changes in Disclosure over the Period 1982 to 1990', *Asia-Pacific Journal of Accounting*, 4(1), June, pp. 103-139.

Mohanty, S. K. (1997), *Universal's Environment and Pollution Law Manual*, Universal Law Publishing Co. Pvt. Ltd., Delhi.

OECD, Directorate for Financial and Enterprise Affairs (2004), 'Overview of Corporate Environmental Management Practices', *Roundtable on Corporate Responsibility: Encouraging the Positive Contribution of Business to Environment through the OECD Guidelines for Multinational Enterprises* [http://www.oecd.org/dataoecd /12/29 /31967893.pdf, visited on 21st November 2006].

Papas, Antonios A. (2002), 'An Assessment of Mandatory Disclosure in the Annual Reports of Greek Companies', *Indian Journal of Accounting*, 32, June, pp. 1-14.

Raffournier, B. (1995), 'The Determinants of Voluntary Financial Disclosure by Swiss Listed Companies', *The European Accounting Review*, 4(2), pp. 261-280.

Repetto, Robert and Austin, Duncan (2001), 'Quantifying the Impact of *Corporate Environmental Performance* on *Shareholder* Value', *Environmental Quality Management*, Vol. 10, Issue 4, pp. 33-44.

Rice, F. (1993), 'Who Scores Best on the Environment', *Fortune*, July 26, pp. 104-111, Quoted in Welford, Richard (1996), *Corporate Environmental Management: Systems and Strategies*, Universities Press (India) Limited, Hyderabad, p. 155.

Russo, Michael V. and Fouts, Paul A. (1997), 'A Resource-Based Perspective on *Corporate Environmental Performance* and Profitability', *Academy of Management Journal*, Vol. 40, Issue 3, p. 534.

Sarantakos, S. (1998), *Social Research*, Macmillan Press, London, 2nd ed., p. 224, Quoted in Ahuja, Ram (2003), *Research Methods*, Rawat Publications, New Delhi, pp. 216-217.

Schaltegger, Stefan and Wagner, Marcus (2006), *Managing and Measuring the Business Case for Sustainability-Capturing the Relationship between Sustainability Performance, Business Competitiveness and Economic Performance*, Greenleaf Publishing [http://www.greenleaf-publishing.com, visited on 21st November 2006].

Seiler, M. J. (2004), *Performing Financial Studies*, Pearson Education, Inc., New Jersey, Quoted in Kaushik, K.P. (2007), 'Determinants of Retained Earnings in Highly Profitable Companies in India: A Comparative Study of Domestic and Multinational Companies', *The ICFAI Journal of Applied Finance*, The ICFAI University Press, Hyderabad, Vol. 13, No. 6, pp. 19-42.

Singleton, R.A. and Straits, B. C. (1999), *Approaches to Social Research*, Oxford University Press, New York, 3rd ed., p. 259, Quoted in Ahuja, Ram (2003), *Research Methods*, Rawat Publications, New Delhi, pp. 216-217.

Sohal, Amrik and Zutshi, Ambika (2006), 'EMS Adoption in the Public Sector: Experiences from Australia', in Sahay, B.S., Stough, R.R., Sohal, A. and Goyal, S. (2006) (ed.), *Green Business*, Allied Publishers Pvt. Ltd., New Delhi, pp. 253-267.

Stanga, Keith G. (1976), 'Disclosure in Published Annual Reports', *Financial Management*, Winter, pp. 42-50.

Takahashi, Takuya and Nakamura, Masao (2005), 'Bureaucratisation of Environmental Management and Corporate Greening: An Empirical Analysis of Large Manufacturing Firms in Japan', *Corporate Social Responsibility and Environmental Management*, Wiley InterScience (www.interscience.wiley.com), 12, pp. 210–219 [http://pacific.commerce.ubc.ca/nakamura/nakamura_csrem_2005.pdf, visited on 21st November 2006].

The Northern Ireland Eighth Environmental Management Survey (2006), *Business in the Community*, ARENA Network, Northern Ireland [http://www.bitc.org.uk/regions / bitc_in_your_region/northern_ireland/programmes/ environment/survey.html, visited on 21st November 2006].

Thornton, D., Kagan, Robert A. and Gunningham, N. (2003), 'Sources of *Corporate Environmental Performance*', *California Management Review, Vol. 46, Issue 1, pp. 127-141.*

Tyteca, D. (1994), *DEA Models for the Measurement of Environmental Performance of Firms—Concepts and Empirical Results*, Unpublished, Université Catholique de Louvain, Belgium.

Wagner, Marcus (2005), 'Sustainability and Competitive Advantage: Empirical Evidence on the Influence of Strategic Choices between *Environmental* Management Approaches', *Environmental Quality Management*, Vol. 14, Issue 3, pp. 31-48.

Wehrmeyer, W., Wagner, M., Pacheco, C. and Schaltegger, S. (2002), *Environmental Management Strategies: Britain and Germany Compared*, Anglo-German Foundation for the Study of Industrial Society, London [http://www.agf.org.uk/ pubs/ pdfs/1336web.pdf, visited on 21st November 2006].

Welford, R. J. and Gouldson, A.P. (1993), *Environmental Management and Business Strategy*, Pitman Publishing, London, Quoted in Welford, Richard (1996), *Corporate Environmental Management: Systems and Strategies*, Universities Press (India) Limited, Hyderabad, p. 152.

West Bengal Pollution Control Board (2004-2005), *Annual Report*, Part II, Annexure IV, pp. 143-160.

Wier, M., Christoffersen, Line B., Jensen, T., Pedersen, Ole G., Keiding, H., Munksgaard, J. (2005), 'Evaluating Sustainability of Household Consumption—Using DEA to Assess *Environmental Performance*', *Economic Systems Research, Vol. 17, Issue 4, pp. 425-447.*

Young, William C. (1996), *'Measuring Environmental Performance'*, in Welford, Richard (1996) (ed.), *Corporate Environmental Management: Systems and Strategies*, Universities Press (India) Limited, Hyderabad, pp. 150-176.

Zhu, Quinghua and Sarkis, Joseph (2004), 'Relationships Between Operational Practices and P*erformance* among Early Adopters of Green Supply Chain Management Practices in Chinese Manufacturing Enterprises', *Journal of Operations Management*, Vol. 22, Issue 3, pp. 265-289.

Zutshi, Ambika (2006), 'Environmental Management System Implementation in Australian Organisations', in Sahay, B. S., Stough, R. R., Sohal, A. and Goyal, S. (2006) (ed.), *Green Business*, Allied Publishers Pvt. Ltd., New Delhi, pp. 311-325.

BIBLIOGRAPHY

Articles/Reports/Journals

Bradford, D. (2000), 'Motivating SMEs towards Improved Environmental Performance', *The IPTS Report, No. 41,* Institute for Prospective Technological Studies, Seville.

Burritt, Roger L. (1997), 'Corporate Environmental Performance Indicators: Cost Allocation-Boon or Bane?' *Greener Management International,* Issue 17.

Chakrabarti, Dr. Snigdha and Mitra, Dr. Nita (2005), 'A Report on Cost-Benefit Analysis of Air Pollution Control Technology—A Case Study of Secondary Lead Smelting Industry', West Bengal Pollution Control Board, Kolkata.

Dehua, W., Chan, Edwin H.W. and Liyin, S. (2004), 'Scoring System for Measuring Contractor's *Environmental Performance', Journal of Construction Research,* Vol. 5, *Issue 1.*

Earnhart, Dietrich and Lizal, Lubomir (2006), 'Effects of Ownership and Financial *Performance* on *Corporate Environmental Performance', Journal of Comparative Economics,* Vol. 34, *Issue 1.*

Epstein, Marc J. and Young, S. David (1998), 'Improving *Corporate Environmental Performance* through Economic Value Added', *Environmental Quality Management,* Vol. 7, Issue 4.

Epstein, Mark (1995), 'A Sound *Environmental* Policy Adds to Financial Success', *Corporate Board,* Vol. 16, Issue 95.

HaBler, Robert and Reinhard, Dirk (2000), '*Environmental*-Rating: An Indicator of *Corporate Environmental Performance'*, *Greener Management International, Issue 29.*

Henriques, I. and Sadorsky, P. (1996), 'The Determinants of an Environmentally Responsive Firm: An Empirical Approach', *Journal of Environmental Economics and Management*, 30.

Howes, Rupert (1999), 'Accounting for Environmentally Sustainable Profits', *Management Accounting: Magazine for Chartered Management Accountants*, Vol. 77, Issue 1.

Ilinitch, Anne Y., Soderstrom, Naomi S. and Thomas, Tom E. (1998), 'Measuring Corporate Environmental Performance', *Journal of Accounting and Public Policy,* Vol. 17, *Issue 4/5.*

Ito, Misako (2006), 'Environmental Consciousness Increases in Japanese Business', *Japanese Economy Division, Topic Report, JETRO Japan Economic Report* [http://www .jetro.go.jp/en/market/trend/special/pdf/jer0606-1e.pdf, visited on 21st November 2006].

Jain, Sanjay K. and Kaur, Gurmeet (2004), 'Green Marketing: An Indian Perspective', *Decision*, Vol. 31, No. 2, July-December 2004.

Madsen, H. and Ulhoi, J. P. (1996), 'Environmental Management in Danish Manufacturing Companies: Attitudes and Actions', *Business Strategy and the Environment*, 5.

Madsen, H. and Ulhoi, J. P. (1999), 'Industry and the Environment: A Danish Perspective', *Industry and Environment*, 22.

Madsen, H. and Ulhoi, J.P. (2001), 'Integrating Environmental and Stakeholder Management', *Business Strategy and the Environment*, 10.

Madsen, H., Sinding, K. and Ulhoi, J. P. (1997), 'Sustainability and Corporate Environmental Focus: An Analysis of Danish Small and Medium Sized Companies', *Managerial and Decision Economics*, 18.

Magrini, Allessandra and Lins, Luiz dos Santos (2007), 'Integration between *Environmental Management* and Strategic Planning in the Oil and Gas Sector', *Energy Policy*, Vol. 35, Issue 10.

Repetto, Robert and Austin, Duncan (2001), 'Quantifying the Impact of Corporate Environmental Performance on Shareholder Value', *Environmental Quality Management*, Vol. 10, Issue 4.

Russo, Michael V. and Fouts, Paul A. (1997), 'A Resource-Based Perspective on Corporate Environmental Performance and Profitability', *Academy of Management Journal*, Vol. 40, Issue 3.

Sawhney, Aparna and Jose, P. D. (2003), 'The Greening of Business Strategy: From Compliance to Competitive Advantage', *IIMB Management Review*, September 2003.

Thornton, D., Kagan, Robert A. and Gunningham, N. (2003), 'Sources of Corporate Environmental Performance', *California Management Review*, Vol. 46, Issue 1.

Tyteca, D. (1994), *DEA Models for the Measurement of Environmental Performance of Firms—Concepts and Empirical Results*, Unpublished, Université Catholique de Louvain, Belgium.

Wagner, Marcus (2005), 'Sustainability and Competitive Advantage: Empirical Evidence on the Influence of Strategic Choices between Environmental Management Approaches', *Environmental Quality Management*, Vol. 14, Issue 3.

Books

Ashford, N.A. and Meima, R. (1993), 'Designing the Sustainable Enterprise Summary Report', *The Greening of Industry Network*, Second International Research Conference, Cambridge, Massachusetts, Quoted in Welford, Richard (1996), *Corporate Environmental Management: Systems and Strategies*, Universities Press (India) Limited, Hyderabad.

Beaumont, J.R., Pederson, L.M. and Whitãker, B.D. (1993), *Managing the Environment*, Butterworth-Heinemann Ltd., Oxford, Quoted in Welford, Richard (1996), *Corporate Environmental Management: Systems and Strategies*, Universities Press (India) Limited, Hyderabad.

Benedetto, C. Anthony di and Chandran, Rajan (2004), 'Behaviours of Environmentally Concerned Firms: An Agenda for Effective Strategic Development', in Polonsky, Michael Jay and Mintu-Wimsatt, Alma T. (2004) (ed.), *Environmental Marketing: Strategies, Practice, Theory and Research*, Jaico Publishing House, Mumbai.

Bhargava, Sangeeta and Welford, Richard (1999), 'Corporate Strategy and the Environment: the Theory', in Welford, Richard (1996) (ed.), *Corporate Environmental Management: Systems and Strategies*, Universities Press (India) Limited, Hyderabad.

Bhattacharya, Jayanta (2004), *Global Corporate Environmentalism*, Asian Books Private Limited, New Delhi.

Bishop, Paul L. (2000), *Pollution Prevention: Fundamentals and Practice*, McGraw-Hill International Editions, Singapore.

Bostrum, T. and Poysti, E. (1992), *Environmental Strategy in the Enterprise*, Helsinki School of Economics, Helsinki, Quoted in Welford, Richard (1996), *Corporate Environmental Management: Systems and Strategies*, Universities Press (India) Limited, Hyderabad.

Business in the Environment and KPMG Peat Marwick (1992), 'A Measure of Commitment – Guidelines for Measuring Environmental Performance', *Business in the Environment and KPMG Peat Marwick*, Quoted in Welford, Richard (1996), *Corporate Environmental Management: Systems and Strategies*, Universities Press (India) Limited, Hyderabad.

Buzzelli, David T. (1991), 'Time to Structure Environmental Policy Strategy', *The Journal of Business Strategy*, March/April, Vol. 12, No. 2, Quoted in Polonsky, Michael Jay (2004), 'Cleaning Up Green Marketing Claims: A Practical Checklist', in Polonsky, Michael Jay and Mintu-Wimsatt, Alma T. (2004) (ed.), *Environmental Marketing: Strategies, Practice, Theory and Research*, Jaico Publishing House, Mumbai.

Cascio, J., Woodside, G. and Mitchell, P. (1996), *ISO 14000 Guide*, McGraw-Hill, New York, Quoted in Bishop, Paul L. (2000), *Pollution Prevention: Fundamentals and Practice*, McGraw Hill, Singapore.

Chaturvedi, Dr. R. G. and Chaturvedi, Dr. M. M. (1998), *Law on Protection of Environment and Prevention of Pollution (Central and States)*, The Law Book Company (P) Ltd., Allahabad.

Davis, J. (1994), *Greening Business: Managing for Sustainable Development*, Blackwell, Oxford, Quoted in Welford, Richard (1996), *Corporate Environmental Management: Systems and Strategies*, Universities Press (India) Limited, Hyderabad.

Dutta, A. K., Agrawal, K. M. and Mitra, Sarbani (2004), 'Trade and Corporate Environmental Management Strategies—An Analysis in Indian Perspective', in Mallikarjun, M. and Chugan, Pawan K. (2004) (ed.), *Managing Trade, Technology and Environment*, 1st ed., Excel Books, New Delhi, Proc. of Nirma International Conference on Management (NICOM – 2004) on *Managing Trade, Technology and Environment*, Institute of Management, Nirma University of Science and Technology, Ahmedabad, January 2-4, 2004.

Edwards, A.J. (2001), *ISO 14001 Environmental Certification Step by Step*, Butterworth-Heinemann, Oxford.

European Green Table (1993), *Environmental Performance Indicators in Industry – Report 3: Draft Handbook*, August, Unpublished, Oslo, Quoted in Welford, Richard (1996), *Corporate Environmental Management: Systems and Strategies*, Universities Press (India) Limited, Hyderabad.

Fava, J.A., Consoli, F., Denison, R., Dickson, K., Mohin, T. and Vigon, B. (1993), *Guidelines for Life-Cycle Assessment: A Code of Practice*, Society of Environmental Toxicology and Chemistry, Pensacola, FL, Workshop Proceedings, Quoted in Bishop, Paul L. (2000), *Pollution Prevention: Fundamentals and Practice*, McGraw Hill, Singapore.

Fiksel, J. (1994), 'Quality Metrics in Design for Environment', *Total Quality Environmental Management*, Winter, Quoted in Welford, Richard (1996), *Corporate Environmental Management: Systems and Strategies*, Universities Press (India) Limited, Hyderabad.

Hart, Stuart L. (2005), 'Beyond Greening: Strategies for a Sustainable World', in Starkey, Richard and Welford, Richard (2005) (ed.), *The Earthscan Reader in Business and Sustainable Development*, Earthscan, London.

Hillary, Ruth (2001), *The CBI Environmental Management Handbook: Challenges for Business*, Earthscan Publications Ltd., London and Sterling, VA.

Hughes, D., Jewell, T., Lowther, J., Parpworth, N. and Prez, Paula de (2002), *Environmental Law*, Lexis Nexis Butterworths Tolley, United Kingdom, 4th ed.

Hunt, Christopher B. and Auster, Ellen R. (1990), 'Proactive Environmental Management: Avoiding the Toxic Trap', *Sloan Management Review*, Winter, Quoted in Benedetto, C. Anthony di and Chandran, Rajan (2004), 'Behaviours of Environmentally Concerned Firms: An Agenda for Effective Strategic Development', in Polonsky, Michael Jay and Mintu-Wimsatt, Alma T. (2004) (ed.), *Environmental Marketing: Strategies, Practice, Theory and Research*, Jaico Publishing House, Mumbai.

Hutchinson, C. (1992), 'Corporate Strategy and the Environment', *Long Range Planning*, 25 (4), Quoted in Welford, Richard (1996), *Corporate Environmental Management: Systems and Strategies*, Hyderabad: Universities Press (India) Limited.

Hutchinson, Andrew and Hutchinson, Frances (1996), *Environmental Business Management–Sustainable Development in the New Millennium*, McGraw-Hill Publishing Company, USA.

Irwin, A. and Hooper, P. D. (1992), 'Clean Technology, Successful Innovation and the Greening of Industry: A Case Study Analysis', *Business Strategy and the Environment*, 1(2), Quoted in Welford, Richard (1996), *Corporate Environmental Management: Systems and Strategies*, Universities Press (India) Limited, Hyderabad.

James, P. (1992), *The Corporate Response*, in Charter, M (ed), *Greener Marketing*, Greenleaf Publishing, Sheffield, Quoted in Welford, Richard (1996), *Corporate Environmental Management: Systems and Strategies*, Universities Press (India) Limited, Hyderabad.

James, P. (1994), *Business Strategy and the Environment*, 3, 2, Quoted in Welford, Richard (1996), *Corporate Environmental Management: Systems and Strategies*, Universities Press (India) Limited, Hyderabad.

Khitoliya, R.K. (2005), *Environmental Protection and the Law*, A.P. H. Publishing Corporation, New Delhi.

Kumar, Arun (1999), *Environmental Problems: Protection and Control*, Institute for Sustainable Development, Lucknow and Anmol Productions Pvt. Ltd., New Delhi.

Little, A.D. (1991), *Seizing Strategic Environmental Advantage*, Centre for Environmental Assurance, London, Quoted in Welford, Richard (1996), *Corporate Environmental Management: Systems and Strategies*, Universities Press (India) Limited, Hyderabad.

Lozada, Hector R. and Mintu-Wimsatt, Alma T. (2004), 'Green-Based Innovation: Sustainable Development in Product Management', in Polonsky, Michael Jay and Mintu-Wimsatt, Alma T. (2004) (ed.), *Environmental Marketing: Strategies, Practice, Theory and Research*, Jaico Publishing House, Mumbai.

Mohanty, S.K. (1997), *Universal's Environment and Pollution Law Manual*, Universal Law Publishing Co. Pvt. Ltd, Delhi.

Nash, J. and Stoughton, M. D. (1994), 'Learning to Live with Life Cycle Assessment', *Environmental Science and Technology*, 28: 236-237, Quoted in Bishop, Paul L. (2000), *Pollution Prevention: Fundamentals and Practice*, McGraw Hill, Singapore.

Porter, M. E. (1985), *Competitive Advantage*, The Free Press, New York, Quoted in Welford, Richard (1996), *Corporate Environmental Management: Systems and Strategies*, Universities Press (India) Limited, Hyderabad.

Ramesh, M.K. (2000), 'Environmental Legislation and Implementation in India', in Chary, S. N. and Vyasulu, Vinod (2000) (ed.), *Environmental Management: An Indian Perspective*, Macmillan India Limited, New Delhi.

Rosencranz et al. (1991), *Environmental Law and Policy in India: Cases, Materials and Statutes,* N.M. Tripathy Private Ltd., Bombay, Quoted in Khitoliya, R.K. (2005), *Environmental Protection and the Law,* A.P.H. Publishing Corporation, New Delhi.

Roy, Dilip (1998), *Environmental Management with Indian Experience,* A.P.H. Publishing Corporation, New Delhi.

Sarkar, Runa (2006), 'Corporate Environmental Behaviour: A Comparative Study of Firms in the Indian Paper Industry', in Sahay, B.S., Stough, R.R., Sohal, A. and Goyal, S. (2006) (ed.), *Green Business,* Allied Publishers Pvt. Ltd., New Delhi.

Shastri, Satish and Trivedi, Manjoo Bala (1997), 'Environmental Laws in India: How Effective it is?' in Sinha, Rajiv K. (1997) (ed.), *Environmental Crisis and Humans at Risk (Priorities for Action),* Ina Shree Publishers, Jaipur.

Sohal, Amrik and Zutshi, Ambika (2006), 'EMS Adoption in the Public Sector: Experiences from Australia', in Sahay, B.S., Stough, R.R., Sohal, A. and Goyal, S. (2006) (ed.), *Green Business,* Allied Publishers Pvt. Ltd., New Delhi.

Taylor, S.R. (1992), 'Green Management: The Next Competitive Weapon', *Futures,* Sept 1992, Quoted in Welford, Richard (1996), *Corporate Environmental Management: Systems and Strategies,* Universities Press (India) Limited, Hyderabad.

The Economist Intelligence Unit (1999), *Best Practices: Environment,* Universities Press (India) Limited, Hyderabad.

U. S. EPA (1992), *Facility Pollution Prevention Guide,* EPA/600/R-92/088, U.S. EPA, Washington, DC, Quoted in Bishop, Paul L. (2000), *Pollution Prevention: Fundamentals and Practice,* McGraw Hill, Singapore.

Vigon, B.W., Tolle D.A., Cornaby, B.W., Latham, H.C., Harrison, C. L., Boguski, T. L., Hunt, R. G. and Sellers, J. D. (1993), *Life-Cycle Assessment: Inventory Guidelines and Principles,* EPA/600/R-92/245, U.S. EPA, Cincinnati, OH, Quoted in Bishop, Paul L. (2000), *Pollution Prevention: Fundamentals and Practice,* McGraw Hill, Singapore.

Welford, Richard (1996), *Corporate Environmental Management: Systems and Strategies*, Universities Press (India) Limited, Hyderabad.

Welford, R.J. and Gouldson, A.P. (1993), *Environmental Management and Business Strategy*, Pitman Publishing, London, Quoted in Welford, Richard (1996), *Corporate Environmental Management: Systems and Strategies*, Universities Press (India) Limited, Hyderabad.

Young, William C. (1996), *'Measuring Environmental Performance'*, in Welford, Richard (1996) (ed.), *Corporate Environmental Management: Systems and Strategies*, Universities Press (India) Limited, Hyderabad.

Zutshi, Ambika (2006), 'Environmental Management System Implementation in Australian Organisations', in Sahay, B. S., Stough, R. R., Sohal, A. and Goyal, S. (2006) (ed.), *Green Business*, Allied Publishers Pvt. Ltd., New Delhi.

Website

http://www.gemi.org/ MET_101.pdf, visited on 21st November 2006.

http://isi.cbs.nl/iama member/CD2/pdf/574.PDF, visited on 21st November 2006.

http://www.oecd.org/dataoecd /12/29 /31967893.pdf, visited on 21st November 2006.

http://goliath.ecnext.com /coms2/summary_0199-3498784_ITM, visited on 21st November 2006.

http://www.greenleaf-publishing.com, visited on 21st November 2006.

http://pacific.commerce.ubc.ca/nakamura/nakamura_csrem_2005.pdf, visited on 21st November 2006.

http://www.bitc.org.uk/regions/bitc_in_your_region/northern_ireland/programmes/environment/survey.html, visited on 21st November 2006.

http://www.agf.org.uk/ pubs/pdfs/1336web.pdf, visited on 21st November 2006.

Index

G

❑❑❑